DECISION-MAKING IN PHYSICAL EDUCATION AND ATHLETICS ADMINISTRATION:

A Case Method Approach

Earle F. Zeigler
Ph. D., LL. D., FAAPE
Professor of Physical Education
The University of Western Ontario
London, Canada

ISBN 0-87563-221-1

Published by
STIPES PUBLISHING COMPANY
10-12 Chester Street
Champaign, Illinois 61820

DEDICATION

TO

Don and Barby

(now both professors in their own right--
and part of the "over thirty" crowd)

PREFACE

The phenomenon of human motor performance in sport, dance, play, and exercise, including organized sport and physical education, is presently so pervasive in our culture that it is impossible to measure its effect on our social system and culture. There is absolutely no question but that this development of the past one hundred years has today become a vast enterprise that demands wise and skillful management. The situation is now such that the appointment of a director of physical education, an athletic director, an aquatic director, a manger of a fitness center, or a person with some combined title is a very ordinary and expected occurrence.

It could be argued that these men and women have taken the first step toward involvement in the profession of management. This statement is based on the assumption that management has now assumed many of the earmarks of a profession. Having said this, we should keep in mind that a recognized profession needs an organized body of knowledge based on research. Further, a profession that is fully worthy of its name must, of course, meet many other criteria. For now, however, we must keep this particular criterion firmly in mind: the existence of an organized body of knowledge based on research. Thus, the perpetuation of our "species"--the physical education and athletics manager--as a profession requires that some organizational structure be developed within educational institutions through which the body of professional knowledge may be transtransmitted to those who follow.

If we grant the above statements concerning the primary criterion of a true profession, we must next appreciate also that there is a continuing need to prepare new administrators or managers in a professional manner so that they will in turn possess the knowledge, competency, and skill to put this "body of knowledge" to work as capable and responsible administrators. It is at this point where so many managers fail to succeed because they have not developed their own conceptual framework for physical education and athletics administration. They have not acquired the decision-making ability in coordination with effective human relations.

The main purpose of this test--which can be used either as a text or a laboratory manual--is, therefore, to assist prospective administrators to obtain a certain level of management knowledge, skill, and competency in decision-making and human relations. This is a tall order to fill, but at the very least we

iii

hope to get the student off to a good start with his or her conceptual framework in two separate but yet interrelated ways: first, by providing an introduction and orientation to the nature of management or administration today (these two terms will be used interchangeably); and, second, by introducing the student of management theory and practice to the case method technique as one technique to use in the achievement of management competency or skill in decision-making and human relations.

We first introduced the case method approach to the teaching of administration and human relations to this field more than twenty years ago (Zeigler, 1959). It has been gratifying to note that this instructional technique has been employed since with health, physical education, and recreation in colleges and universities all over the continent. We anticipate that the 1980's will witness a resurgence of interest in this highly effective technique as one of a number of such instructional approaches available to assist the prospective manager to acquire some of the skills needed for successful management.

When a class employs this teaching/learning technique, all concerned read, analyze, and then discuss "real life" administrative problems similar to those they will face in their future careers. There is no question but that this is a sound approach, as the emphasis is on careful analysis and digging for facts. Although the instructor is still very important, he is urged not to dominate the discussion, or to seek a predetermined goal. The instructor may serve as a resource person, an evaluator of progress, an informed member of the group, a discussion chairman, and a summarizer--in these five ways.

Many who had administered programs, and who had perhaps taught "the administration course" within the physical education and sport major program, had felt the need for a new approach. We ourselves had played with the concept of "democratic administration,' and in our courses we had tried group discussions, committee work, group projects, different kinds of readings, policies and procedures manuals, and term papers. All of these techniques were helpful, to be sure, and they did serve to break away from the traditional, monotonous, unilateral type of teaching in which lectures followed by a short question-and-answer period predominated. However, we discovered that the introduction of the case plan of instruction served as the "missing link" insofar as involvement of students in the discussion and the decision-making process was concerned.

Thus, with the introduction of the case method of teaching in our field in the late 1950's--really an ideal teaching technique in an evolving democratic country permitting pluralistic philosophies of education--students were given the opportunity for the first time to apply their knowledge, understanding, and imagination to management problems that had actually been faced by teachers, coaches, and administrators on the job. With this technique the student takes part actively in the search for a rational course of action based on the relevant, concrete facts available. The class member develops attitudes; he learns to analyze problems critically, and he may ultimately develop the self-reliant judgment necessary for success as a physical education and athletics administrator.

There is an important point to be made at this juncture of this discussion. Despite the fact that we still believe all of the above statements strongly, we are also aware of the fact that some people who adopted the case method approach abandoned former teaching techniques completely. We are now absolutely convinced that such a change of approach is unwise if one course experience embodying this approach is all that the student will have in administrative theory and practice in his or her program. This is why this text has been developed in such a way that other experiences can be combined with it. Ideally, we recommend that each week there should be one lecture, one case discussion, and one group project where students are given an opportunity to subdivide into discussion and work groups involving from three to six people (e.g., working on the development of a policies and procedures manual). Of course, this is an individual matter for decision based on the knowledge, competencies, and skills that are planned for the entire course experience (or within a specialization in sport and physical education management).

In our opinion it is now most urgent that management be viewed as a developing social science (a behavioral one). In the early 1960's, with the help of some other professors and a number of exceptionally good doctoral students, we were able to mount a theoretical thrust to the area of administration as it applied to physical education and athletics. For us this movement culminated with the publication of a text containing the results of many of the doctoral and master's theses completed during that decade (Zeigler and Spaeth, 1975).

At the present, changing curricular patterns are everywhere in evidence in our field because of strong social influences, some of which are characterized by the knowledge explosion and what has been called the administrative or managerial revolution. Our programs of professional preparation have been

v

challenged sharply at both the undergraduate and graduate levels by critics both outside the field and from within it as well. It is now very clear that the former "one-semester administration occurs" is simply not adequate for the prospective physical educator/coach regardless of whether he or she ends up with a workload that involves a significant amount of managerial responsibility. At the very least, there should be some sort of a laboratory experience along with the theoretical phase of the course experience. It is at this point that a volume such as this could be invaluable because of the use of the case method as an important instructional aid.

If our physical educator/coach does indeed become the administrator or manager, the course experience being described here is really only a bare minimum--i.e., as one part of the sub-disciplinary and sub-professional core experience that the student undergoes during the first two to two and one-half years of the university experience. There seems to be no doubt but that a substantive amount of knowledge and a variety of professional choices that are now becoming available to the young practitioner in today's society--a period that is characterized by an increasing amount of role differentiation.

It is interesting to note, further, that the last few decades have been a time in which there was steadily greater realization and implementation of what might be called the social science and humanities (or perhaps socio-cultural and behavioral) aspects of sport and physical education. Thus, keeping the focus on this new development, along with the necessary and ever-present bio-scientific aspects of our field, we are finding also that we must keep the so-called sub-professional aspects of the profession firmly in mind too as we operate in the 1980's and thereafter. We can look back for guidance, but we should never turn back if we hope to be permitted to make our potential contribution to human development in the world. It is obvious that we will need wise management to help us achieve this long range objective.

Before closing this preface, a few more thoughts about the course experience itself are in order. Initially, it would be a good idea to ask the student to determine his/her own administrative philosophy by means of a (admittedly subjective) self-evaluation checklist (see Appendix A). Following this-- and it would be wise to have a class discussion about the results--we believe that the student should be introduced to the background and current status of management theory and practice in related fields as well as in his own. The instructor's lectures on Mondays, if this approach is followed, can very nicely revolve around the material included in the first three chapters of the book. On the first Wednesday, after giving students an assignment to read the chapter on "learning by the case method," we think that the instructor would be wise "to dive right in" with a case discussion on the second Wednesday. This would mean that Fridays, or the third hour that the group meets, can be tied in with the group projects, committee meetings, or whatever the instructor wishes to accomplish in regard to the accrual of knowledge and competency within this particular course experience. Supplementary reading that relates directly and indirectly to the particular case that has been assigned for a specific week will enhance discussions by giving the students more confidence that they have something authoritative to offer.

Of course, as students discuss the various cases, they (and the instructor) will realize that their knowledge is far from complete. The interest generated by the discussion (and post-class discussion) of these cases will encourage all concerned to read more widely and completely than previously. Furthermore, instructors are urged to recognize and reward by praise those students who refer to what appears to be sound source material in the discussions and written case analyses. The bibliographical material offered at various points throughout the text should serve as an excellent reading guide.

The author owes a debt to the many friends, colleagues, and students who have worked with him in the management area at the Bridgeport (CT) YMCA, Yale University, The University of Western Ontario (in the late 1940's and 1950's), The University of Michigan, University of Illinois at Champaign-Urbana, The University of Western Ontario (for the second time in the 1970's and early 1980's)--and finally those at Columbia Teachers College, Arnold College (now part of the University of Bridgeport), and the former Department of Education at Yale University, where he took a graduate minor in physical education, and undergraduate minor in physical education, and a doctoral program in the history and philosophy of education (and the equivalent of a master's degree in professional education as well). (I did not mean to forget Bates College above, where I took my undergraduate A.B. in 1940. Also, I should mention those who helped me achieve the M.A. in German at Yale in 1944.) To all those real people who have been described anonymously in the various, no malice was intended. To Robert Watts of the Stipes Publishing Company--and, of course to Mr. R. A. Stipes, Jr.--I with sincere pleasure record my gratitude for their sage advice and continuing support over the years with seven other publications in 1965, 1966, 1968, 1971, 1973 and two in 1975. Ms. Marie Mayer, who assisted with the preparation of the manuscript, should be recognized for her invaluable assistance as well. Finally, to my wife (Bert), who serves as my chief proofreader, literary critic, and disgruntled creator of occasional indexes, I express my continuing love and gratitude.

Earle F. Zeigler

DECISION-MAKING IN PHYSICAL EDUCATION AND
ATHLETICS ADMINISTRATION: A CASE
METHOD APPROACH

Contents

PART 1
INTRODUCTION AND ORIENTATION

CHAPTER 1
A MANAGEMENT OVERVIEW

Administration or management--terms that will be used interchangeably here--has become a challenging profession that can be studied profitably and practiced with increased understanding and skill. However, the complexity of educational administration, at <u>any</u> level in both public and private schools and universities, has become increasingly well known even to the layman. In this book we are concerned specifically with the the administration of physical education and athletics. Our approach will be one in which we argue that there are many ways in which teachers, coaches, supervisors, physical directors, and directors of physical education and/or athletics are all managers--but to varying degrees.

Because of the complexities in modern administration occasioned by what has been termed the "managerial revolution," myths, taboos, insularity, the development of a language of administration, and changing values in our society, the administrator today is increasingly faced with the necessity of welding action and theory together--what has been called the action-theory alliance. This means further--although it has been scarcely recognized in physical education and athletics--that there is an urgent need for a different emphasis in the preparation of managers.

In educational circles, and here we necessarily include the sphere of physical education and athletics, administrative positions are now of such a nature--what with shrinking budgets and a "management of decline" syndrome--that a number of people seem to be fleeing from the "assumption of the administrative risk." This trend, if it may be called that, appears to be more evident in the United States than in Canada. In the latter country such managerial posts are typically not regarded as lifelong assignments and are often only for a three- or five-year term. The fact that management at the university level, if not in the high schools or elementary schools, is a "rotating responsibility" may have to a degree avoided the malaise of management in Canada, whereas the increasing complexity of management and the often seemingly untenable status of the middle manager has tended to exacerbate the problem in the States.

2

Interestingly enough, within sport and physical education there seems to be an ever-ready supply of candidates for managerial posts when they are advertised. We trust that it is simply not a question of "fools rushing in where angels fear to tread," but, of course, it is one way to get a secretary (perhaps the only one!). Somewhat more seriously, due to the lack of authoritative evidence, we can only conjecture as to why this may be so. We have argued earlier that there are probably several reasons why physical educator/coaches are often ready to apply for managerial posts (Zeigler and Spaeth, eds., 1975, pp. xi-xii). For example, such positions do pay higher salaries, and it is true that salaries in academe have not kept pace with rising living costs. It could be argued further that people in this field are better suited constitutionally for administrative leadership of a certain type. We are often accused of a "blow the whistle" mentality as a leadership technique designed to exert power effectively. Finally, the steady routine of teaching and coaching can indeed wear a person out in short order unless a somewhat restricted routine is soon discovered.

Decision-Making in Administration

The centrality of the decision-making process in administration is a major focus in this text. We are not for a moment arguing here that the approach being recommended here is the only approach, and that it is suitable for all situations. However, through long experience we do believe that the use of the case method approach in teaching human relations and adminsitration has much to offer. This statement may well be especially true for people who have been functioning in an environment characterized by highly competitive sport where coaches expect people to accept orders readily in what is often treated as a "do or die" environment. We have discovered further that many people haven't the faintest idea of the possibilities of that which we blithely call "democratic administration." Or to put it another way--perhaps more kindly--there appear to be a great many different definitions of the concept! (As we look back, it can be stated unequivocally that the "democratic administrator" who opts for a more authoritative stance typically is much more acceptable to us than the person who "takes votes on everything and anything at the drop of a hat," and then proceeds to do whatever he or she wanted to do originally with seemingly absolutely no feeling of guilt!)

The Development of Administrative Thought

Decision-making is nothing new, of course, and we have ample evidence that for thousands of years much thought has been given to the governance of organizations. The great

3

organizational achievements in the history of the world belong to the actual history of administration. Thus, the present status of administrative thought may be more clearly understood through a review of the major development which have occurred, and also through an analysis of the perennial problems that managers have faced. Much of the underlying administrative thought may be found in diverse fields such as philosophy, religion, political science, history, and economics.

Social change has been such that a term like "administrative revolution" was needed to describe what transpired in the late nineteenth and first half of the twentieth centuries. However, it has only been through organizational management that science and technology have been able to create the modern world. In recent decades significant steps in administrative theory have been taken in public administration, business administration, and educational administration, as well as in the behavioral sciences. Administrative practice of a trial and error nature may have sufficed for many up to this point, but it should now be a thing of the past. As Gross has stated, "modern man has no escape from the complexities of organizations and their management" (1964, vol. 2, p. 808).

There is now a great quantity of knowledge about human behavior, but administrative theory has not yet developed to the point or a level of generalization at which it may be called systematized knowledge about organizational phenomena. There is a need for clarification of terms and concepts. Future research should be value-free, and it may well be rooted in the behavioral sciences primarily. There is a need for emphasis on processes more than on correlation.

Interest in theoretical concepts began in the field of educational administration during the late 1940s. At the same time the American Association of School Administrators became concerned about the state of the profession. During the period from 1947 to 1957, the National Conference of Professors of Educational Administration provided an increasing amount of interdisciplinary contact. Since then an allied professional group, the University Council for Educational Administration has also exerted significant leadership. The UCEA was a direct outgrowth of the Cooperative Program in Educational Administration (CPEA) that had gotten its start with direct financial assistance from the Kellogg Foundation (Halpin, 1958, p. 2).

Thought, theory, and practice in administration or management has mushroomed in a seemingly disproportionate manner in recent years to the extent that one cannot keep up with the

4

multitude of books, magazines, journals, conferences, and seminars on the subject. Many has been disappointed in the inability of administrative theorists to achieve a level of generalization that would enable all managers to carry out their responsibilities and duties as effective social scientists. It has now been more than twenty-five years since Litchfield stated, "We seem to be saying that there is business administration, and hospital administration, and public administration; that there is military administration, hotel administration, and school administration. But there is no administration" (1956, p. 105). We believe that it can now be truly said that there has developed a steadily increasing awareness of the social-science quality of management.

Various Approaches to Administration

What might be called a "trend toward unity" of the various fields concerned with administration has been slow in coming, to be sure, but as early as 1966 Gordon (pp. 6-23) suggested a conceptual framework which "permits the incorporation and comparison of many approaches as well as the joining of values, substance, and process". At the same time he indicated that there have been four approaches to administration in the United States (traditional, behavioral, decisional, and ecological) that we will discuss very briefly before returning to his plea for unification.

The Traditional Approach. The traditional era was characterized as being composed of the "mother sciences"; rationalized views of administration; and what has been termed the scientific management movement. The "mother sciences" approach viewed the activity of the organization as being basically economic in the case of business; as being fundamentally political if government was in question; or as being social if institutions were under consideration. The "broad rational view" was one in which administration was regarded as a separate recognizable field of study. Managerial behavior was seen as a function, composed of sub-functions such as planning, organizing, staffing, directing, and controlling. The "scientific management movement" included stress on rational study and improvement in the efficiency of administration. The performance of workers in a bureaucratic structure was studied carefully.

The Behavioral Approach to Administration. Whereas the traditional (or scientific) approach began in the latter half of the nineteenth century, it can be argued that the behavioral approach was an early twentieth-century phenomenon that was to a certain extent a reaction to the earlier efficiency-oriented movement. The behavioral emphasis is directed toward the way

5

that people live and behave in organizations. The "behavioral-
ists" sought to prove their contentions empirically, and their
contributions often were identified as "human relations." Organization is viewed as a social system not always within the control and understanding of the administrator. Thus, the task
of the human relations-oriented manager is to so arrange the
work situation and the people in it that the achievement of cooperative relationships and a high level of production will be
realized. The contributions of psychology and sociology undoubtedly received considerable attention with this approach.

The Decision-Making Approach to Administration. What
has been called the decision-making approach emerged in a
rather distinctive fashion after the behavioral approach--al-
though it must be explained that all of these approaches did--
and undoubtedly still do--overlap to a greater or lesser degree.
With this approach--that began in the late 1930s and the early
1940s--the task of the administrator is largely that of a deci-
sion-maker. Administration or management is accordingly a
process, and it is concerned primarily with the relationships
among objectives, strategies, and competition. The goal is
achieving objectives under competitive conditions. Information
is gathered, and then one or more of a variety of techniques
and/or methodological applications are brought to bear on it so
that the best decisions may be made under the circumstances
that prevail. Thus, the quantification of data served as input
for complex decision-making to an extent never before employed. Today many management theorists see the decision-making
process as the central process in management.

The Ecological Approach to Administration. Even though
it can be argued that Gordon was not really able to gain sufficient historical perspective when he identified an ecological approach to administration in 1966, such identification now appears
to have been correct (1966, p. 17). The ecological approach is
based on relationships among the internal and external environments of the organization. Central to the ecological viewpoint
of management is the organization's "ability" to adapt to change
and to thereby strengthen and develop itself. Here the term
"organizational growth does not necessarily mean growth in
terms of size, but also from the standpoint of strength, efficiency, and competitive ability." The ecological approach could
be called eclectic to a degree, because it may include where
possible and when desirable elements of other approaches to
management. The main goal is, therefore, survival in a rapidly
changing world.

6

A Transcending Approach to Administration (Gordon)

The four viewpoints about (or approaches to) administration are important and basic, and they can undoubtedly serve in the building of an overall conceptual framework or theory of management. Of course, it has not yet been determined what all the variables are, and which of them are dependent or independent. Also, greater analysis of the external and internal environments is needed. Most certainly as well, the place of societal and individual values in a conceptual framework is basic. This is especially true in the final analysis when decisions are made and administrative action is to be taken. A "process concept" in which sub-processes are entered and possibly amalgamated can assist management theorists to visualize what actually might take place. This could eventually become the "scientific method" of the organizational theorist. Such a flexible synthesis should eventually provide a provisional working theory of administration (Gordon, 1966, pp. 19-23).

Administration in Physical Education and Athletics

Institutions and organizations in North America, in similar fashion to developments everywhere, are increasing in size, number, and complexity. The term "Big Business" can now be applied to government (despite any efforts to reverse this trend), labor, science, agriculture, religion, education, and no now even sport and exercise. Although this volume is designed primarily for those who will administer programs in educational institutions, we can't forget that sport and exercise--not to forget dance--have literally become "womb to tomb" affairs in modern society. Further, it is very difficult to say where so-called professional and semiprofessional sport leave off--that is, the fading definition of the amateur in university circles in North America particularly--when we consider the perennial problems of sport as a money-making activity. Thus, in the case of our gate-receipt competitive sports, the problem seems more specifically to be a question of business within education, the latter a pivotal social force that we have sought to set apart from the society's commercial establishments. Many have felt that business within education was incompatible, especially as this applied to highly competitive sport. However this may be, the physical education and athletics administrator has been placed in an untenable position when he or she has been expected to finance a program almost completely through gate receipts, but the values and norms of the educational enterprise mitigated against the use of what has been termed "sound business practice."

7

And so we now have a situation in North America where organized physical education and athletics during the past one hundred years has gradually but steadily become a vast enterprise that demands wise and skillful management. Daily we see advertisements for an open position as director of physical education and/or athletics (or some variation thereof) at all educational levels. The people who hold these posts have assumed many of the earmarks of a "profession within a profession within a profession." This may sound ridiculous, but managers do now have professional associations within a larger group of people that has professional associations--and yet we are often considered members of the teaching profession (a really gigantic group of largely professional people).

Having said this, it is important to keep in mind that a recognized profession should have an organized body of knowledge based on research. This is only one of the necessary criteria, of course, but it is fundamental to the perpetuation of our "species"--the administrator or manager of physical education and athletics. It is basic, therefore, that some organizational structure be developed within educational institutions through which a body of professional knowledge can be determined and then transmitted to those who express a desire to choose this field as a career.

If the above statements are reasonable, then let us review briefly how managers of physical education and athletics received their preparation for this often demanding and tenuous position in the past. Generally speaking, many, if not all, of these men and women worked their way up through the ranks in some sort of an apprenticeship scheme (especially if we can consider the position of head coach in a gate-receipt sport as fitting into this category). One basic prerequisite seems to be that they themselves were interested and active in sport and related physical activities. Quite often, as well, they were physical education majors and took at least one course at both the undergraduate and graduate levels that were of an administrative nature. In some cases, and especially in the case of men, they were not physical education majors in college (perhaps because such a program was not offered), but later decided to cast their lots with our field because of successful competitive athletic experiences. Especially important, furthermore, has been the fact that these people often demonstrated what were recognized then as fine personality and leadership traits. They knew how to get along with most people, they made fine appearances, they knew how to get things done, they were willing to work very hard when the occasion demanded, and they believed strongly in the importance of sport and related physical activity.

It is important to understand that the "preparation" of
managers in this fashion is not unique to the field of physical
education and athletics. If we were to trace the history of
professional programs in many other fields, a similar circum-
stance prevailed--whether we are considering medicine, law, or
engineering earlier or other fields where administrators are
needed regularly to manage the many programs in existence
then and now (e.g., business, education, hospital administration). Interestingly, we find a contrast here when we examine
the recognized academic disciplines in colleges and universities.
Administrators are picked typically on the basis of scholarly
and research endeavor--and more recently because they choose
to be available for one or more reasons. Often they possess
certain desirable personality traits as well, but it must be
stated that search committees by their very make-up seem to
disagree on the nature of the basic "desirable traits," or else
select administrators based on insufficient evidence.

Mistrust of Administrative Theory

Despite the efforts of a small but dedicated cadre of individuals within the field during the past fifteen years, there is
very little evidence at the time of this writing that administrators of physical education and athletics, either in practice or in
administration courses, are truly concerned with the theoretical
aspects of administration or management. (To put this statement in perspective, we would define management as the execution of managerial acts, involving conceptual, technical, human,
and conjoined skills, while combining varying degree of planning, organizing, staffing, directing, and controlling within the
management process to assist an organization to achieve its
goals.)

Thus, we find a very peculiar situation in existence at
the present. Many people seem to be ready to apply for managerial posts, but they somehow don't see any necessity for
formal preparation prior to the acceptance of a position that
would seem to require administrative competency. In fact, a
further paradoxical situation arises in our field at the college or
university level primarily when one is imprudent enough to discuss such a thing as "administrative theory." The paradox
arises because the field seems very definitely to be divided into
two groups--a situation that we fervently hope will change during the 1980s because of the various social forces impinging upon us--neither of which can see the need or importance of such
a subject as management. These two groups might be labeled
as the "practitioners" and the "scholars and scientists." The
practitioners can't see the need for management theory (the old
"sounds good in theory argument, but it would never work in

9

practice gambit"). Conversely, the scholars and scientists would relegate it to limbo for its "softness" and nonscientific quality. To put it another way, the practical administrator will make an approach work whether it's sound theory or not, while the scholar tends to view management as merely vocational in nature and suggest that research in this field is basically "second-class stuff."

A Revised Approach to Management Education

This volume is predicated on the belief that the field of physical education and sport is long overdue to revise its approach to management education. Twenty-five years have now elapsed since we began to develop a text in which the case-method approach of teaching human relations and administration was introduced to the profession for the first time. At that point we recognized that change and improvement was needed, but we had not yet fully understood what the impact of the behavioral sciences was going to be. Now we are fully convinced that we should be preparing people carefully and thoroughly for the "assumption of the administrative risk," but within higher education especially we are not seeing sufficient awareness on the part of selection committee members that a candidate for a managerial post should meet certain criteria before being permitted to manage a department, division, school, or college. The trial-and-error management approach in which the leader functions by habit, hunch, and common sense--sometimes called the "seat of the pants approach"--has not yet become a thing of the past. A field such as sport and physical education should truly decide that it is vitally important to prepare men and women professionally as managers. Presently we view it as almost a cardinal sin the way scholars and researchers--fully developed or prospective--are "drained away" from sorely needed academic endeavors to often become inadequate, "seat-of-the-pants, paper-shufflers."

As we move ahead with improvements in our pattern of management education, it is necessary that we strive for agreement of the meanings of administrative concepts that appear regularly in the developing body-of-knowledge that is mushrooming in related disciplines investigating administrative theory and practice. More than a decade has passed since Penny's study showed that significant differences (with respect to the meanings associated with selected concepts typically employed in management literature) existed between professors of educational administration and physical education and sport administrators-- and even those who taught administration courses in physical education and athletics. Improved ordinary language and more sophisticated professional language terms will be needed to express the basic concepts precisely. Obviously, this need will become even more urgent as systematized knowledge about organizational phenomena is developed (Penny, 1968).

Further, as we examine the occasionally appearing reviews of physical education and sport research, administration has typically been included within the article or monograph. Even today much of the literature still reflects the traditional (normative) era of administrative thought which stressed the teaching of "principles" of administration. Typical theses and dissertations have been peripheral insofar as behavioral, decisional, and ecological approaches are concerned. Still further, various inventories of scientific findings about human behavior, leadership, problem-solving, and decision-making are available to us, but somehow they are not typically being used either by practicing managers or by those who are teaching the undergraduate or graduate courses in management theory and practice in the field. Finally, if there are hypothetical (theoretical) statements that may be shown to be true about the most effective means of organizing and managing programs in physical education and athletics, it seems quite safe to say that the validity and reliability of these statements has not yet been demonstrated to any reasonable degree by this profession. Value-free investigation of an applied nature is needed to give tenable management theory in this specialized field to those who are actually administering the various programs of a public, semi-public or semi-private, and private nature--and perhaps also to make our contribution to the growing body-of-knowledge about the subject generally.

Management Education in "Third Wave" Society

At this point, you may not be fully convinced about the need for greatly improved management education in this field. If this is true, it seems wise at this point to mention briefly Toffler's 'Third Wave' concept that has been spawned as an aftermath of his earlier futuristic volume. Paradoxically, just when we are criticizing this field for its lack of orientation to what he identifies as "The Second Wave," along comes his prediction that Second Wave society will be gradually but steadily-- and undoubtedly too rapidly for some--be superseded by "the Third Wave of change." He states that,

> Today, as the Third Wave of change begins to batter at this fortress of managerial power, the first fleeting cracks are appearing in the power system. Demands for participation in management, for shared decision-making, for worker, consumer, and citizen control,

11

and for anticipatory democracy are welling up in nation after nation. New ways of organizing along less hierarchical and more ad-hocratic lines are sprung up in the most advanced industries . . . All these are merely early warnings--indicators of the coming upheaval in the political system (Toffler, 1981, pp. 67-68).

It is impossible to predict what the future will be like, of course, but at this point all indications are pointing toward greater involvement of all concerned in the decision-making process. For example, we have recently witnessed the gradual introduction of more, not less, involvement of workers from the lower echelons in decision-making in such productive countries as the Federal Republic of Germany and Japan (the so-called Theory Z approach in the latter case). Thus, as we mentioned earlier, in our opinion the introduction of the case plan of instruction can serve as the "missing link" insofar as involvement of students in the discussion and the decision-making process were concerned.

Concluding Statement

The success of the case method of teaching human relations and decision-making in managment would appear to negate considerably the value of a deductive approach to the study of this subject. Rather than starting with established principles and prying into their nature to arrive at the identity of the specific facts, the case method of decision-making works more from facts, half-facts, and opinions to general truths or concepts. Alternative courses of action are postulated, and then a course of action is selected, based on the best evidence available and a weighing of the pro's and con's of the course of action chosen. Finally, currently useful generalizations can be determined that are carried forward for orientation to similar problems that arise in the future. (Of course, these can never be applied precisely or exactly.)

Our field has not yet discovered for itself whether management is an art or a science; consequently, we have covered only superficially the "energizing" forces used by the administrator. The main idea of this volume is to suggest how greatly the administrative process is governed by the personality of the administrator. Further, we believe that decision-making through the case method approach offers an approach to the teaching of human relations and management that will indeed be appropriate for the rest of this century--and possibly on into Third Wave society about which Toffler has alerted us. Certainly there have been deficiencies in the "traditional" approaches, and it is also quite possible that the question of human relations may rule out forever a completely scientific treatment of management. From what has been stated to this point, it should be completely obvious that we are recommending that the the reader give serious consideration to the employment of this approach to decision-making in sport and physical education management. That which follows will offer you a sound beginning and, if you give it a fair chance, we believe that you will find the experience most enjoyable as well. Good luck/bonne chance.

References

Gordon, P. J.: Transcend the current debate on administrative theory. Hospital Administration, 11, 2:6-23, 1966.

Gross, B. M.: The Managing of Organizations, vols. 1 and 2. New York: Crowell-Collier Publishing Company, 1964.

Halpin, A. W.: The development of theory in educational administration. In Administrative Theory in Education. A. W. Halpin (Ed.). Chicago: Midwest Administration Center, The University of Chicago, 1958.

Litchfield, E. H.: Notes on a general theory of administration. Administrative Science Quarterly, 1, 7, 1956.

Penny, W. J.: "An analysis of the meanings attached to selected concepts in administrative theory." Ph.D. diss., University of Illinois, Urbana, 1968.

Toffler, A.: The Third Wave. New York: Bantam Books, 1981.

Zeigler, E. F., and Spaeth, M. H. (Eds.): Administrative Theory and Practice in Physical Education and Athletics. Englewood Cliffs, N. J.: Prentice-Hall, Inc., 1975.

CHAPTER 2

CURRENTLY USEFUL GENERALIZATIONS ABOUT PHYSICAL EDUCATION AND ATHLETICS

As an approach to the actual analysis of the cases in this book, it seems advisable to categorize to some extent the various administrative problem areas that may be encountered. To put forth firm principles for guidance in the solution of the many problems with which teachers, coaches, sport coordinators, athletic directors, and others will be confronted would be a mistake. This would convey the idea that there are pat answers, immutable and unchangeable. Although it may sound "wishy-washy" to some, we believe it is much more practical and realistic to describe here what we have chosen to call "currently useful generalizations." (This term was used more than a quarter of a century ago by M. P. McNair and A. S. Hersum, the editors of a volume called The Case Method at the Harvard Business School. New York: McGraw-Hill Book Co., Inc., 1954, p. 10.)

This chapter concisely summarizes "currently useful generalizations" concerning the management of physical education and athletics (or sport and physical education--a newer term). If this material seems reasonable, generally speaking, the credit should go to the author to a limited degree, but it belongs largely to the many administrators and managers working in this field whose experience and insight have enabled them to gather and report a large body of knowledge upon which this chapter is based. Those deficiencies which may seem apparent when the reader attempts to apply these "generalizations" to specific problems may be caused by this author's inability to reflect correctly what others have said or written, by his own inability to generalize personal experience adequately, or by the peculiarities of the particular situation to which they are being applied at present. The following statements may sound authoritative and definitive, but they should be challenged by the manager as he or she applies them to problems that arise on the job (or to the extent that they are used in the analysis of the cases that follow).

Consider the total program of physical education and athletics. You may be able to suggest additional categories, or to combine or eliminate some of the following areas recommended as a point of departure:

1. Aims and Objectives
2. Medical Examination
3. Classification for Physical Activity
4. Relationship to Health Education (an allied profession)
5. Relationship to Safety Education (an allied profession)
6. Relationship to Recreation (Education)--(an allied profession)
7. Relationship to Dance (an allied profession)
8. Instructional Program (sport, dance, and exercise required or elective)
9. Special Physical Education (including therapeutic exercise and adapted sports)
10. Intramural Athletics
11. Voluntary Exercise and Physical Recreation Program
12. Sport Clubs
13. Interscholastic and Intercollegiate Athletics
14. Undergraduate Professional Programs
15. Graduate Study and Research Programs
16. The Managerial Process (planning, organizing, staffing, directing, and controlling)
17. A Systems Approach to Management
18. Internal and External Environments (including organizational climate, public relations, instructional methodology, discipline, etc.)
19. Various Technical Concerns (including finance & budget, legal matters, facilities & equipment, etc.)
20. Professional Ethics
21. Evaluation and Measurement

Aims and Objectives

The determination of aims and objectives seems basic. A philosophy of life and/or religion should coincide with a philosophy of education and with a philosophy of sport and physical education. In the latter instance, developmental physical activity includes human motor performance in sport, dance, play, and exercise from the beginning to the end of the human's life.

Thinking should be logical and consistent, and the beliefs of a professional manager in this field should not conflict in any fundamental way with professional practice in public, semi-public or semi-private, or private agencies. A recognized professional person in this field should be operating on the basis of the "currently useful generalizations" for which he or she stands. These generalizations should coincide with the generalizations that have been accepted for professional practice by the recognized professional society. It is on this basis that a person is certified as a professional practitioner by the state or province in which he or she resides.

If one calls principles "generalization," this does not mean that he or she does not believe anything--far from it! It does mean that this individual will guide his or her actions according to what appears to be best at the moment, realizing that it is most often practical to work from specific objectives toward general aims. Expediency may cause a sport and physical education manager to sidetrack some of his less vital beliefs momentarily, but this does not mean that he or she must perforce lose sight of what is believed to be ultimately right.

In this culture it is obviously impossible for those in the field of sport and physical education to agree on one basic philosophy. Obviously, there will always be at least several leading schools of thought and a number of lesser ones. Although our individual sets of beliefs should be expressed by us explicitly, and we convey them implicitly by our daily actions, truly definitive sport and physical education philosophies are very rare. In the United States in this century, outstanding leaders like C. H. McCloy (Iowa), J. F. Williams (Columbia), and J. B. Nash (New York University) accomplished a great deal in helping to crystallize professional thinking. The times being what they are, leaders of this calibre are not being permitted to emerge in any field of endeavor today.

Although physical education and sport as a field is making an effort to achieve a stronger scholarly and scientific base, this greater thrust that really started in the early 1960's has not been given sufficient backing from any quarter. Ultimately, of course, science and philosophy should have complementary roles to play in aiding the field to find its proper place in the educational system, as well as in the society at large. Thus, in addition to its function of analysis whereby philosophy can serve science in what some might consider to be a "handmaiden" fashion, a philosophic orientation should help the field to consider its basic problems in a systematic fashion. For example, it is especially important at present that the professional practitioner in sport and physical education view the field as a whole. We should be seeing ourselves not merely as athletic coaches, gymnasium instructors, exercise scientists, aquatic specialists, sports administrators of various types, commercial fitness promoters, or what have you.

We are arguing, therefore, that a philosophical orientation experience at the undergraduate level would help the aspiring professional to fashion a mental image of what the field should be. It should be prospective, in the sense that it forms a vanguard, leading rather than following actual practice. Although many view the conscious assumption of a philosophy about anything as being too highly theoretical for their level of intelligence, such thought has actually become a "snare and delusion" for the majority. We all start to develop implicit philosophies about the world at some point in the wombs of our mothers, so why should we be so frightened at the thought of striving for an explicit expression of our beliefs? Such a philosophy must ultimately be practical, of course, or it would be worthless in the final analysis. An instrumental philosophy would necessarily imitate science in part, but only as it serves a plan for action. Science can strive to describe the field as it is; philosophy should aim to picture it as it should be. With this idea firmly in mind, philosophy can be an excellent complement to science; it reaches and points toward the world of tomorrow.

At this time it appears most urgent that the sport and physical education profession take strong, positive steps to achieve a significant amount of consensus among the various philosophies of sport and physical education extant in the world. This seems especially important because the field is bound to be caught up with the communications revolution taking place in the last half of the twentieth century. Some possible common denominators are as follows:

1. That regular physical education and sport periods should be required for all children and young people through sixteen years of age (approximately).

2. That sport and physical education professionals should cooperate with those serving in the all allied profession of health education to help children develop certain positive attitudes toward their own health in particular and toward community hygiene in general. Basic health knowledge should be taught in the school curriculum by qualified personnel.

3. That purposeful human motor performance in sport, dance, exercise, and play, as taught by qualified professional practitioners in sport and physical education, can make a worthwhile contribution to the use of leisure throughout a

person's life. (In this regard the profession of sport and physical education should work cooperatively with the allied recreation profession.)

4. That physical vigor is important for people of all ages. Such activity should be integrated in a program that includes activities promoting circulo-respiratory endurance, flexibility, muscle tonus, and segmental alignment of bodily parts (when the body is at rest or in motion).

5. That boys and girls at some stage of their development should have experience in competitive sports (varsity, intramural, or adapted).

6. That therapeutic exercise should be employed to the greatest extent possible to correct remediable physical defects. (Here the field should work cooperatively with the allied professions of medicine and physiotherapy.)

7. That character and/or personality development may be fostered through fine programs of physical education and athletics. (Adapted from Zeigler, 1977)

Viewed as explained above, sport and physical education philosophy can be one part of an overall education (which in turn can be part of overall life philosophy. Many hold the view that a philosophy of life is basic to a philosophy of education. It can be considered also as basic to a philosophy of sport and physical education, be this part of the educational system or a part of one's total life process. With this approach the establishment of a person's fundamental beliefs is part of the experience an individual should undergo. One's implicit philosophy of life is gradually but steadily made more explicit as a vital element of the maturation process. A philosophy of education, as one subdivision of the total stance, should develop similarly and flow from this undergirding set of beliefs. A blended series of beliefs about the place of sport and physical education throughout a person's life cannot help but be roughly analogous as it flows from fundamental beliefs while being applied to the role of purposeful human motor performance in the developmental physical activities of sport, dance, play, and exercise. A field that now appears to have so many sharp divisions should search mightily for philosophical consensus that will permit the profession to fulfill its potential in society. All can readily agree that the physical education and athletics administrator will not be in a position to exert his or her greatest influence, if this person occupying a key role in the organization does not have as logical and consistent a set of aims and objectives as possible for the field--as part of an overall philosophy of life.

Medical Examination (Relationship with Medicine, an allied profession)

For our purposes in physical education and athletics, the medical examination is essential before anything else is attempted. In a sense, therefore, the entire program of sport and physical education or any part thereof should hinge on the findings of a medical examination. It is at this point that a vital relationship begins with the medical profession and the 'health sciences' concept. Basically, our profession can only proceed to provide its services if the results of a complete medical examination have been made available. In an intelligently conceived program of physical education and athletics, the selection of any activities to be included must be determined after an assessment of the person's health status has been made. For the safety, protection, and well-being of all concerned, some basic items of medical information should be on record before any strenuous physical activity is begun. We hold no brief as to whether the board of education or a duly appointed board of health has the responsibility for this aspect of health services. We do believe, however, that the responsibility for the health of the child should not be divided because of inherent weaknesses in such an arrangement.

The medical examination itself serves more functions than is generally realized. In addition to diagnosis of defects, and the subsequent notification of the individual, parents, guardian, etc., the school or university health authorities should strive to secure correction of remediable defects where possible by careful guidance of the person involved. Each individual should be helped to develop a scientific attitude toward bodily ailments. Our profession's relationship with health education, as an allied profession, will be discussed below. At this point we merely wish to stress the need for a comprehensive medical examination of sufficient depth so that the physician may inform the physical education and athletics administrator how assignment for physical activities may be made. Further, this is especially important where there is a physical education and sport requirement. Of course, it is not possible to dictate to members of another profession the exact way in which the individual must be classified for assignment or involvement with physical activity that comes under the jurisdiction of the physical education and

19

athletics unit, but it is usually possible to arrange for some rating scheme similar to that which follows:

A ---- No defects (unlimited physical activity)

B ---- Minor defect (unlimited physical activity, but consideration should be given to the defect)

C ---- Moderate defects (may or may not be disabling; restricted activity)

D ---- Serious defects (either exempt from activity or highly specialized, reconstructive activity)

Students given the rating of A or B would be considered fit for normal activity and would subsequently be scheduled for the series of physical education and sport classification tests that have been planned by the department. Students with a C or D rating would be assigned to Special Physical Education and individual counselling.

In addition to the suggested rating scale for the consideration of the school or university health service--a scale that is based on the intensity of physical activities offered--it would be desirable to employ an additional scale based on type of activity. Such a scale might be employed to aid the teacher/coach to make an even finer distinction of activities for use in individual exercise prescription as follows:

I ---- Unlimited competitive activity
II ---- Competitive activity (non-contact)
III ---- Individual or dual, non-competitive activity
IV ---- Therapeutic exercise
V ---- Aquatics only

Still further, if it is possible to have the person examined orthopedically, some sort of a static postural rating might be assigned as follows:

a ---- Excellent posture and mechanics

b ---- Good posture (minor mechanical defects)

c ---- Fair posture (one or more observable defects that require remedial or therapeutic exercise)

d ---- Poor posture (serious postural problem requiring the attention of an orthopedic surgeon)

It should be kept in mind, of course, that a static body mechanics examination only tells part of the story. An analysis of segmental alignment while the body is in motion would provide a much broader base upon which more sound advice might be offered.

Obviously, the availability of a composite of three types of ratings described above would place the physical education and athletics administrator in an ideal position to plan a fine overall program of human motor performance based on a reasonably detailed appraisal of the medical status of all involved.

Classification for Physical Activity

After the examining physician has informed the physical education and sport teacher if the student is completely healthy (A), almost healthy (B), in need of special physical education (C), or capable only of highly specialized, perhaps reconstructive activity (D), the teacher should test and classify those in the A and B categories (and perhaps those in C where advisable and/or possible) according to the objectives of the school, college, or university program concerned. Testing, measuring, and evaluating are necessary in order to prove to administrators, supervisors, students, and the public that many of our children and young people are physically "illiterate" (a misnomer, of course, but one that seems to make the point). Why do we evaluate through the use of classification or proficiency tests? Franks and Deutsch explain that "the purpose of tests and measurements is much broader than grading. Besides being administered to assess student performance and/or progress, test scores also give the teacher insight into the validity of his methods" (1973, p. 3).

At this point, of course, we are thinking of the testing that should occur at the outset of the program. These purposes were enunciated clearly and specifically many years ago by Williams and Brownell in their classical text as follows:

1. To serve their individual needs.
2. To promote fair competition between individuals and groups.
3. To facilitate instruction.
4. To assemble individuals of like interests as well as like abilities.
5. To insure continuity in the program from year to year (1951, p. 101).

A battery of physical education and sport classification tests should include items which the department considers that most students should be able to pass within the time allotted by by the school to physical education and sport requirements. Every effort should be made to select the tests used on the basis of such recognized, desirable standards as validity, reliability, objectivity, simplicity, standardization of procedure, availability of duplicate forms, and worthwhileness. Certain test items are often considered to be of greater importance to the development of the individual than others. If the student is not able to meet the minimum standard set for any part or all of the test battery, he/she might be required to select activities in the order that the department recommends as best for him or her as a person. For example, if a person were "below standard" in swimming, body mechanics, motor fitness, self-defense, and basic movement skills, it might be required that these deficiencies be corrected in that specific order which the department of physical education and sport deems best. The department's philosophy should reflect the thinking of the best leadership in the field, as well as that of educational administration, boards of education, the staff of the department, the parents, and the students themselves. The ultimate responsibility in North America rests with the state or province in which the program is offered, but it should be expected that the profession itself would set high standards by which the political unit would be guided.

The department should consider classification and proficiency tests in the following categories:

1. Age-height-weight tests
2. Circulo-respiratory tests
3. Body mechanics tests
4. Motor fitness tests
5. Leisure sports (indoor and outdoor)
6. Self-defense tests
7. Rhythmic movement skills tests
8. Health and sports knowledge and appreciations tests

Obviously, the work of the physical education and sport administrator has only begun when a battery of tests has been selected and administered. When the tests have been carefully scored, rated, and appraised, the program needs of all the students can be evaluated. An ideal program would provide counseling sessions as soon as it is practical so that the students will be able to understand and interpret the results. Such testing should take place at appropriate intervals so that the progress of the student can be measured and evaluated.

While a new student is being oriented to the program, he or she could be permitted to begin immediately with some form of enjoyable physical recreational activity. In this way the student may well develop good attitudes concerning the continuing value of this type of activity. Of course, it is possible that the activity the person chooses could coincide with some deficiency demonstrated by the classification tests. Even if a decision is made that the student will be required (as a result of a certain classification test) to take certain basic conditioning work for developmental purposes, it is strongly urged that the individual be given instruction and the chance for enjoyable participation in a sports activity at the same time.

Relationship to Health Education (an allied profession)

It has now been clearly established in the United States, and there is steady movement in the same direction in Canada, that there is a developing health education profession separate and distinct from physical education within the educational system. This is not to say, of course, that in many places all over the continent people don't think of health and physical education as being relatively synonymous. Further, is every likelihood that physical educators will for some time to come be asked to assume the "health education responsibility" in certain elementary and secondary school systems. However, for a number of reasons there is strong logic behind the change of the name of the American Association for Health, Physical Education, and Recreation to the American Alliance for Health, Physical Education, Recreation, and Dance--i.e., a number of allied professions working together with both common goals for all, and yet maintaining their development as separate professions.

The field of school health education, as part of a larger health education movement, moved ahead rapidly and soundly since the stage was set initially by the draft statistics of World War I. It was realized by many that sound preventive health measures during the school years might have warded off both physical and mental health defects. To help matters along, the 1920's were years in which there was enough money available to begin to remedy the situation. School health education was accepted in the curriculum rather widely, and its inclusion was bolstered by early research and publications.

The total educational program suffered a severe setback in the 1930's because of the financial depression. As so often happens, subject matters most recently added to the curriculum are eliminated first. Fortunately, for health education at least, understanding of the relatively low level of physical and mental health brought support to school health education as the country began to emerge from its financial plight. Professional preparation in school health education grew stronger in the 1930's, and increased stature was the inevitable result as better-prepared teachers appeared in the field.

Since 1940 there has been, generally speaking, steady expansion and consolidation in the area of school health education. No matter which educational philosophy is being espoused, it is difficult to argue against the idea of a positive approach to the matter of individual and community health. As the United States moved from war to war (and crisis to crisis), deficiencies of all types in the national health picture came to the fore. There has been a continuing array of national conferences held to meet matters of urgent concern which arose. Separate health education curricula have been established in colleges and universities, as opposed to the earlier (almost automatic) combination health and physical education major programs. (It must be stated, however, that many physical educators continued to minor in school health education, or at least elected a few courses from school health education options because they knew that there was a strong possibility that they would be asked to assume some responsibility in this area if they accepted teaching positions.)

Recently the idea has emerged that health should be a separate and distinct subject in the school curriculum, rather than a subsidiary subject "tied to the apron strings" of the physical educator/coach (a man or woman who has typically been a generalist and not truly qualified to teach what has become a most complex subject if taught adequately). Additionally, it has become obvious that specialized options or areas of specialization within the burgeoning field of health should be offered. The question of the alignment of these educational offerings with the health sciences entity of universities demands further consideration. This type of thinking appears to be leading to independent professionalization, separate and stronger state legislation to include health education in the curriculum, and different types of alliance and federation with the field of sport and physical education and the field of recreation and parks management (Zeigler, in Read, 1971, pp. 70-71).

a. Health services. Health service today implies determining the student's health status, informing parents of any defects that exist, educating parents and offspring in the prevention of common defects, aiding the teacher/coach to detect symptoms of illness, and helping to correct defects which are remediable.

Although it took many years for boards of education to realize that schools must be concerned with more than illiteracy, as the educational philosophy pendulum swings back and forth there are still those who demand a return to the "good old days" when reading, writing, and arithmetic dominated the curriculum completely. Obviously, the achievement of a certain level of competency in these subjects is basic, but the situation has become ever so much more complex than previously. The new educational era demands that the school take unto itself practically all of the child's problems. Today, if conditions are ideal, the physician, medical specialist, nurse, dentist, school psychologist, psychiatrist, nutritionist, teacher/coach, and janitor all have a part in the over-all job of keeping the child healthy (not to forget the all-important fundamental role of the parent/guardian).

It is difficult to know where board of education responsibility for health services leaves off and where board of health control begins. Cooperation between these two public agencies is most important, of course, but any such arrangement usually has its weaknesses either because of the managerial table of organization or the personalities involved. The fact that it is not possible for either agency to set policy which encroaches on the other's sphere of operation indicates that the responsibility for the health of the child (from the standpoint of the society-at-large, that is) should not be divided at this level.

"Medical inspection" was the term formerly used for the medical examination of today. What is the school's responsibility for health appraisal? Will such responsibility change if and when universal health insurance programs are adopted? What type of medical examination should there be? How often should it be carried out? Who should look after the correction of remediable defects? What should the relationship be between school psychological services and the overall school health program? Who should maintain the health and accident records? What is the best plan for emergency care?

The medical examination itself serves more functions than is generally realized. In addition to diagnosis of defects and subsequent notification of parents in an official manner, the school health authorities should strive to secure correction of remediable defects by careful guidance of the children involved. Each child must be helped to develop a scientific attitude toward bodily ailments and their possible correction.

Having established the importance of the medical examination, we should ask ourselves some questions about the actual examination that the children receive. Is the parent invited to be present so that the physician can explain at least some of the findings at that time? Is the homeroom teacher present at some point to learn more about the child for future guidance? Is the examination sufficiently complete and detailed? Too often, physicians are placed in situations where they are so rushed in the performance of their duties that the child receives only a more-or-less perfunctory check-up.

It cannot be argued that a carefully maintained health record is superfluous in the development of a child. To be sure, limited budgets may restrict the adequacy of any such record to a degree. On the other hand, it is extremely important that the child receive the services of various health and educational experts. To get a complete picture of the child, many things must be known about his/her environment, disease record, scholastic ability, social adjustment, and health practices. Health services should be involved with the appraisal, correction, and continuing protection of children throughout their years in the educational system.

b. Health instruction. Health instruction is the second of the three subdivisions of school health education. Should health instruction be a separate, distinct subject-matter area within the school curriculum? What should a course in school health education include? What about the introduction of controversial topics such as explicit sex education instruction? What type of articulation should be developed among the elementary school, the middle school, and the high school? What should the role of the physical educator/coach be (e.g., who should teach school health education--the physical educator/coach, a health education specialist, a physician, a bio-science teacher, a school nurse?). How much time should be devoted to what is known as mental health? Is a health coordinator necessary in a school?

The health instruction class is a perennial problem that has rarely been resolved adequately in the past. Facts about personal and community health have undoubtedly become a considerable part of the knowledge of how to live. Most important, of course, is that school health education should be a positive influence on behalf of what might be termed "vibrant health." For example, although the large majority of people know that regular medical examinations are advisable, a large percentage of the population maintain their bodies in much poorer conditions than they do their automobiles. Most people have their cars' oil and filters changed regularly, but they persist in waiting for pain before going to the physician or dentist.

Down through the years, health instruction has generally been taught somewhat poorly. Just as in the case of a certain amount of physical education, parents realized that even a larger number of health education courses were next to useless. This is not to say that the health knowledge itself was unimportant, inaccurate, or out-of-date--although it often was--it was more a question of the way it was taught, and the lack of enthusiasm that resulted from what should have been a useful experience. As a result of this, now people must be convinced that school health education deserves a priority when curriculum decisions are being made. No matter who teaches this important subject, its importance can be proved only if positive attitude change results. A modern problem-solving approach should be incorporated as an important teaching technique. For example, here is one area where the case method of instruction could be employed to advantage.

To conclude, health instruction must be more than just the teaching of the so-called principles and facts of healthful living. For example, the drawing or exhibition of the various systems of the body and the blackboard or wall with subsequent superficial explanation will simply not do. Youngsters are typically far too healthy to sense the need for mastery of health facts. School health education should have as its goal the integration of updated book-knowledge with actual living achievement. This is no mean task, and it deserves the full-time attention of a well-prepared school health education specialist. The curriculum objectives should be spelled out from the standpoint of specific knowledge, competencies, and skills to be achieved during the entire public education experience. Our ultimate goal is the motivation of children and young people to motivate them to employ such knowledge and attitudes so that they will live life to its fullest individually. At the same time we need adults who will subsequently use this healthful vigor to serve society to the greatest possible extent.

c. Healthful school living. Healthful school living itself can be subdivided into three categories; the conditions of the school environment, the conditions of the classroom experience, and the conditions of school organization. As we usually find school construction in all stages of development, the school building itself demands serious, ongoing consideration. The taxpayer and parent must be shown that the demands of health and those of architectural beauty do not inevitably clash. And if they do, the students themselves should have first priority. The school plant must be both hygienic and beautiful if the student is to have the best educational opportunities. Although plans should be made for schools to be as close to the geographical center of population as possible, due thought should also be given to adequate size of building and surrounding area, as well as to hygienic environment and the student's safety.

Conditions of the classroom experience are important, a also. For example, what about the problem of discipline? Should the teacher attempt to dominate the students by sheer will power, as some seem to believe it is necessary to act in this fashion? We often hear people say that "such-and-such" needs a strong leader? What do they mean by that--someone who seeks to "strike fear into the hearts" of the children or young people? What responsibility do we have to help young people develop their own standards of behavior? Can we agree that the end of all discipline is intelligent self-direction--and even that the possession of such competency has an important place even in much of the work of the armed forces? Further, don't we need to consider such factors as undue fatigue, success and failure, noise and excitement, sedentariness, the hygiene of reading, and individual differences?

The actual conditions of school organization plan an important role in healthful school living. Is there a proper balance in the school among work, play, rest, and the taking of nourishment? For example, to what extent have we realized the educational potentialities of the school lunch by considering the adequacy of the cafeteria, time allowed for eating, economics of the project, student participation in conduct rules, and health supervision of lunchroom employees?

Is the school curriculum properly divided, keeping in mind that most students are more efficient mentally in the morning? (There may well be a relationship to the climate here, of course.) Should the general tone of the young person's day be "hurry"? For example, are students expected to change into gym clothes, experience a meaningful period of instruction with some time for practice and free play, and take a soap shower and dress--all in thirty-two minutes? Do teachers and administrators seem hurried and often a bit frantic? What supervision is there over the health of teachers and others so important to the entire school experience? Modern society is so rushed that a conscious effort should be made to slow down the daily tempo of the entire school program.

Relationship to Safety Education (an allied profession)

Few people would argue against the concept of 'safety' and all that this implies in a school or university setting. It is difficult to know where to place the responsibility for the safety program within the educational system. We have often heard the term "healthy and safety education" used in connection with programs or departments at the school or college levels. The responsibility for driver education often rests with the public schools, and yet there are many situations where private agencies are most active in this regard. Somehow safety education has been quite closely identified with the field of physical education during this century, although it can also be said that the field has gradually but steadily achieved recognition and independent status. Logically, except for the fact that many sport and developmental physical activity areas provide opportunities accidents, there is probably no more legitimate justification for attempting to place the responsibility for safety instruction on the physical educator/coach than on the chemistry instructor or the instructor in what has been called industrial arts. The teacher in any subject-matter area ought to know first aid as well, and could presumably be as well prepared for driver training work as any other person involved.

It should be understood that these preliminary statements are in no way intended to demean or ascribe lesser importance to safety education or driver training--far from it. In our highly complex society, there is most certainly a place for placing the field of safety education on a par with the recognized professions (all of which have achieved greater or lesser status based on their determination, acceptance, and achievement of certain established criteria). Thus, even though the word "safety" does not appear in the title of the American Alliance for Health, Physical Education, Recreation, and Dance, we are fully prepared to accord its status within our group of allied professions. The administrator or manager of physical education and athletics ignores the development of a full-fledged safety program within his or her departmental or divisional structure at the risk of great harm to young people in some phase of the program (not to mention claims for liability against himself/herself or the system because of lack of foresight and/or actual negligence).

All of this adds up to the fact that the administrator of physical education and athletics has a direct responsibility in this aspect of the school's program as at least a member of the school's health and safety council (and occasionally serving as chairperson of such a council if the school does not have a pro-professionally prepared specialist in these areas). It is simply not reasonable to expect that a school safety program can be carried out in a hit-or-miss fashion. Accidental deaths of school age children from five to fourteen years of age total more than 10,000 each year. The leading cause of death for children from ages one to fourteen is accidental injury, and undoubtedly many of these deaths occur because of inadequate or non-existent school safety programs. Further, with the exception of respiratory infections, accidental injuries are the leading cause of disability in this age group. About three out of five school accidents occur in organized activities, with the classroom, physical education and sport areas, and the streets as the typically sites on an overall basis (Oberteuffer, et al., 1973, pp. 339-340).

A safety council should include administrators, teachers, staff members, and students. Its responsibility extends in a variety of directions and includes emergency care, fire drills, traffic safety and supervision, safety education, visual materials, building and grounds inspection for hazards, the school bus program, rules and regulations regarding the safe use of buildings and grounds, and the driver training program. All employees need to understand exactly what constitutes safe practices in all areas in which the school has responsibility and what constitutes negligence on their part. Adequate liability insurance is an absolute necessity, and this program should be reviewed each year. From this brief discussion, it should be evident how vitally important it is for the development of an adequate safety program in every school and university. It should also be apparent that the administrator of physical education and athletics should be knowledgeable in this important area, but should hardly be expected to be an authority or to exert unusual leadership. Safety education has indeed become an allied profession of the sport and physical education profession, and we in this field look forward to an ongoing, developing relationship with this important field in our society.

Relationship to Recreation (an allied profession)

Before leisure could be used in North America, it had to be earned. Furthermore, certain prevailing ideas about idleness had to be broken down. Neither of these occurrences took place overnight. Recreational patterns have gradually emerged as the United States and Canada have grown and prospered. Inititally, people oriented their own recreational pursuits in an unorganized fashion. Following this, all types of commercial recreational opportunities were made available, some of dubious value. And, finally, public and voluntary agencies were created to meet the recreational needs and interests of the populace. These patterns of recreation are now proceeding concurrently in the latter years of the twentieth century, and careful analysis is most difficult.

Despite steady inflation, from an economic standpoint we now find ourselves in a much more favorable situation than previously. The average work week has been cut almost in half since the turn of the century, although rising costs have forced many people to "moonlight" with a second job. In other instances, because of inflation and changing life styles, wives have become breadwinners to keep total income at a level where a "reasonable" level of material prosperity could be maintained. The above notwithstanding, many people--earlier or later in their lives--are now choosing leisure instead of more work because they want to "enjoy life." Many others, often disadvantaged and/or displaced, are forced to accept an increased amount of leisure along with welfare and/or unemployment benefit payments, although they do not have all of the material possessions of life that they might wish to have.

For some countries, including the United States and Canada, the twentieth century has been characterized by the greatest surplus economy the world has ever seen. We have accordingly witnessed a vast new development that may now be called an organized recreation pattern. In the past fifty years the development of public and voluntary agency recreation, not to mention commercial recreation, has been absolutely phenomenal. As these social and economic changes have taken place, professional recreation associations have developed; professional preparation for recreational leadership has mushroomed; and municipal recreation and parks programs along with community centers in schools form a network across the United States and Canada (adapted from Zeigler, 1968, pp. 98-99).

The relationship between physical education and athletics and the recreation profession merits ongoing consideration and nurture. Here again we truly are allied professions and cooperation is highly desirable and often absolutely necessary. The strength that can be gained from alliance is enormous. However, we must take every precaution with our public images, so that the public do not get the idea that we are "fighting for the use of the same bodies." The physical educator/coach has no right to practice anything in the recreation profession but sport and physical recreation--unless he or she has specific preparation and accreditation in recreational leadership. The recreation director or superintendent should not attempt to administer parks unless, through experience, training, and certification, he or she is prepared to cope with such a task. The reverse of this is just as true.

Further, with changing times, we have noted a greatly increasing emphasis on competitive sport within the recreation profession, a position that would have somehow been almost repugnant to many recreation personnel a decade or so ago (despite the fact that the earlier experiences of many had been in highly competitive sport). As state, provincial, and federal governments have become more interested in competitive or elite sport, the recreation profession has moved to fill a void as funds have been made available and physical education and so-called educational athletics have not extended their profession's boundaries beyond the educational establishment.

To promote inter-professional and inter-disciplinary co-operation and alliance in the future, each professional group should remind its members regularly where the boundaries lie-- what they are and what they aren't. Sport and physical education (or sport and developmental physical activity) should be concerned with the art and science of human movement (human motor performance) in sport, dance (?), play, and exercise. The recreation profession encompasses all of those activities or interests, except the life-sustaining ones, that people of all ages take part in during leisure to enrich the quality of life. This includes social interests, communicative interests, aesthetic and creative interests, physical interests, and so-called learning interests (hobbies, etc.). Obviously, the professional recreational administrator has an enormous responsibility that might be compared (in a certain way) to the mammoth responsibility of the anthropologist--the study of man! Thus, it would appear that the field of recreation and the field of sport and physical education have some overlap, but it is definitely to the advantage of both professions--not to mention the advantage to the people of the larger society--if and when a strong working relationship and alliance is forged between the two fields. We can help each other greatly through such co-operation because we are both "playing on the same team"--the team that serves mankind through development physical activity and through wholesome recreational pursuits of all kinds.

Relationship to Dance (an allied profession)

The relationship of dance to the field of physical education and sport (or whatever name one wishes to ascribe to the profession) is not a simple one to resolve. Within a university, for example, dance could have separate departmental status with the other fine arts in a humanities division; however, most often it has been housed with departments or schools of health, physical education, and recreation. At one major university, at least, there is a department of physical education and dance within a school of education. All sorts of organizational arrangements are possible and, if one looks around sufficiently, a large number of arrangements could be discovered. At the junior or community college level, the high school level, the middle school level, and the elementary school level, however, dance has been situated for better or worse within the same unit or department that houses physical education and athletics. In many ways such an arrangement is highly desirable for physical education and athletics because dance represents an aesthetic curricular component that all too often is completely lacking from physical education and sport. Further, the idea of human movement in sport, dance, play, and exercise being represented by one department seems organizationally sound. However, whether such an arrangement is ultimately in the best interests of the dance profession is being questioned in many quarters today.

Dance is now recognized as one of the allied professions within the American Alliance for Health, Physical Education, Recreation, and Dance. This appears to be one more stage in the development of another allied profession, and it would be wise for the field of sport and physical education to work out an acceptable policy in regard to what stand ought to be taken in this matter at the various educational levels. Obviously, such a position statement could have far-reaching ramifications. Thus, it could well be worked out in cooperation with dance personnel representing the various facets of the dance profession. Dance, physical education, and sport could well function under one overall administrative unit on into the indefinite future, but only if certain developments were to be carried out. For example, a departmental name such as human movement studies or human motor performance could conceivably be workable if separate recognition were given to sport, dance, and exercise within such a unit. However, if we in sport and physical education persist with our present tendencies and don't make it clear to our dance personnel that we welcome their presence and will provide them opportunity for reasonable growth and development, there is no question but that we will in short order force those women and men with a major interest in dance to turn away from our units at the first viable opportunity. This would slow dance's development only temporarily, but in our opinion it would do irreparable damage to the overall image of what has been known as physical education and athletics in the past. Certainly the time is ripe to improve and strengthen our relationship with the dance profession.

Instructional Program (sport, dance, and developmental physical activity--required and/or elective)

    a. The conditioning program. If the student has not met the standards of the circulo-respiratory and motor fitness tests, it is necessary to raise his or her general level of condition. Forcing an individual to follow a long, routinized conditioning program, including calisthenics, pulley-weight exercises, barbell training, Nautilus machine exercises, and jogging or running may frighten some people to such an extent that they will shy away from such physical activity forever. On the other hand, merely allowing the student to engage in any sport or game, no matter what the intensity of a particular selection might be, may result in a continuation of the ineffectiveness displayed in the classification tests. It would seem logical to follow the middle road by permitting some election from a combination of activities that cover the various categories included. The emphasis should be placed on motivating the student to participate with interest in a complete program of motor performance in sport, dance, and exercise.

What are the student's needs that may be met through a program of developmental physical activity in sport, dance, and exercise? Briefly, they might be listed as follows:

1. General body contidion and physical strength
2. Endurance to accomplish strenuous tasks
3. Coordination and reaction time
4. Knowledge about the employment of correct body mechanics (static and dynamic)
5. Skill in selected indoor and outdoor individual and team sports
6. Skill in aquatics and water safety
7. Skill in self-defense
8. Skill in rhythmical activity (adapted from unpublished article by T. E. Blesh, pp. 1-2).

A conditioning program for a definite period of, say, six to twelve weeks might include activity in at least three phases of the above. Much depends, of course, on whether daily activity for a reasonable period of time is prescribed. Further, the department will need to decide what an "irreducible minimum" consists of in any one or all of the areas prescribed.

b. Sports and dance instructional program. Students who demonstrate a level of achievement designated as the "irreducible minimum" in the endurance and motor fitness classification tests might be referred immediately to sports and/or dance instruction, but only for the first six weeks of the academic year. Such assignment would help to generate interest and develop favorable attitudes. In subsequent time or instructional units, sports and dance instruction can be coordinated with the other areas of instruction where classification testing may have shown students to be deficient.

In the sports and dance instructional program, it is wise to schedule a yearly plan for all the various individual, dual, and team sports that the department feels are needed and for which the necessary funds are available. A unit in a sports or dance activity should be a planned sequence of learning and should take from twelve to thirty lessons for completion, depending on the difficulty of the activity and the level to which it is offered. In planning a teaching unit, consideration should be given to objectives, learning experiences, subject matter, instructional methods, equipment and facilities needed, and adequate means of evaluation.

Keeping in mind that in this plan we are dealing with students who are meeting a developmental physical activity requirement, let us assume that individuals were divided into two basic groups as a result of the classification testing experience. Those who met departmental standards could be automatically scheduled into the elective program (within the requirement) where they would be given considerable leeway in the selection of the sports and dance activities they might wish to pursue. Those who did not meet the irreducible minimum standard would be assigned to the prescribed program within the requirement for a greater or lesser amount of time depending upon the program objectives for that academic year.

What we are stating here, for example, is that all students in each of these basic groups must meet a developmental physical activity requirement. Here we are assuming that it is a two-year requirement (for example, at either the high school or college level), three periods each week, forty or fifty minutes each period and, we have to assume, that the term extends anywhere from a quarter (ten weeks), to a trimester (twelve weeks?), to a semester (fifteen weeks), or perhaps up to twenty weeks each "half year" at the high school level. We are taking it for granted also that each student must carry out a program which meets the specifications typically laid down for a credit course in a department (i.e., it is planned; it offers instruction; it is supervised; and achievement is evaluated the same way other courses are graded).

Thus, those who are placed in the prescribed program will find their activities arranged for them so as to promote knowledge about and competency in endurance, strength, flexibility, and functional body mechanics. This phase of the program would include developmental activity in the fundamental skills as well, and an effort should be made to allow some leeway if possible in the selection of activities from a prescribed list. On the other hand, those students who are placed in the elective program within the overall requirement of two years would have considerable leeway regarding the activities they select and the time of the day or week that they wish to take them--to the extent that this is possible, of course. We wish to stress that the department has a guidance function in relation to this matter and, therefore, instructors should feel a professional responsibility to prevent a student from using poor judgment in his or her election of course experiences. (Nevertheless, the individual should probably be allowed to make the these decisions except for exceptional instances when a special consultation should be arranged among the student, the instructor, and the supervisor.)

Students who have achieved such elective status within the department requirement should become quite proficient in several of the activities that he or she elects during the four semesters of enrollment in the program. A long range departmental aim would be that a deep interest and subsequent knowledge, competency, and skill would result for lifelong use.

It is not advisable to go into great detail about a sports or dance instructional unit at this point in the discussion, but let us assume that the first-level basketball unit is elected. This unit might involve a six- to ten-week period of instruction in basketball for a high school or college freshman class in developmental physical activity. A general objective of the course might be stated as follows: to perform the individual and group fundamentals of basketball well enough to obtain enjoyment from participation and also from watching advanced-level competition. Some specific objectives might be stated as follows:

1. To develop ability to pass and catch the basketball with a fair degree of proficiency using basic passes.

2. To develop ability to move around the court in a game situation using proper footwork.

3. To develop the ability to dribble the ball under a game situation.

4. To develop some ability in the lay-up shot, the two-handed set shot, a one-handed set shot, and a foul shot.

5. To demonstrate an understanding of the fundamentals of individual offense and defense in a game situation.

6. To demonstrate the ability to play with others in a team offense and a team defense situation.

7. To demonstrate a working knowledge of the basic rules as shown in performance and written examination (as adapted from an unpublished outline prepared by C. A. Berry).

Lesson plans would be developed for each class session. The grade for the basketball unit would be determined for each individual taking part in relation to the specific course objectives stated above. This grade should be made available to the student as soon as possible, and should be combined with grades from other units elected in determining a final grade for the semester or academic year.

c. The elective program (post-requirement). This program is to be distinguished from what might be called the required-elective program described immediately above. There "elective" meant that a student who had met all of the departmental standards set for the two-year required program would be permitted at some point during that two-year period to select from suggested activities a developmental physical activity plan to suit best his or her needs and interests.

The post-requirement elective program would be available to students--as funds permit--during the third and fourth years of either high school or college. In this phase of the total program, no matter whether any or all standards had been met during the two-year required period, students would be encouraged to elect some type of developmental physical activity according to his or her needs and interests. With the exception of intramural athletics and the voluntary exercise and physical recreation program, credit should be granted for this experience. This recommendation is based on the assumption, once again, that definite guidance, instruction, supervision, and evaluation are provided.

Students should register for a course experience within the elective program in the same way as he or she does with all other academic courses. An adviser should assist the student to determine personal objectives based on what transpired and the level of achievement during the two-year required period. We recommend that all members of the physical education and athletics staff assume some responsibility for the elective program, especially from a guidance standpoint so that students will come to look upon this experience as a individualized undertaking.

The following are some of the objectives which might apply more specifically to this elective phase of the department's total offerings:

37

1. Teach skills to all participants which will permit them to enjoy their present physical activities while preparing a sound basis on which to plan lifelong continuation of this type of sport, dance, and/or exercise.

2. Teach a discriminate choice of activities to those in the program for later life use.

3. Inculcate a knowledge and appreciation of developmental physical activity that will lead to a cooperative attitude toward the profession.

4. Provide standards of conduct in keeping with the values and norms of the society.

5. Present opportunities for pleasurable experiences.

6. Enhance the desire to maintain vigorous, positive health.

7. Permit students to advance as rapidly as their abilities and desires will permit (in keeping with available departmental resources).

Special Physical Education (including therapeutic exercise and adapted sports)

This phase of the total physical education and athletics program has undoubtedly been the most neglected, although recent legislation in both the United States and Canada may change this situation markedly in coming years. There is a definite need for this type of remedial work, but in the past most administrators and boards of education have not felt it important enough to merit a sufficient appropriation. This activity was called medical gynmastics around the turn of the century, and subsequently corrective exercise. The latter was shortened to correctives. More recently, this specialized area of physical education was called the individual program, the adapted program, adaptive physical education, or special physical education. The name special physical education now seems to have caught on and may be with us in the foreseeable future.

Down through the various decades of the twentieth century there have been articles and reports of investigations indicating that many children and young men and women have a variety of postural defects that might have been avoided or could be corrected to some degree at least by body mechanics

38

instruction and special physical education. It was often recommended that this task should be handled in a cooperative manner by physicians and physical educators. As long aso as 1942, Lowman urged administrators to consider the deleterious effects of many of their activities on the posture of students. He stated that "they should remember that at least seventy per cent of the students have faults in posture and consequently are using bodily machines out of line" (Lowman, 1942, p. 510). He stressed further that the typical posture of athletes is bad as well, and that teacher/coaches should explain to them that their performance can be improved through normal joint alignment. Of course, it is most important that youngsters at the elementary school level get off to a good start in regard to what have been called static (fixed or stationary) body mechanics and functional (while in movement) body mechanics. In fact, one of the strong criticisms of the earlier correctives movement was that too much of the postural work was largely static in nature. Body mechanics analysis of functional movements is, of course, extremely important. It should also be stressed that in addition to the possible benefits in physical efficiency and health, one's appearance will also be improved through normal joint alignment. This latter point lends an aesthetic component to this aspect of developmental physical activity that is often overlooked.

At this point it is not appropriate for us to describe the various aspects of a special physical education program in detail. However, a few necessary points will be made. It will be recalled that the student, as a result of the medical examination, may be placed in Groups A, B, C, or D. Those in Groups A and B were considered fit to take part in the Classification for Physical Activity testing. Group C includes those students who have moderately serious defects, which may be disabling. Those in Group D have serious and disabling defects. Group C students should have restricted activity with a modified program of therapeutic exercise where this chould help. Group D students may be exempt from all physical activity based on a physician's recommendation. If any physical activity is permitted, it would be part of a highly individualized program. Ideally, as mentioned earlier, all students should be examined orthopedically to determine if therapeutic exercise is recommended.

A special physical education program has several basic objectives. After the student has received a diagnosis and prognosis of his or her case, there should be help so that the condition can be improved to the extent possible. At the same time that the person is learning about his or her deficiency from all aspects of the problem, some form of interesting modified physical activity should be offered. If a condition exists in which there is no possibility of improvement, care should be taken to insure against the possibility of physical or mental retrogression. This might be possible by providing a modified program which will allow the student a maximum amount of participation with what we call normal groups in normal developmental physical activity. Such mainstreaming would enable the individual to develop skills and any and all concomitant interests to guarantee some degree of participation throughout the person's life.

From what has been said, it should be evident that the field of physical education and athletics--and in this instance we are really talking about developmental physical activity-- must either do something constructive about special physical education, or inform educational administrators and the public that it cannot do anything, or hasn't been allowed, or hasn't the training, or hasn't the facilities and equipment, or isn't interested in this phase of the work.

(continued in the next chapter)

References

Berry, C. A.: An unpublished instructional outline made available to the author, Columbia Teachers College, 1947.

Blesh, T. E.: Suggestions for physical education in preparatory schools. The Physical Educator. 15,1:6-9, 1958.

Franks, B. D., and Deutsch, H.: Evaluating Performance in Physical Education. New York: Academic Press, Inc., 1973.

Lowman, C. L.: Physical education counseling. The Journal of Health and Physical Education, 13, 9:510, 1942.

Oberteuffer, D., Harrelson, O. A., and Pollock, M. B.: School Health Education, fifth ed. New York: Harper & Row, 1973.

William, J. F., and Brownell, C. L.: The Administration of Health and Physical Education, fourth ed. Philadelphia: W. B. Saunders Co., 1951.

Zeigler, E. F.: Problems in the History and Philosophy of Physical Education and Sport. Englewood Cliffs, N. J.: Prentice-Hall, Inc., 1968.

Zeigler, E. F.: Physical Education and Sport Philosophy.
    Englewood Cliffs, N. J.: Prentice-Hall, Inc., 1977.

Zeigler, E. F.: The health teacher needs a philosophy. In
    New Directions in Health Education. D. A. Reed (Ed.).
    New York: The Macmillan Co., 1971.

CURRENTLY USEFUL GENERALIZATIONS ABOUT PHYSICAL EDUCATION AND ATHLETICS
(Continued)

In Chapter 2 we began the discussion of what are being called currently useful generalizations in physical education and athletics. There we began with the topic of aims and objectives, and we progressed as far as treatment of the topic special physical education (including therapeutic exercise and adapted sports). In this chapter (Chapter 3), we will begin with a discussion of intramural athletics and conclude with consideration of essential evaluation and measurement.

Intramural Athletics

A fine intramural athletics program is most important in the achievement of a balanced program in school health, physical education and sport, recreation, and dance. There is no question but that intramurals have made great strides at the college and university level, but at the high-school and middle-school levels, the surface has barely been scratched. More help is needed in this area to do the job even reasonably adequately. If the average student has a sound experience in competitive sport, he or she is likely to have a favorable "image" of sport and physical education. High school boys and girls are the "public of tomorrow" that will decide whether physical education and athletics is worthy of financial backing at all levels of the educational system.

We contend that competitive sport is a desirable part of the overall program of physical education and sport. We believe that through this means students can be confronted with situations that are "physically desirable, mentally stimulating, and socially sound" (Columbia Teachers College class notes from the 1940s!). We feel that every student who is able should have an opportunity to participate in some phase of this program.

In addition to long range aims, there are many specific objectives for the intramural athletics program. As well as providing healthful exercise that contributes to the individual's growth and development, sport can provide an opportunity social contacts that foster and promote group spirit and loyalties. This physical recreation that occurs during leisure tends to develop an appreciation of and lasting interest in sport of all types, but primarily the participant becomes acquainted with and skillful in games and sports that have carry-over values to later-life participation.

There are many possible units of competition within intramurals, from dormitories, fraternities, sororities (all living units of any size) to classes designated by year of graduation, to weight classification teams, and to campus or school clubs. A great variety of sports are possible from touch or flag football, soccer, and cross-country running in the fall; basketball, swimming, and volleyball in the winter, and softball, tennis, golf, and track & field in the spring. Not to be forgotten are games and sports that are somewhat less "physical" in nature (e.g., horseshoes, bowling). Of course, this program should be expanded to include as wide a variety of sports as student demand and the budget will bear.

We recommend that all students who are enrolled in the intramural athletics program be required to have a medical examination at the beginning of the academic year. Thus, the individual student's classification at that point would decide whether a person would be permitted to take part in a particular sport from the standpoint of his/her health status. Of course, the intramurals program is on an elective basis entirely, and any such participation should be based on a person's interest and desire--and not on pressure that might be applied from representatives of the competitive unit (e.g., dormitory or fraternity). Typically, no regular class credit would be given for intramural participation, but in the elective phase of the instructional program, participation in a contest may be substituted for one period of class attendance by special arrangement with the class instructor.

The question of eligibility often arises at certain educational levels in relation to the student's academic standing. We recommend that any student who is enrolled in the school or university on a regular basis be permitted to take part regardless of current academic standing. By this we mean that intramural sports are to be considered in the same vein as any other co-curricular activity. (Some individuals may require special counselling, of course, in an effort to assist them with overall planning of their daily schedules. For example, for several reasons a student would be wise to limit participation to one sport during one season.) No varsity squad man or woman should be permitted to participate in that same sport within the intramurals program.

There are a number of other matters that will need to be considered in some detail, but we will just mention them briefly as follows: coaches, practice sessions, officials, awards, equipment, finance, records, publicity, managers, handbook, type of competition, etc.

There will be great variation in the matter of providing coaches for the many intramural sports teams. At the high-school and middle-school levels, it may be possible to get some assistance from teachers, parents, or varsity athletes. At the university level physical education majors and/or varsity athletes are good sources for coaching assistance. Every possible means should be used to provide adequate instruction for the players. Physical education and athletics staff members should supervise and aid the coaches to the extent that this is possible.

With team sports especially, every effort should be made to provide qualified officials, whereas in the individual and/or dual sports the participants themselves must assume responsibility (e.g., golf, tennis, bowling). This means that officials for team sports will need to be trained and receive some sort of compensation.

In keeping with the spirit of intramural sports, no awards of significant intrinsic value should be given either to individuals or teams. Inexpensive certificates suitable for framing are recommended. Participation can be encouraged through careful organization and administration, adequate instruction, and the publishing of individual and team achievement records.

The intramurals program ideally would be financed in the same manner as are all other parts of the physical education program, but admittedly there is great variation in the way this is being handled currently at the various educational levels. Because we envision this as a co-curricular program--as we also view intercollegiate athletics--rather than as an extra-curricular program, we believe that ideally there should be no special fee required for participation. If this were to be the case, it could be argued that regular physical education and sport equipment be used. For example, various colored jerseys could be furnished by the department, as could adequate safety equipment necessary for certain sports (e.g., ear protectors for wrestlers, face mask for hockey goalie). Obviously, if there a separate budget for intramural sports, the equipment situation would change significantly. This would be especially true if a student fee were assessed to all students in the institution. Whatever the situation, the provision of expendable equipment for individual sport participation (e.g., squash racquets) can be a great drain on any budget.

In intramural sports, we recommend that a round robin plan be used typically, although double elimination tournaments are to be preferred to single-elimination ones if possible. Students might not consider it worthwhile to go through practice sessions for a reasonable training period if they would then play only one or two contests. A consolation bracket is always desirable.

Finally, complete records should be kept on all aspects of the program, and informative publicity should be made available to the various communications media. The appointment of team managers can be of great help here, and they can also assist with other necessary managerial duties and responsibilities. At the beginning of each year, an intramurals handbook should be made available and distributed widely. In addition to its value in the several promotional aspects of the program, it can be a regular source of information and guidance to all concerned.

Voluntary Exercise and Physical Recreation Program

This is an area in which the department can make a truly lasting contribution. Here we are talking about that phase of the program of exercise, sport, and dance that not only contributes to health and fitness, but also assists people to become "artists in living." Viewed from the standpoint of the recreation profession, these "physical recreation" activities represent that facet of the total recreational offering which is closest to the department of physical education and sport, and which is steadily becoming increasingly popular with people of all ages. Thus, this phase of the program would include those who undertake individual weight training programs, jogging routines, casual racketball or squash racquet matches, swimming of laps in the pool, instructional classes in some phase of sport, dance, or exercise (non-credit), etc.

Sport Clubs

For several reasons the number of sport clubs has increased significantly in recent years. Of course, it can be argued that sport clubs preceded both intramural sports and intercollegiate athletics on college campuses, but the development that we are discussing here is the present-day rise in interest in these activities due to students' specialized interests on the one hand, and the elimination of certain varsity sports due to present budgetary constraine at the university level especially. A consensual definition of a sport club (as provided by Cleave, 1978, p. 5) is "a more or less organized group of persons who wish to participate in a sport, or at a particular level in a sport, not provided for in the intramural or intercollegiate program." Thus, a sport club program serves as a supplement to the physical education, intramurals, and intercollegiate programs by (1) providing instruction at all skill levels, (2) providing increased opportunities to participate at a wide range of ability levels, and (3) expanding the extra-mural competitive program. Sport clubs, particularly at the college level, are student-initiated, student-organized, and student-administered organizations--preferably with a faculty advisor. At present the most popular types of sport clubs are those that offer instruction and experience in martial arts, outdoor activities, and life-time skills (Cleave).

Interscholastic and Intercollegiate Athletics

Interscholastic and intercollegiate athletics, along with entire intramurals program described above under three separate categories, should be viewed as an integral part of the entire physical education and sport program. Under ideal conditions, this program should be regarded as at least co-curricular in nature, because participation under sound educational leadership can provide an opportunity for fine educational experiences for both men and women at all levels starting with the middle school (or junior-high level). We recommend that the chairperson or head of the department of sport and physical education should be ultimately responsible for the program, which should be financed by institutional funds (or at least in this fashion to the greatest possible extent). It is recommended that all gate receipts be placed into the general school or college fund from which monies are allotted each year for instructional purposes and general maintenance (usually for the following year).

Although it has ever been thus--or at least so it seems --there are a great many problems that will continue to harass the athletic director in the years immediately ahead. What is the present status of the inter-institutional program at each of the educational levels? Are more stringent controls needed and, if so, how are they to be implemented carefully and effectively? Who should have the ultimate control over policies and procedures governing the program? Are the health, safety, and overall educational experience of the participants being fully considered? Are any or all of recruiting, subsidizing, and proselyting to be permitted? Shall scholarships be granted to bonafide students based on financial need? Is insurance coverage adequate for any emergency? How should athletics be financed (i.e., from gate receipts completely, partially, or not at all)? Where shall the funds for capital expenditures be obtained? Who shall determine policies and procedures in relation to the communications media? Are tournaments serving an effective purpose? On what basis does a student become eligible or ineligible for regular athletic competition? What constitutes "equal opportunity" for girls and women in inter-institutional athletic competition? What about gambling, semiprofessionalism, and the role of alumni? To what extend should interschool competition be encouraged at the middle-school and high-school levels? How should the program be evaluated? These are but a few of the questions that arise perennially and which merit answers on a continuing basis.

Participating in interscholastic or intercollegiate athletics is, of course, entirely elective. Ideally, class credit for physical education and sport should be given for team participation, but this should never take the place of the existing required program as described above. In other words, team participation should not take the place of the required activities unless duplication is involved (e.g., a member of the wrestling team should not be required to take combatives).

Students who have earned their living fully as a professional in a sport should in all probability not be eligible to compete in that same sport at the college level, but should be allowed to compete in other sports. If a student were to fall below the normally acceptable standards for progression academically, he or she might be asked to discontinue athletics just as an individual might be asked to curtail other "extracurricular" activities. Each student's case should be considered individually. What we have recommended here is the ideal, of course, and we appreciate that there are usually conference standards that apply in such cases.

All sports should ideally be regarded as major sports, but we do appreciate that circumstances and tradition often place one or more sports in a special category. Each sport should have a varsity team and a junior varsity team with sound coaching. We appreciate the financial problems that have arisen in highly competitive sport, but we believe that teams for first-year students should be operated with limited schedules involving very little traveling. The orientation needs of the first year at university for both men and women must be taken into consideration.

We would argue further that organized practice should be held only during the season in which the sport is played. However, in both the United States and Canada for reasons of expediency

47

and because football in such a unique phenomenon on the North American scene, spring practices in that sport may be held only on the college level. This is not a problem in Canada, and at certain other institutions with shorter academic years, but in any case spring practice should be limited to a maximum of thirty sessions.

Coaches should be regular members of the school or university faculty, typically in the physical education and athletics division, with salaries and tenure similar to those of other teachers or professors. Because of his or her ability as a teacher in the sport(s) coached, the coach at the college level should also serve as an instructor for any such sports in the major program of the division or in coaching options, etc. A coach at the university level should over a period of time make a scholarly contribution to his or her area of expertise in similar fashion to the standards applied to all other professors.

Undergraduate Professional Program

This topic, of course, is the primary task of the university teacher, as is the next one treating the graduate study and research program. On the other hand, elementary, middle school, and secondary school teachers, coaches, and administrators--not to mention the public that is being affected further by the many graduates entering alternative careers--are experiencing the results of the product that is being produced by the large number of professional programs throughout the United States and Canada.

As matters stand now, we know that our professional programs are far from perfect. From time to time we make curriculum changes often based on the opinions of staff members that are formed in a basically unscientific manner. In other words, we are not truly aware of what our neighboring institutions are doing, what the demands of the job are, what our alumni feel that the strengths and weaknesses of the program were, what the present body of professional students think about their experiences, and what a study of contemporary society seems to indicate.

What is a physical educator/coach? Certainly there appears to be considerable confusion from all quarters today. The public seems to believe that anyone with a good personality, a fair educational background, and some adequate sports, dance, and exercise skills can teach and coach. The status of the physical educator/coach must be raised in the minds of the public and other teachers. By and large, physical education and sport majors need a broader educational background. This deficiency shows up in many ways. However, this problem has developed partially because there is too much knowledge and skill to be mastered within four undergraduate years. First, a broadly based general education is required that includes a variety of course experiences in the humanities, social sciences, and natural sciences. In recent years there has been general agreement that at least one half of the undergraduate program ought to be able to be classified as "general education."

Second, if a person wishes eventually to teach and/or coach in the elementary, middle, or secondary schools--and to some extent at the junior college and/or community college level --he or she is faced with meeting state or provincial certification requirements for teachers. The implication here is that teachers should possess certain knowledge, competencies, and skills about the teaching and coaching act itself. It seems reasonable, therefore, to recommend that prospective teacher/ coaches should have excellent course experiences in the following areas: social foundations of education, educational psychology, educational administration, instructional methodology, and student teaching and coaching.

Exactly how much specialized professional preparation in physical education and sport should be required within a degree program? This is not an easy question to answer today (and probably it was difficult earlier, too). Initially, we contend that there should be a "core experience" that all must take regardless of later specialization at either the undergraduate or graduate levels. Our thinking on this subject has been developing over many years. We now recommend that this core experience should be delimited to physical education and sport only, and that only terms related to our own field should be employed. For example, our professional courses should not be called physiology of exercise or sociology of sport--let them teach those courses if they wish in the respective departments concerned. Thus, with thanks to Professor Laura J. Huelster, we recommend that the core series of courses in physical education and sport should be identified as follows:

1. Background, Meaning, and Cross-Cultural Significance
2. Functional Effects of Physical Activity
3. Socio-Cultural Aspects of Sport and Physical Activity
4. Motor Learning and Development
5. Mechanical and Muscular Analysis of Physical Skills
6. Management Theory and Practice in Sport and Physical Education

7. Program Development in Sport and Physical Education
8. Evaluation and Measurement in Sport and Physical Education

In addition to the above, as part of the core, we recommend an irreducible minimum of professional activities courses in sport, exercise, and dance.

To continue with our second major point, then, a brief comment is necessary about the areas of specialization that have developed within the traditional major program in physical education during the 1970's. Formerly the physical education major was spread so thinly among the various allied professions with his required and elective courses that he or she was apt to finish the college program as a "jack of all trades and master of none." Paradoxically, as these allied professions have proceeded to separate (e.g., recreation and parks administration), the tendency to elect individual professional courses (or minor programs) from their subject-matters has remained while at the same time a number of specialization areas have sprung up with physical education and sport. Here we are referring to such specializations as fitness specialist, coaching specializations, sport management, athletic therapy (training), special physical education, as well as sub-disciplinary specializations (e.g., sport psychology) and, of course, the traditional physical education teaching major program. Our conclusion is that we must work to discover ways to bring the people involved in various specialties within the profession (sport and physical education) into a closer relationship, while at the same time maintaining the position of the allied profession within our orbit, so to speak. Of course, we hope to remain as their "allied profession within their orbit" too.

Third, we are facing a serious problem at the present that we--and all of higher education--have barely come to grips with as of this time. Here we are referring to the need for experimentation with a "competency approach" to determine the extent to which it might help to eliminate the present, relatively ineffectial, repetitive teaching with which the typical professional course has been charged. We believe that the traditional subject-matter approach to learning has often stifled initiative. The professional student takes a set number of courses and attends university for a required number of years. Upon graduation, the "teacher/coach" is presumably sufficiently educated and competent to engage in his or her profession. Unless we introduce some sort of competency approach, how can we be certain that our graduating students will be able to function satisfactorily as intelligent citizens and competent teachers and coaches of sport and physical education? We must have a more effective way of measuring their ability as determined by specific competencies developed through selected experiences with subject-matters as resource areas.

Graduate Study and Research Program

The present status of graduate study and research programs in physical education and sport, considered on a North American basis, is difficult to ascertain (Zeigler and Paton, 1974, p. 101). No one was making any great claims for the calibre of graduate study and research programs in the 1950's, but there was a general feeling that programs were gradually improving. Thus, it was a shock when Conant in 1963 recommended that graduate programs in physical education should be abolished (Conant, 1963, p. 201). McCloy had warned us in 1957 that graduate study was of a poor quality. Specifically he deplored the all-too-frequent elimination of the thesis requirement; the lack of prerequisites for graduate study in the field; the fact that many graduate faculty members were themselves not engaged in scholarly work; and the gradual elimination of reading competency in foreign languages as a definite requirement (McCloy, 1957, pp. 33-34).

A subsequent Conference on Graduate Education, sponsored by the then American Association for Health, Physical Education, and Recreation in early 1967, designated the five purposes of graduate study as follows:

1. To add to the store of human knowledge through basic research.

2. To extend the range of nonverbal expression (dance, games, sports, etc.) through encouragement of human invention and imagination.

3. To prepare scientific research workers and humanistic scholars.

4. To provide advanced preparation for practitioners (teachers, coaches, supervisors, activity specialists, and administrators) at various levels of competency.

5. To develop leaders who have the ability to think and to employ their rational powers in gaining understanding, aesthetic sensitivity, and moral responsibility (AAHPER, 1967, p. 21).

The 1960's was a decade in which a disciplinary emphasis became a prominent influence in physical education. Unfortunately, just at the time when this scholarly thrust was being mounted, including the social science and humanities aspects of the field to an already heavily professional-preparation-oriented graduate curriculum, the financial outlook for higher education took a sharp turn for the worse at the turn of the decade of the 1970's. This occasioned an urgent need for both consolidation and innovation. In a number of instances this forced a period of self-evaluation on a local, state (provincial), regional, national, and continental basis. For example, local and regional needs should be served by universities within that geographical area, but no one will thank--and continue solid support indefinitely to--an institution that becomes a "diploma mill for tired teachers and coaches."

Whether one or more types of degree program patterns are implemented, it is highly desirable to preserve a common core experience of physical education and sport knowledge at the graduate level too which all must possess prior to elective course experiences. There should be a reasonable amount of articulation among the competencies, skills, and knowledge required at the undergraduate level and the common core experience of knowledge required for all at the master's level. This common core should include from twelve to fifteen semester hours of course work involving (1) research methods (including statistics); (2) background, meaning, and cross-cultural significance of sport and physical activity; (3) human motor performance; and (4) thesis or project seminar (credit or no credit).

In addition to consolidation--i.e., a graduate program where a disciplinary oriented program has its various offerings combined into two options (e.g., humanities and social science option and bio-science option)--there is a need for at least three different types of master's programs being offered at universities situated in one region of a state or province. The greatest demand would naturally be for a master's program to prepare a more qualified teacher and/or coach. A second type of program or degree pattern that should be available to a considerably smaller group within a state or province would be the disciplinary oriented master's program leading to the traditional M.A. or M.S. degree. A third type of program deserves early consideration as well--a master's degree program where the student may specialize in the theory and practice of selected types of human motor performance (e.g., dance, gymnastics, aquatics). This idea is recommended on the assumption that we should be moving positively to establish sport as a legitimate part of our culture which merits scholarly study at the university level.

Graduate programs in North American universities have traditionally been superimposed gradually on undergraduate programs. As a result they have grown organizationally in a relatively haphazard manner with often inadequate management policies and procedures. Chairpersons of graduate programs in this field would be well-advised to develop manuals of their own that include the following: (1) those policies and procedures which the graduate school insists on; (2) those policies and procedures that the physical education graduate faculty have decided upon--over and above those of the graduate school; and (3) those policies and procedures which the graduate chairperson implements because they seem to be in the best interest of all concerned. We recommend further that whenever possible graduate programs should be constituted with a separate budget.

Moving from the assumption that both consolidation and innovation are necessary which involve both new program emphases and combination of former options, managers and their executive or advisory committees are urged to allocate money for equipment and facilities for scholarly endeavor and research to those who give every evidence of possession of the required knowledge, competency, and skill (and attitude!) to carry out investigation. A "proven track record"--not promises or talk about what is underway--is undoubtedly the best recommendation as to where money should be invested. We urge administrators to encourage young scholars with interests in the social science and humanities aspects of the field and the sub-professional aspects of the profession (e.g., curriculum, management, evaluation), as well as in the bioscience aspects of our work.

No matter where one turns, problems and difficulties confront those who would improve graduate study and research programs in physical education and sport. The focus of the various degree programs needs to be sharpened. The scholarly experience needs to be strengthened for some, while the internship experience necessary for others should be improved immeasurably (or in many cases begun for the first time). No matter in which direction one looks, there is an obvious need for quality control. "A better mouse trap can be built," if the profession will simply set itself vigorously and intelligently to the task!

The Managerial Process

In 1955 administration (or management) was described as "the total of the processes through which appropriate human and material resources are made available and made effective for accomplishing the purpose of an enterprise" (Amer. Assoc.

of School Administrators, 1955, p. 17). Writing more than twenty-five years later, we are now stating that managerial achievement at a given time results from the execution of managerial acts, involving conceptual, technical, human, and conjoined skills, while combining varying degrees of planning, organizing, staffing, directing, and controlling with the managerial process to assist an organization achieve its stated goals. With this description in mind, we then reasoned further that the aim of the manager is to create an organizational climate wherein people work cooperatively, effectively, and efficiently with ideas and resources to accomplish a desired percentage of individual and group goal achievement. As accurate as either (or both) of these definitions might be, it is seemingly difficult for most people to think in such abstract terms. For this reason we have developed a taxonomical model of the management process that should actually depict a never-ending series of managerial acts in a successful organization (see Figure 1 on page 55).

Coupled with this, we have also developed after investigation a second model to describe management development and process in regard to the knowledge and skills that may be obtained through a competency-based approach. In this schemata we began with the three categories of skills postulated by Katz in the 1950's and added two further categories that we felt rounded out the model more fully (Katz, 1955). Katz re-examined his delineation in the 1970's and re-affirmed his earlier conceptualization (Katz, 1974). (See Figure 2 on page 56.)

Additionally, in our explanation we decided to employ the managerial functions that have been handed down during this century as described originally by Henri Fayol. This were then delineated extremely well by R. Alec Mackenzie in his administrative model entitled "The Management Process in 3-D" (Mackenzie, 1969, pp. 80-87). Working with colleagues at The University of Western Ontario and elsewhere, we conducted a study that resulted in an adaptation of these categories and appropriate statements to the field of physical education and athletics (see Figures 3-7 on pages 57-61).

A Systems Approach to Management

As we delved further into the arrangement of the various components of the entire process, we envisioned the formation of an equation with mathematical symbols to explain administrative activity from both a theoretical and practical standpoint. However, it became obvious that a schematic model for managerial achievement could be arranged logically--as elements of a set, so to speak--within the steps or components of a systems

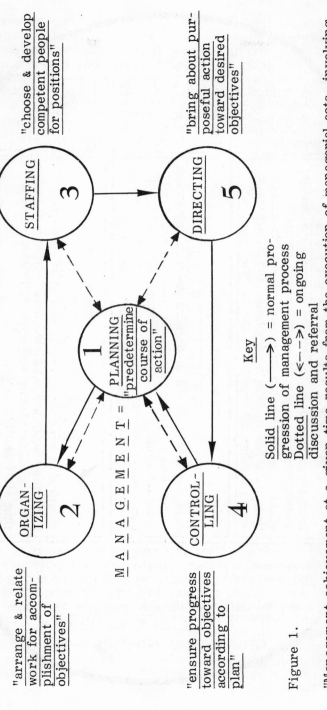

A TAXONOMICAL MODEL OF THE MANAGEMENT PROCESS

("Depicts a Never-ending Series of Managerial Acts in a Successful Organization")

"arrange & relate work for accomplishment of objectives"

"choose & develop competent people for positions"

STAFFING
3

DIRECTING
5

"bring about purposeful action toward desired objectives"

PLANNING
1
"predetermine course of action"

M A N A G E M E N T =

ORGAN-
IZING
2

CONTROL-
LING
4

"ensure progress toward objectives according to plan"

Key

Solid line (——→) = normal progression of management process
Dotted line (◄--→) = ongoing discussion and referral

Figure 1.

"Management achievement at a given time results from the execution of managerial acts, involving conceptual, technical, human, and conjoined skills, that combine varying degrees of planning, organizing, staffing, directing, and controlling in the management process. The aim is to create an organizational climate wherein people work cooperatively with ideas and resources to accomplish a desired percentage of individual and group goal achievement." E. F. Zeigler

M A N A G E M E N T   D E V E L O P M E N T   A N D   P R O C E S S : ---
(The Knowledge and Skills Obtained Through a Competency-Based Approach)*

("Employing Basic Skills
in Combination Toward Goal")

C O N J O I N E D   S K I L L S

Planning a budget; creating a unit that is active professionally; managing change; developing leadership skills; evaluating organizational operations and outcomes, etc.

("Formulating Ideas")

C O N C E P T U A L   S K I L L S

Predetermining course of action; planning for change; understanding variety of organizational concepts; visualizing relationship to various clients; learning to think in terms of relative emphases and priorities among conflicting objectives and criteria, etc.

("Managing Details")

T E C H N I C A L   S K I L L S

Using computer as aid in decision-making; employing verbal and graphical models for planning and analysis; developing a feedback system; developing policies and procedures manuals; developing a pattern for equipment purchase and maintenance, etc.

("Influencing People")

H U M A N   S K I L L S

Relating to superiors, peers, and staff members; counseling staff members; handling conflicts at various levels; developing employee motivation; combating staff mobility, etc.

P E R S O N A L   S K I L L S

("Developing One's Own Skills")

Learning self-management; developing life goal planning; building one's communication skills; maintaining total fitness; improving personal skills in perception, analysis, assertiveness, negotiation, motivation, etc.

Figure 2.

* Three of the categories were taken from A. L. Katz's "Skills of an Effective Administrator."

56

ELEMENTS OF THE MANAGEMENT PROCESS--Planning*

Planning
(predetermine course of action)

1. Determine needs of society
2. Establish long-range organizational goals
3. Set immediate objectives for the organization
4. Establish priorities
5. Determine sequence & timing of program implementation
6. Allocate necessary resources
7. Develop policies on important recurring matters
8. Devise strategies for effective program development
9. Decide on procedures for standardization of practice
10. Forecast tentatively where present course of action will lead

Figure 3.

* These categories and statements were adapted from R. Alec Mackenzie's "The Management Process in 3-D," Harvard Business Review, Nov.-Dec., 1969.

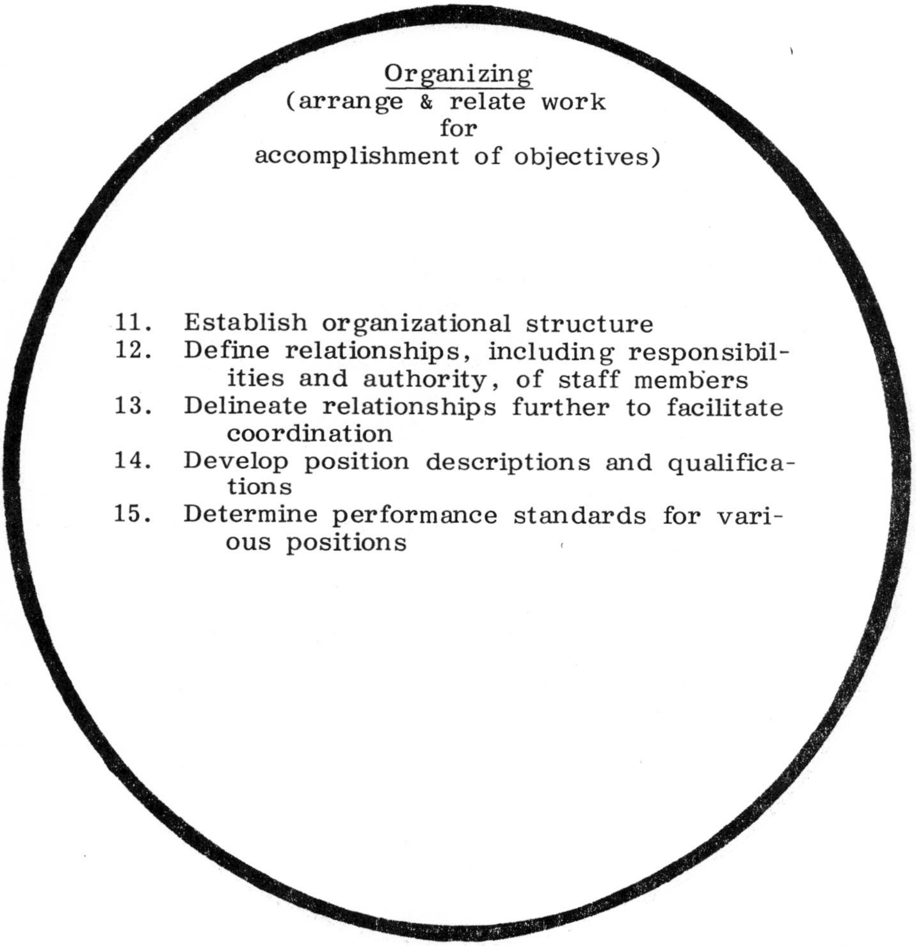

Organizing
(arrange & relate work
for
accomplishment of objectives)

11. Establish organizational structure
12. Define relationships, including responsibil-
    ities and authority, of staff members
13. Delineate relationships further to facilitate
    coordination
14. Develop position descriptions and qualifica-
    tions
15. Determine performance standards for vari-
    ous positions

Figure 4.

ELEMENTS OF THE MANAGEMENT PROCESS--Staffing

Staffing
(choose and develop the most competent people for positions)

16. Recruit and select the best-qualified people for positions.
17. Assign responsibilities and accountability for results
18. Orient staff members to their positions
19. Provide special training where need is obvious
20. Develop staff members gradually through improvement of knowledge, attitudes, and necessary management skills

Figure 5.

Directing
(bringing about purposeful
action toward desired
objectives)

21. Review performance standards individually and collectively
22. Motivate staff members to carry out duties
enthusiastically
23. Coordinate effects of staff members as effectively as possible
24. Stimulate creativity and innovation in
achieving objectives
25. Resolve conflicts when necessary through
concerned, democratic mediation

Figure 6.

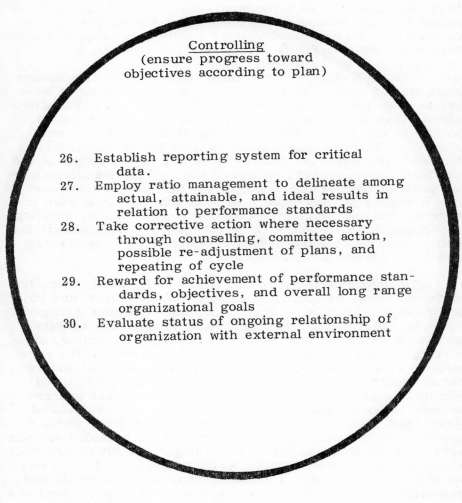

Figure 7.

Note: Appreciation is expressed to my colleagues, Professors P. Chelladurai, T. Haggerty, and S. Cleave for their assistance with this particular aspect of the investigation through careful review and helpful suggestions.

approach. Such an analysis is available to the education profession, for example, based on one systems perspective developed within the behavioral sciences (Milstein and Belasco, 1973).
Here the concern is with the input, thruput, and output, each
aspect strongly related to the other. For the purpose of our
own work, therefore, we developed a schematic model of a systems approach (see Figure 8 on page 63).

The implications for sport and physical education management are, of course, no better or worse, no stronger or weak-
er, no more practical or theoretical (for sport and physical education) than for any other aspect of, or organization within,
society at any level. The complexity of management is well-
known, if not fully appreciated, even by the layman today.
However, the layperson and the large majority of people in the
profession have not yet appreciated the need for the strong promotion of a 'total system' concept. In our opinion there are
now a number of reasons why we must take a holistic view in
regard to the many interacting components of a dynamic, evolving
highly complex situation. The promulgation of such an evolving
entity could provide the needed perspective for a systems approach to managerial achievement.

To summarize the model described in Figure 8, then, the
manager, armed with external demand and the human and physical resources supplied at the input phase, executes managerial
acts that involve conceptual, technical, human, and conjoined
skills. Such acts combined varying degrees of planning, organizing, staffing, directing, and controlling based on the para-
meters, constraints, and opportunities of the internal and external environments. The aim is to create an organizational
climate wherein people work cooperatively with ideas and resources to accomplish a desired percentage of individual and
group goal achievement. If all of this is considered within a
systems perspective, the users of the service provided will present feedback that will permit the manager and his or her associates to take corrective action where necessary. In this way
an ongoing relationship, including accompanying demands and
resources, with the external environment will be maintained in a
viable state. We believe that the time is past due when the
field of sport and physical education should adopt a total management process as explained above including the implementation
of a systems approach that will help in the achievement of the
profession's stated goals.

Internal and External Environments

Consideration of the "environments" of the administrator
involves an analysis of the social forces that impinge on the

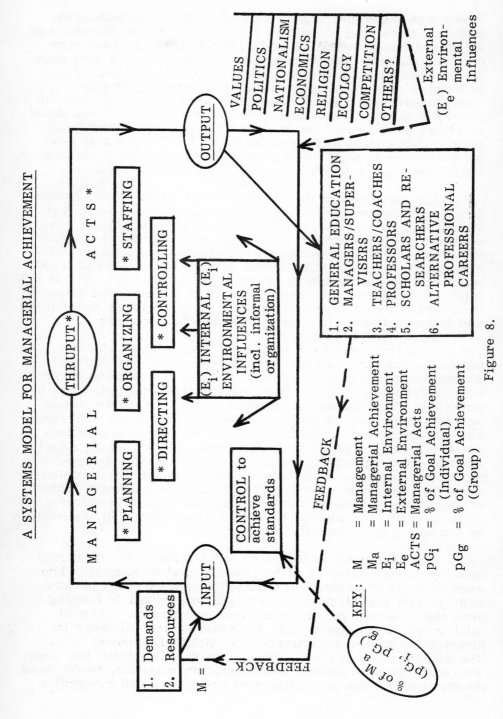

A SYSTEMS MODEL FOR MANAGERIAL ACHIEVEMENT

MANAGERIAL   THRUPUT*   A C T S *

* PLANNING   * ORGANIZING   * DIRECTING   * CONTROLLING   * STAFFING

OUTPUT

VALUES
POLITICS
NATIONALISM
ECONOMICS
RELIGION
ECOLOGY
COMPETITION
OTHERS?

External (E$_e$) Environmental Influences

(E_i) INTERNAL (E_i) ENVIRONMENTAL INFLUENCES (incl. informal organization)

1. GENERAL EDUCATION
2. MANAGERS/SUPERVISERS
3. TEACHERS/COACHES PROFESSORS
4. SCHOLARS AND RESEARCHERS
5.
6. ALTERNATIVE PROFESSIONAL CAREERS

Figure 8.

FEEDBACK

CONTROL to achieve standards

INPUT

1. Demands
2. Resources

M =

FEEDBACK

% of M$_a$ (pG$_i$; pG$_g$)

KEY: M   = Management
      M$_a$ = Managerial Achievement
      E$_i$ = Internal Environment
      E$_e$ = External Environment
      ACTS = Managerial Acts
      pG$_i$ = % of Goal Achievement (Individual)
      pG$_g$ = % of Goal Achievement (Group)

63

leader and his or her organization (Zeigler and Spaeth, eds. 1975, p. 399 et ff.). Prior to any overview of the internal and external (immediate and general) environments, we cannot escape the thought that there are human beings at the very core of the administrative process whose purposeful behavior may bring about the goal realization of the entire organization. These individuals possess many and varied interests, and each person is inescapably unique. Furthermore, conflicts are almost inevitable as they function in a definite and specific environment. This phenomenon does appear to be true because people's behavior is so often characterized by the lack of rationality of one type or another (Gross, 1964, chapter 14).

The structure of the organization in which human beings function is explained as a pattern or framework in which individuals and parts or units of the department, school, or company fulfill a variety of roles so that the purposes of the enterprise may possibly be achieved. In the process a number of hierarchical and polyarchical relationships are often established which function according to prevailing codes of behavior. It is vital to understand that there is typically a formal and informal structure in every organization, both of which exert significant and influential amounts of power on specific occasions.

Here there will be a very brief discussion of the manager's internal and external environments. The internal environment includes the organizational clients, suppliers, advisers, controllers and controllees, adversaries, and publics with opinions. The external environment is made up of the organization's resources, its social organization, the power structure, and a structure of values and norms. Further considerations are the need for the administrator to develop a working knowledge of social theory; to assist the larger community by assuming some direct responsibilities for the society's welfare; to understand that the "world family of man" displays recurrent themes of rationality, activism, humanism, and concern with values; to comprehend the concept that the rate of change in the world is increasing at a geometric ratio.

Organizations, as a type of social collectivity, do ascribe primacy to the matter of rather specific goal-attainment. They seek to exert environmental control through excellent performance so that certain desired goals will be realized in keeping with the value system of a particular organization. The administrator should appreciate, for example, that his organization's value system is different, but ultimately derived from, the societal value system. Thus, a university, which has been characterized as a pattern-maintenance organization, would "tend to select only those goal-attainment, adaptive, and integrative alternatives which contribute to the maintenance of the pattern of its units" (Hills, 1968, p. 65).

Organizations function within a society, of course, and a society is the most nearly self-subsistent type of social system. Societies seem to have four basic types of functional problems that have been met through the development of four subsystems technically designated as pattern-maintenance, integration, goal-attainment, and adaptation. The economy of a society is its adaptive subsystem, while the society's form of government (polity) has become known as its goal-attainment subsystem. The integrative and pattern-maintenance subsystems, which do not have names that can be used in everyday speech, consist actually of a set of series of processes by which a society's production factors are related, combined, and transformed with utility--the value principle of the adaptive system--as the interim product. These products "packaged" as various form of "utility" are employed in and by other fundamental subsystems of the society (Johnson, 1969, p. 50).

As can be readily understood, different organizations within a society have different goals and are typically organized with this purpose in mind. Organizations accordingly may well have goals which are primarily adaptive, goal-attainment oriented, integrative, or pattern maintenance-oriented in nature. Whereas some organizations have goals related to economic production, others of a governmental nature work toward the achievement of group goals. A third type of organization is directed or oriented to the function of integration (e.g., legal services which assist in the resolution of conflicts or political parties which organize support for interest groups within the society). A fourth classification of organization correlates to the functional problem of pattern-maintenance and here, as mentioned above, the university may be categorized. Schools, churches, and even the family can be placed in this fourth category or classification.

Once the administrator understands that any organization has both external and internal functions, he/she is next confronted with the fact that the four functional problems (e.g., goal-attainment) have both external and internal aspects. If we keep in mind that "since organizations are defined by the primacy of a particular type of goal, the focus of their value systems must be the legitimation of that goal in terms of the functional significance of its attainment for the more inclusive system" (Hills, 1968, p. 67). Viewed more specifically or precisely, if the primary function of the public schools is to socialize young people so that they can function successfully in their

65

respective societal roles in the future, they need to develop
(1) the competency to fulfill those roles; (2) the capacity to <u>be-
have interpersonally</u> in ways appropriate to their ascribed roles;
(3) a commitment to live up to generally perceived and accepted
<u>normative patterns</u> of the society; and (4) an understanding
and acceptance of the primary <u>values</u> of the social system. Obviously, no organization can for long completely neglect other
system problems with which any organization is confronted (Ibid.,
p. 68).

Several points need to be made as this extremely brief
treatment of the "environments" of the manager draws to a close.
In the first place, an administrator should plan to assist the
larger community (his/her <u>external</u> environment) by assuming
some direct responsibility for society's welfare over and above
his or her own immediate task as a professional. Second, keeping in mind that the <u>external</u> environment relates to the still
broader social environment within the society typically, at present there is no escaping the fact that this external environment has now become culture-wide and even world-wide in scope.
Finally, the concept of 'future shock'--our collision with the
future, so to speak--as we move toward some sort of "Third-
Wave" society is one which the administrator should make every
effort to comprehend in all of its ramifications.

Various Technical Concerns

As we draw near to the end of these two chapters cover-
ing what we have termed "currently useful generalizations"
about physical education and athletics, we will touch briefly on
what have been termed the "various technical administrative concerns" (Zeigler and Spaeth, eds. 1975, p. 13). Here we are
referring to such concerns as legal liability, facilities and equipment, personnel administration, instructional supervision, curriculum development, finance and business management, microcomputer literacy, etc.

First, there is the question of legal liability, a problem
that appears to have grown larger and more complex during the
past decade. Moriarty points this out forcefully in "Physical
Activity & Legal Liability," a monograph published by the Research Council of the Canadian Association for Health, Physical
Education and Recreation as follows:

> The increase in legal action in the sporting world has
> been followed by an explosion in both the public and
> professional literature . . . The entire number of
> single articles dealing with sport and the law in America

and Canada in the 1960's has been more than dupli-
cated by entire issues devoted to sport and law in the
1970's . . . (Moriarty, 1980, pp. 2-3).

Obviously, the physical educator/coach needs to know how to
avoid legal litigation; what to do in case of a lawsuit; and the
various aspects of liability for injuries in sport and physical
education activities.

The matter of facilities and equipment for physical education and athletics is often a vexing one. Unfortunately, the
recommendations of various national conferences on this subject
are often overlooked or disregarded by local officials despite
the remonstrations of the sport and physical education administrator. We are not suggesting for a minute that we in this
field know all the answers about the engineering and architectural problems that arise in connection with our facilities. However, people outside our field rarely if ever understand the
problems that we are likely to encounter after the gymnasium,
the pool, or the exercise room have been in use for some time.
The task seems to be one of developing ways of tactfully but
definitely calling such information to the attention of all involved in the planning, and then working assiduously--with a
bit of prayer on the side--to ensure that the best possible facility with the most adequate equipment is provided.

We appreciate that communities face almost insuperable
odds in their attempts to finance education at all levels. This
means that we must be careful to avoid unreasonable demands
when new facilities are to be constructed. However, the needs
cannot be underestimated either as we are indeed building for
the present--and the future! Economy and adequacy are two
words that will in all probability cause conflict unless we make
our needs known in such a way that all concerned will appreciate the problems.

Finally, in this section, we must mention briefly the matter of so-called "microcomputer literacy," an area that is undoubtedly affecting all levels of education increasingly. Granting that few people in our field have yet acquired extensive
competency in this educational and research tool or device, the
administrator of physical education and athletics cannot afford
to allow himself or herself to be caught in a position where the
services that can be made available in this way are not fully
utilized or utilized in the overall program. Even if we as individuals do have the personal competencies needed to work in
this area, it is vital that we develop positive attitudes toward
the inherent possibilities in this technological advancement. As
administrators we should at least know the limitations of the

various systems available and where to turn for assistance as we seek to gain the advantages of this technology for our work.

Professional Ethics

Because a person is a social animal, and because physical activity--often including sports and games--are typically part of everyone's life, we should give careful consideration to the problem of helping the young person to bridge the gap from an early sense of life with its embryonic, amorphous value integrations to the making of ethical decisions in competitive sport and similar types of physical activity. We should be helping that person--the intramural, sport-club, or varsity athlete often involved in highly competitive situations charged with strong emotions--to develop conscious convictions in which the mind leads and the emotions follow to the greatest possible extent. It is at this point also where wise educational leadership can by example and precept serve as the best possible guide for the young person often confronted with difficult ethical decisions involving both speech and conduct.

The term "ethics" is typically employed in three different ways, each of which has a relation to the other. First, ethics classifies a general pattern or "way of life" (e.g., Muslim ethics). Second, it refers to a listing of rules of conduct, or what is often called a moral code (e.g., the "fair play" ethics of an athlete). Last, it describes an area of inquiry about ways of life or rules of conduct (e.g., that subdivision of philosophy now known as meta-ethics).

History substantiates that ethics is a description of "irregular progress toward complete clarification of each type of ethical judgment" (Abelson, 1975, p. 82). By this is meant the "search for the meaning and standards of good in general, and of well-being, right conduct, moral character, and justice in particular." How does one judge exactly, or even generally, how much "irregular progress" has been made since the development of Greek ethics began in the fifth century B.C.? One may argue that the changing political, economic, and other social forces of that time required the introduction of a new way of conduct--just as today there appears to be an urgent need for altered standards of conduct during this evidently transitional period.

It would be an obvious exaggeration to say that there are as many approaches to ethics and/or moral philosophy today as there are philosophers. Conversely, however, there is no single, non-controversial foundation stone upon which to build the entire structure of ethics. This is not to say that there are not some aspects of this branch of philosophy upon which there has been fairly wide agreement. In the past moral philsophers offered general guidance as to what to do, what to seek, and how to treat others--injunctions as to what to do, what to seek, and how to treat others--injunctions that we could well keep in mind in the consideration of sport ethics and ethics for physical education and athletics administrators.

As a rule philosophers have not tried to preach to their adherents in the same way as theologians have felt constrained to do. Nevertheless, many philosophers have offered practical advice that included pronouncements on what was good and bad, or right and wrong. Still, many have persistently searched for a true moral code--a normative ethical system upon which all people could and should base their conduct. More recently, however, the advent of philosophical analysis as a distinct approach during this century in the Western world has thrust the contemporary analytic philosopher right into the middle of the struggle between what has been called ethical objectivism and ethical subjectivism (the argument that truth is independent of person, time, and place as opposed to the idea that moral judgments about people relate only to the way we think or feel about people and their actions). Thus, at the very time when the world is in such a turmoil with "hot" wars, "cold" wars, terrorists--at the very time when people of all ages want to know about "what to do, what to seek, and how to treat others"--the large majority of scholars in the field of philosophy are almost completely silent, avoiding the rational justification of any type of moral system, and analyzing the meaning and function of moral concepts and statements only occasionally.

What we find, therefore, is that the dispensing of ethical wisdom in life is generally left to people who have given the subject much less scholarly thought than those related professionally to the discipline of philosophy. What we have as a result is a situation where theologians, dramatists, novelists, poets, medical doctors, politicians, sport figures, educational administrators--in no special order of importance--offer an amalgam of opinions ranging from suggestions to dogma about all aspects of life including sports and games. Most notable among these amateur philosophers are scientists and comedians--people who may have earned justifiable fame, or even notoriety. We believe strongly that at least part of the professional output of sport and physical education philosophers ought to be pointed directly in an applied manner to what might be called the lay public and also to their colleagues in educational circles and closely related fields.

Those of us concerned with the administration of physical education and athletics should be working toward the elimini- nation of irrational ethical beliefs while attempting to discover the soundest possible ethical system for our evolving society. We recognize that the task of normative inquiry can be most difficult, especially when complex issues and conclusions stray into the realm of metaethics. However, it is precisely at this point where the sport and physical activity philosopher ought to be offering his or her services and working cooperatively with the administrator. If we ever hope to be able to justify ethical theory in competitive sport, we need to be able to state correctly, elucidate sufficiently, and defend adequately any moral or ethical claims and arguments that may be made--and codified into rule books--about participation in competitive sport.

Evaluation and Measurement

Evaluation and measurement is an aspect of physical edu- cation and athletics administration where many managers falter. What is there to evaluate, to measure? If measurements were taken, what should we measure? With the undergraduate pro- gram would we measure the number of graduates and their class averages--including those who make the dean's list? With the graduate program should we also count the number of mas- ter's degrees awarded, or similarly the number of doctoral de- grees? Should we find out what our graduates are doing, if they are all gainfully employed in the promotion of sport and physical activity in both the public and private sector? Or should we attempt to assess the impact that our field, including our graduates, have had on that region of the society in which they are serving? Is there sufficient demand for our "pro- ducts," at least as we evaluate the situation? Are we being provided with sufficient resources of all types? How good is our intramurals and physical recreation program, including the many sport clubs we sponsor? Is our intercollegiate athletics program meeting its goals--by the way, what are its goals? What do we consider to be our "general education function" at all educational levels? How well are we fulfilling that function? How much of an opportunity are those in our allied professions receiving to carry out their professional programs? Are we co- operating sufficiently with them? Are our teachers teaching well; are our coaches exerting effective educational leadership? Are our professors publishing both sub-disciplinary and sub- professional articles and monographs (i.e., material to help teachers and coaches in the field and research to add to our field's body of knowledge about what it is that we do)? Are our offerings well regarded by our colleagues in educational in- stitutions--perhaps to the extent that our physical education grades are figured in with "academic" averages? These are all

questions that we might well ask ourselves about our work--
and, of course, there are many others--but we can rarely if
ever find answers to these questions that are both sufficient
and satisfactory.

We know that sport and physical education, or whatever
it is that we call ourselves, has many of the earmarks of a profession, but we continue to be perplexed about whether we
have stronger ties inherently with the humanities, the social
sciences, or the natural sciences. We believe that human motor
performance in sport, dance, play, and exercise is inescapably
unique, and that it does not fit neatly into any category. Our
field was once one of the liberal arts, but at one point in the
Middle Ages it was torn from this lofty perch. Purposeful human movement appears to have deep roots in all three of the
above areas, depending on the angle from which it is viewed.
One group stresses that it belongs more to the humanities, because the basic aim is to help people of all ages achieve certain
attitudes and appreciations that will enable them to lead richer,
fuller lives. A second faction will say that this field has a
greater role to play in the social sciences--that is, we help children and young people to acquire desirable personality traits
through participation in various types of physical activities that
are educationally sound. Then, too, our activities provide an
opportunity for people to grow within the group as interrelated,
interdependent people; we foster the right balance between
competition and cooperation, they say.

Those who emphasize the natural scientific aspects of the
field (i.e., the functional effects of physical activity, motor
learning and development, and mechanical and muscular analysis
of physical skills) are anxious to gather as much systematized
knowledge as possible through all possible avenues and types of
research. In this, of course, there must be continuing (and
continual?) borrowing from mathematics, all of the natural sciences (with special emphasis on the bio-sciences), and the more
laboratory-oriented phases of psychology. Certainly there must
be borrowing from everywhere possible to get all the facts, but
there may well be some aspects of life and living not accessible
to science or even factor analysis. Immediate concern about an
improved place for physical education and athletics in the curriculum hierarchy of education is important, but in the final
analysis we should have as our aim to inculcate attitudes in our
population so that people of all ages will take part in healthful,
enjoyable physical activities throughout their lives. This we
cannot--we dare not--forget as we evaluate and measure our
various programs.

A Final Word

It has not been possible to cover all of the currently useful generalizations possible within this chapter and the previous one. Please understand that the opinions expressed here are not intended to serve as an indoctrination. Although many of the thoughts and facts offered may represent what appear to be some of the better current judgments, they must be made to stand the challenge of close scrutiny and investigation--especially as they may apply to discussions of the various cases that follow.

In closing we must say a few words about organizational decline and so-called "cutback management" that you may well experience as future administrators. By this we are referring to the management of organizations where spare resources are not available to assist with growth, innovation, possible uncertainty, and the granting of regular raises--not marginal cost-of-living increments. Many of us in the older generations knew very little and hence were unprepared with the necessary knowledge and attitudes to cope with the necessary management cutback of the 1970's. This topic ties in with evaluation and measurement inevitably, because we can no longer afford the luxury of snap judgments, intuition, and similar informal analysis without putting our programs into jeopardy.

This is a highly complex topic, with which we cannot hope to deal in detail here and now. However, a few points will be made in the hope that an opportunity will be provided for you to pursue this topic further. For example, Levine tells us that there are four causes of public organization decline as follows: (1) problem depletion, (2) environmental entropy, (3) political vulnerability, and (4) organizational atrophy (Levine, 1978, pp. 318-319). Problem depletion simply means that the problem for which the organization was started has been met or alleviated. Environmental entropy is a situation or state in which the organization finds itself when capacity for public support has lessened. The explanation for political vulnerability can be understood more readily; certain factors are present in the situation which make the organization vulnerable to waves of political change (people think the organization is not "doing the job"). There are many reasons, of course, for what is called "organizational atrophy" (e.g., poor evaluation and measurement, inadequate management).

Obviously, when an administrator is faced with a "management of decline" situation, he or she should be ready to face it with sound knowledge and attitudes that will assist him or her to survive. Strategic choices will need to be made to face

72

the four causes of decline listed above. The management team
and the staff members must be fully informed about desirable
cutback management tactics. Steps will have to be taken to re-
sist decline or to make the decline as smooth as possible. If
you are ever confronted with an administrative problem of this
magnitude, we urge you to seek counsel at the first opportunity as you plan for the future (Ibid., p. 321).

We simply do not know what the future holds in store for
us as physical education and athletics managers. When the
"hard" decisions must be made, there is always the possibility
of a strong, authoritarian solution. We feel that the case method approach to the teaching of human relations and administration in this society is more appropriate; through this technique
the management team can be "tough-minded," and yet there is
the distinct possibility that democratic rights and processes may
be carried on into the twenty-first century.

References

Abelson, R. and Friquegnon, M.: Ethics for Modern Life.
New York: St. Martin Press, 1975.

American Association for Health, Physical Education, and Recre-
ation: Graduate Education in Health Education, Physical
Education, Recreation Education, Safety Education, and
Dance. Washington, D. C.: AAHPER, 1967.

American Association of School Administrators: Staff Relations
in School Administration. Washington, D. C.: The
Association, 1955.

Cleave, S. L.: "An Analysis of the Organization and Administration of Sport Club Programmes in Ontario Universities."
M.A. thesis, The University of Western Ontario, 1978.

Conant, James B.: The Education of American Teachers. New
York: McGraw-Hill Book Company, 1963.

Gross, B. M.: The Managing of Organizations, vols. 1 and 2.
New York: Crowell-Collier Publishing Company, 1964.

Hills, R. J.: Toward a Science of Organization. Eugene,
Oregon: Center for the Advanced Study of Educational
Administration, 1968.

Johnson, Harry M.: The relevance of the theory of action to
historians. Social Science Quarterly (June 1969).

Levine, C. H.: Organizational decline and cutback management. Public Administration Review, 38, 4:316-315, 1978.

Katz, R. L.: Skills of an effective administrator. Harvard Business Review, 33, 1:1955. (See below).

Katz, R. L.: Skills of an effective administrator. Harvard Business Review, 52, 5:90-102, 1974. (An updated version of the above article.)

Mackenzie, R. A.: The management process in 3-D. Harvard Business Review, 47, 6:80-87, 1969.

McCloy, C. H.: Current trends in graduate study. Journal of Health, Physical Education, and Recreation, 28 (November 1957), 33-34.

Milstein, M. M., and Belasco, J. A.: Educational Administration and the Behavioral Sciences: A Systems Perspective. Boston: Allyn and Bacon, 1973.

Moriarty, R.: Physical Activity & Legal Liability. Ottawa, Canada: Canadian Association for Health, Physical Education and Recreation, 1980. 39 p.

Zeigler, E. F., and Paton, G. A.: Consolidation and innovation in graduate study in physical education and sport, in Proceedings, 77th Annual Meeting, National College Physical Education Association for Men. Chicago, IL.: Office of Publications Services, Univ. of Illinois, Chicago Circle, 1974, 101-107.

Zeigler, E. F., and Spaeth, M. J., eds.: Administrative Theory and Practice in Physical Education and Athletics. Englewood Cliffs, N. J.: Prentice-Hall, Inc., 1975.

PART 2

AN EXPERIENTIAL APPROACH -- THE CASE METHOD

CHAPTER 4
TEACHING AND LEARNING BY THE CASE METHOD

The primary objective of a course in management theory and practice such as this is undoubtedly to increase each prospective manager's capacity to work effectively with others. The ability to lead on many occasions, to follow in other situations, and to cooperate at all times is essential. Students can be helped to develop an attitude and a theoretical point of view toward managerial practice. The case method of instruction will help you to determine a frame of reference in which you can develop your administrative skills. In this way you will actually be preparing yourselves for positions of responsibility in physical education and athletics at any level of the educational system, not to mention the many alternate careers that are becoming increasingly available. You will be learning to work with others in a plan to accomplish objectives on the way toward the realization of long range aims, all of which have been devised through group effort.

Students and teacher alike, all of whom have had experience at some level in team sports, can realize much more fully than others that group effort means, literally, "team effort." A team can best achieve its goal by unselfish, cooperative play by each of its members. Each individual has to carry out his or her duties to the best of his or her ability. You may well desire personal prestige and gain, but, above all, it is most desirable for you to make your own interests secondary, striving to do your share--and a bit more--in the drive for eventual team victory.

At the outset we wish to stress that the importance of factual knowledge cannot be minimized. An administrator must possess a large store of facts about his or her work and must also know where to find information quickly. Such knowledge, however, is not the main attribute of a good manager. The important qualities are the ability to work cooperatively with others; the ability to think and act responsibly; and the ability to provide an "atmosphere" where co-workers will have opportunities to work effectively and with true satisfaction as members of the group.

Developing an Administrative Frame of Mind

Students need to develop an "administrative or managerial frame of mind." This cannot be achieved by mere reading
and discussion of the various assignments, although this technique certainly gives some increase in understanding. Through
the case method students and instructor will meet new situations
constantly. These situations cannot help but be characterized
by facts, half-facts, and opinions.

If you hope to find "the answers" in this case book, you
will be disappointed. You will find a certain number of opinions, which may be correct in those situations to which they apply. Your answer may be an answer, but you cannot state unequivocally that it is the answer. Mature administrators can
probably recall many of the problems they have encountered.
Many of them came up through "the old school" where they
were offered what were called "principles" texts. Although the
term principles has almost vanished when used this way, a number of the present texts still include material presented in this
manner. It would be next to impossible to lift these "principles" out of context and apply them directly to the problem at
hand without considerable adjustment. Thus, how many of these
principles were they forced to by-pass because of the practical
considerations of the moment? The administrator may start action "according to the book," but what happens thereafter depends upon the many unforeseeable factors which always enter
any situation.

A Supplement to Experience

Of course, the case method of teaching human relations
and management is not an infallible substitute for experience.
But it does expose the student to a variety of cases taken
from the field which he or she is preparing to enter. As the
group faces these concrete, true-to-life (but disguised) situations, it is the responsibility of the instructor to guide each
member in such a way that he or she arrives at a solution by
constantly examining and re-examining all the relevant facts
that are known.

With this approach you are not asked what you believe
about the importance of athletics in the educational system.
Answering from your background in what amounts to a principles course, you might say that "competitive athletics under
competent leadership should be an integral part of every
school's educational program." Has such "experience" really
helped you to act in a given situation? Consider the following
example.

You are presented with an actual case situation where a particular principal had made the statement that "athletics are all right in their place." Furthermore, this principal has control of the budget, and he tells the athletic director that no "regular school funds" are going to be diverted to leisure activities, the beneficial result of which is questionable. To back his stand further, the principal knows that certain influential members of the school board agree with his position 100 per cent. Certain other relevant facts, half-facts, and opinions are made known to you about this school in question. Now, what do you think? If you were in charge of men's and women's athletics, to whom would you turn for support? Would you resign on the spot? Not if you want another job! Would you begin to criticize the principal publicly at every opportunity? Would you try to curry favor with the chairperson of the school board, whose daughter happens to be captain of the girls' volleyball team? What can you do? It is certain that you cannot spout your principles of sport and physical education or what chapter three of your university management text said was the place of athletics in the secondary school. Furthermore, although you might want to, you can't "play God" and fire the principal summarily in order to clear the way for your plans. This is a difficult, real-life problem.

No Fixed Formulas

A word of warning is necessary here, particularly if you are beginning to believe that the case method of teaching administrative decision-making has merit. Possibly no other method of learning is more demanding of your time, effort, and interest. There are no ready-made general theories one can apply to all situations. A certain amount of confusion and frustration will often result from your efforts. The instructor also may have certain misgivings as you all struggle with a particular case. You may ask, "what kind of a technique is this case method in the final analysis?"

However, after a month or so--perhaps even sooner--you will begin to "see the light." Perhaps for the first time you will feel the satisfaction of independent, concrete, responsible thinking. You will realize that fixed formulas and established principles are next to useless in specific situations. What is generally needed in each situation, on the other hand, is a step-by-step pattern to bring the various factions at least partly into harmony so that some progress can be realized.

An instructor may find the need to exercise restraint, because he or she may "know the answers." That is, this person may think this to be true because of greater experience.

It is difficult for an instructor steeped in the traditional pattern to realize that he or she can't fall into the trap of giving you the answer to the problem being discussed, because there probably isn't any one solution at all!

Preparing the Administrator/Manager

Between the teacher and the researcher, there stands a third important category of educational employee that has developed as institutions have grown tremendously in complexity --the administrator/manager. For example, many colleges and universities choose their administrators from among the ranks of successful teachers or researchers. Occasionally the administrator is chosen because of excellent business experience, or perhaps even because of personality or "connections"--and has excelled at neither teaching or research endeavor.

The thesis of this book is that administrators can be best prepared by the case method plan of instruction. Certainly, they cannot become qualified for these important duties because of their eminence as teachers in the traditional pattern, where intelligent statements and "practical advice" are offered to students for consumption. And it is self-evident that research specialists are only occasionally interested in diverting their time from research pursuits to administrative work. Furthermore, it goes almost without saying that a person who has not excelled at either endeavor does not have much to offer unless he or she has a "gift" for dealing with people or has had special training. It could be that this latter individual might have just the sort of intelligence and personality that would lend itself to preparation through the case method approach for a managerial position. Of course, one would not recommend that maladjusted "teachers" and "researchers" be drawn into administration--although this does seem to happen at the lower supervisory levels too often.

No matter whether we are considering administration or management at the higher, intermediate, or lower levels of education, all faculty and staff members have administrative responsibilities to varying degrees. This is one more reason why the case plan of instruction seems particularly good. In our opinion we believe that it represents the best possible method of implementing the concept of "democratic administration" that has been brought to the fore in this field in recent years.

Traditional Approach Found Wanting

It could be argued that those responsible for professional preparation should simply choose their teacher/coaches more carefully, and then give them the knowledge, skills, and principles which the experts have gathered and included in the many texts available. In principle this approach appears to have considerable merit, but educational psychology has shown that reading assignments and related lectures do not prepare them to manage programs. For that matter, typical tests, term papers, curriculum syllabi, occasional brief discussions, trips to swimming pool filtration plants, or any of the other devices employed have also failed to meet this need satisfactorily. Why is it that graduating professional students often approach their first positions with more than ordinary misgivings?

It was probably such shortcomings which led to the introduction of student teaching and field work experience into the various professional preparation curricula. These brief experiences help, but rarely do they give students the opportunity to think and to reason about administrative problems. We can argue about the amount of time spent in management theory and practice courses, but it is simply too wasteful of time and money for our students to learn everything through the "school of hard knocks."

Orientation to Respective Roles

Many instructors have an innate urge to tell their juniors just what the score is. They have been "through the mill," and they want to tell students what they will encounter on the job. Consider the case of the young teacher/coach who complains that the principal doesn't listen to his solution for a problem connected with scheduling. The instructor would generally suggest that the young person should try the principal's plan and give it a good chance to work out, or, better still, suggest that the teacher/coach "ad-prac"[1] his way through the situation by praising his superior and then indirectly leading him to adopt the teacher's idea as his own. These thoughts may arise in the instructor's mind because people told him or her what was "right" at an earlier time. Perhaps the instructor's older friends have suggested ways of obtaining objectives by flattery and other devious means. Now, the instructor wants to play the role of elder wise man.

Naturally, better teachers really do have a sound background of facts and experiences. They have faced most of the problems which students will encounter. Many times teachers do know what students should do or say in a given situation.

---

[1] A slang phrase that was used to mean "polishing the apple."

In fact, the teachers must have been typically successful earlier in their methods of solving problems, or they probably would not be holding their present positions.

Nevertheless, the sad fact remains that no amount of theoretical or factual knowledge passed on by a competent teacher can give the student wisdom and judgment about how to act most effectively as an administrator. You must develop and use your own knowledge, your own wisdom, and your own insight to penetrate a difficult situation involving human relations.

Let us assume that the young teacher mentioned above heeds the well-meaning advice and tries a devious approach to get his superior to come around to his opinion. What are the chances that the principal will accept the teacher's advice? Would you wish to bet on the chance that the recommendation will be accepted?

Instruction by the case method has a democracy-in-action flavor that can never be approached by the more dictatorial method of "telling." Students, as members of the class, begin with the same facts as the instructor--the case at hand. Your task is to analyze the known facts and arrive at a solution systematically. Each one of you has exactly the same opportunity to offer a solution to the administrative problem area under discussion. All contribute to the development of a set of "currently useful generalizations" that will goven policy formation in this particular case. Actually, not even the instructor knows the answer. There is no set of answers that can be consulted. It is quite possible that, because of the way the case has been presented, or for some other reason, the best answer has not yet come to light.

Through this method of instruction, a new set of personal relations precepts will appear to each participant. The spotlight does not fall on the teacher as the star performer. You begin to transfer your attention to all the other personalities in the group. In this class all are equals; hence, you must know what each is thinking. To achieve this there must be the chance for freedom of expression. Only through this means is there a hope of arriving at a mutually satisfactory solution. Because each student realizes that he or she is a part of this process, the individual thinks more and is anxious to "try his or her wings." You begin to realize that others will come up with suggestions that you had not even considered. You acquire experience in expressing your own thoughts to an extremely critical audience.

You may wonder just what the instructor does in this approach. There is no set formula for conducting classes by this method. The instructor generally introduces the method and assigns the cases to be read for class discussion. He or she becomes an important member of the group and asks pertinent questions. Also, the instructor offers considered opinions occasionally, perhaps when his or her contribution is asked for by some class member. If the students have many logical arguments and opinions to offer, the instructor must be alert to understand and evaluate each contribution. He or she may be hearing certain reasoning about a particular problem for the first time. You, the student, are in a position where you don't necessarily have to parrot the instructor's views to get an "A" in the course. But you do have to justify your stand against all comers. If you fail to win your point, you must be ready to accept a compromise or even to act on the basis of majority opinion.

There does not appear to be any set remark for an instructor to make to open discussion. If a case seems to be very complicated, the instructor might ask, "What is the main issue in this case?" Or simply, "What did you think of this case problem?" might be sufficient. After some experience, students begin to look for the main issue at the outset--then determine the sub-issues. At times the instructor will be tempted to redirect the thinking of the group, but he or she must decide if such action is appropriate. Even when a student appears to have misinterpreted some of the facts, the instructor must make a choice again whether to speak out or to wait for others to challenge.

With a mature group the instructor may want to give individual students the opportunity to chair certain discussions. The instructor might even choose to sit outside of the "traditional circle." (Students generally sit in a circle, or have swivel chairs, in order to face each other when speaking.) Some students who lead discussions for the first time tend to become quite "directive" or even dictatorial in their approach-- but the rest of the class will usually not be denied. They tend to take over and make it a real group discussion. The chairperson should be careful to see that each person has a chance to express his opinion. Hand-raising is perhaps the best means to let the chairperson know that a person wishes to speak, although this may not be necessary in a small class. The chairperson should keep track of the order in which three or four hands were raised. Coffee-drinking and/or smoking may help in the creation of an informal atmosphere, but the latter practice has become offensive to some and is often against fire regulations.

The Role of Lectures

Most students have come to expect that the answers will be handed to them in some form or other. Thus, the case plan of instruction will come as rather a shock to them. They may find that they have no background from which to draw material. In fact, the strain of such active thinking may be great, especially when their arguments are generally challenged--if they choose to speak. Instructors may find that group opinions are not forming, even though there has been much heated discussion. At that point he or she is best advised not to lecture, especially when the group does not appear to be arriving at the instructor's conception of the "correct answer."

There is, however, a place for lecturing in the case plan of instruction. If case discussions are confined to the usual fifty-minute period (eighty minutes is much to be preferred), the instructor may want to deliver a brief "lecturette" at the end of the period to pull some of the loose ends together. In such lecturettes, he or she must remember the relationship that is being encouraged between the instructor and the students. There should be nothing of significance in the presentation that has not come out of the class discussion.

If the instructor and the group decide that a second session is desirable, the instructor could then deliver the remarks at the beginning of the second fifty-minute period. This technique is reinforced by Dearborn's earlier analysis of the five-fold role of the instructor in the case method course (discussion leader, resource person, helpful expert, evaluator or summarizer, and judge of performance (in McNair, 1954, pp. 128-132).

Gragg points out that the student new to the case method approach typically undergoes three clearly recognizable phases. First, she realizes his inability to think of all the suggestions that will come from his fellow students. She has read the case carefully and prepared her answers or solutions, perhaps in written form. Sometimes she (or he) types out the solution to a case on one page and lists the "currently useful generalizations" arising from this situation on another. To her surprise, in class she encounters a multitude of opinions and interpretations that she hadn't even considered (in McNair, 1954, pp. 12-13).

About the end of the first eight to ten weeks, students can generally accept help from others in good grace. Realizing that they can't know it all, they draw more heavily on the ideas of others. Although competition for grades is as keen as ever, no one seems too worried about giving or receiving assistance to a reasonable extent.

If all progresses well, intelligent students should realize toward the end of the course that their instructor may think that he or she has the answer, and it may indeed even turn out to be the best answer. But what is most important, they understand that they are entitled to their own opinions, so long as they are ready to substantiate their facts and to argue their opinions logically. The aim in this approach, of course, is the development of a wise administrator, capable of intelligent self-direction and ready to accept advice from his fellows without having to fall back on the authority of his or her position to achieve sound results.

Case Method Not Perfect

Although fine development can be expected from the case plan of instruction, it is not perfect. There is a great difference between thinking about an administrative problem constructively and cooperatively on the one hand, and being responsible for a decision that may radically affect the success of an important school program of physical education and athletics on the other. We believe, however, that this approach is the best substitute for actual experience that has yet been devised. Understanding, judgment, and independent thought are the rewards to be gained from a careful application of this plan.

The "atmosphere" in the class is all-important. This point cannot be stressed too much. It involves such intangibles as the relationship between you, as student, and the teacher. The instructor may quickly begin to call you by your first name. Although it is not necessary that you address him or her so familiarly, we always tell a new group of students to call us by whatever name they feel comfortable with--first name, last name, Dr., Professor, Mr., Ms., but not "Hey you!" The main point is that you both feel that you are discussing a problem as equals. Only then will the student feel free to express all his or her ideas about a subject. Occasionally, generally when asked, the instructor will state some opinions too. Each time he or she does this, keep in mind that these ideas are only those of one person analyzing a situation--albeit an intelligent, experienced observer. Thus, you will learn to express your own ideas. Equally important, you will gain respect for the opinions of others. Everyone in the class, including the instructor, can't help but gain from this interaction.

Students Learn to Analyze

It is very important in this plan of instruction for you to learn how to analyze situations carefully and completely. Some may do this automatically, but many in the class will read through a case quickly and rather carelessly. Some may even wander far from what appear to the majority to be the central issues of a problem, but the instructor will try to ask "leading" questions to keep the class on approximately the right track. Your instructor may ask you to "write up" cases of different types that you may have observed or experienced. This is extremely valuable experience in many ways. Perspective is developed which can be most helpful. In writing a case, you may give an over-all interpretation after the basic "reporting" has been finished. It is advisable to interpret the case from the standpoints of the various people actually involved in the situation. Such a case writing assignment is best concluded with a summary statement of your own proposed solution to the problem. (For a further discussion of the writing and analyzing of a case, see pp. 102-106.) The general complaint of beginning students is that they do not have enough facts to arrive at a reliable solution. This may be, but often you will get a different slant on the problem when your instructor inquires if you have really utilized those facts that you do have at hand.

Beware of "Story-telling"

When you are analyzing a case orally, or writing up an analysis as an assignment, do not waste any more time than necessary in story-telling. All involved are supposed to have read the case carefully several times, and the instructor may have practically memorized it! Of course, you do not have to memorize anything, because you may refer to the written facts of the case at all times. You could make such a reference in a regular life situation, so why not here? If you aren't prepared when the instructor calls on you for an opinion, he will quickly pass on to someone who is ready to speak. Many instructors give grades for class participation, and a consistent lack of preparation will surely be noted. If you are not ready to speak--and keep in mind that some instructors will allow you to make that choice--be as frank as possible in your response. It makes little sense to offer an ill-considered opinion to cover up for poor preparation.

Some cases will have happened in such a way that definite stages are readily apparent. Chronological sequence of occurrences is usually very important in a report. After a preliminary analysis, it is possible to consider the relationships among the various participants in the case. At this point the class is ready to examine any strong attitudes or beliefs of the people involved as evidenced by their statements or actions. The group can also try to determine what changes have taken place in a pattern of incidents and what caused these changes to occur. Each student might then be ready to postulate his or her own solution to the case problem, if such a solution is possible. Don't be afraid to use your imagination at this point. It will often lead you to new interpretations of the facts that you had not previously considered.

Subjective Opinions vs. Objective Facts

Keep in mind that you must judge between a subjective opinion and an objective fact as well as between relevant and irrelevant material. If a coach states, for example, that the athletic director was unreasonable to think that the team could get along with such poor equipment, you, as a careful analyst, must determine if the director really was being unreasonable. Could it be that the coach used poor judgment in making such a remark? When asked to penetrate more deeply into such statements, some cynics in the class may feel that time is wasted in such imaginative speculation. Gathering together the various possibilities and re-examining the fragmentary evidence in the situation may assemble into a pattern just the sort of material you will want to have at hand later, when facing an actual life situation.

The truism "things are never as simple as they seem to be" is at the heart of the case plan of instruction. Each person involved in a case problem is inescapably unique, for no two people see the same situation in exactly the same way. When you realize this, your own discernment will greatly improve. Then you will be on the way to a better understanding of human relations in this increasingly complex human world.

When a Case Is Not What It May Seem to Be

This leads us to the conclusion that a case if typically not what it may seem to be on the surface. Every student will analyze the problem through the "colored glasses" of his or her own background and present attitudes. One student may look at things as either black or white. In one case, the coach will be his fair-haired boy, while the principal is the "rat." Such a student's opinion is generally that if the principal is fired, everyone will live happily ever after. Another student may be accustomed to having the instructor think for her. If this student offers an opinion to which the instructor nods and smiles, she feels she has the right answer. Still a third student may be looking for the approval of his classmates. Instead of expressing what he really feels, he says what he thinks the class wants to hear. An occasional student will go to the other extreme, "wandering off into the night." At first, his feelings may be hurt when group opinion tends to force him back onto the well-lighted street of accepted fact. Of course, such a person may become stubborn and even disrupt the class. Students and teacher alike must ask themselves whether students who appear to be going off on a tangent should be held in check (if at all).

One of the facts that we discover upon beginning this method of instruction is that some students talk a great deal more often than others. Does this mean that these people are the most intelligent and wise members of the group? It soon becomes apparent that this is definitely not so. Many times these students are only the ones who, by nature, tend to express themselves more than others, or perhaps they grew up in a family situation where they were encouraged to speak freely at all times. When the first set of written case analyses are returned, you might be surprised to find that the young woman who spoke in class only when spoken to actually wrote the best paper. You might be further somewhat surprised to learn that the student who was always ready with a quick answer has analyzed the case problem only superficially.

It is difficult for instructors who are leading a discussion for the "umpteenth" time to avoid directive teaching and strong class guidance. We simply cannot direct the discussion to follow a specific pattern because last year's class came up with a certain proposed solution to the matter that seemed excellent. There is not any reason to believe that a pre-determined solution would work best. Thus, there is no "pat" answer! Two groups discussing an identical case may decide on diametrically opposed solutions. We don't recommend that the instructor look for and encourage this sort of result. We do suggest that you let the "cards fall where they may."

Practical Suggestions for the Student

1. Don't try to copy a friend's solution to a case simply because he or she is known as a good student.

2. Find out what the problems--the main problem and the sub-problems--are before you try to give any answers.

3. Don't reject a classmate's idea summarily if you disagree. Conversely, don't accept his theory at once if you concur.

4. Work at developing your powers of perception and discrimination.

5. Develop a point of interest if it seems important to you.

6. Pay attention to what is said--it may prove worthwhile.

7. It is often easy to detect the biases of others; to be able to realize your own prejudices is most difficult.

8. If you feel discouraged and frustrated with the case method approach, discuss your feelings frankly and fully.

9. Don't force the instructor to give an answer, just so that you will go away "happy."

10. When all else fails, read the case again.

Practical Suggestions for the Instructor

1. Do not try to copy someone else's formula for the teaching of a class by the case plan of instruction.

2. Be certain that you, as the instructor, understand just what point the student is trying to make. Do not accept or reject his or her idea quickly.

3. When a student asks you a question, your best answer may be to ask another question.

4. Later on in the course, the instructor may suggest some approaches which the students seem to have missed in a particular case. To do so at first may be disastrous.

5. Remember that your task is to help your students develop their powers of perception and discrimination.

6. Try to keep the discussion related to the case in question; but don't cut a student off abruptly if he or she seems to be wandering off the topic a bit.

7. A student will talk about those points of interest that seem important to him or her. Soon most of the class will realize that they should pay attention to what the individual is saying.

8. Instructors can help a great deal by tactfully holding unwarranted assumptions up for inspection by all.

9. If you feel that you must make a point, do it in a matter of fact way and be done with it.

10. When students refer back to actions or words of a person involved in an earlier case, make sure that the class understands that there is no such thing as a principle that can be applied to help solve all problems of a similar nature.

11. Don't come to class prepared to lecture on a certain aspect of a case to be introduced for the first time that day.

12. Despite any insecurity you may feel, don't fall into the trap and give them your answer.

13. If a student seems to be discouraged and frustrated about his or her progress, try to get several students with similar feelings together out of class and have a bull session about the problem.

References

Anderson, C. R., Menning, J. H., and Wilkinson, C. W.: Writing for Business. Homewood, IL.: Richard D. Irwin, Inc., 1960.

Andrews, K. R.: The Case Method of Teaching Human Relations and Administration. Cambridge, Mass.: Harvard University Press, 1953.

Bauer, R. C.: Cases in College Administration. New York: Teachers College, Columbia University, 1955.

Charan, R.: Classroom techniques in teaching by the case method. Academy of Management Review, July, 1976, 116-123.

Dooley, A. R., and Skinner, W.: Casing case method methods. Academy of Management Review, April, 1977, 277-289.

Fraser, C. E.: The Case Method of Instruction. New York: McGraw-Hill Book Co., 1931.

Leenders, M. R., and Erskine, J. A.: Case Research: The Case Writing Process, second ed. London, Ontario: School of Business Administration, The University of Western Ontario, 1978.

McNair, M. P., ed.: The Case Method at the Harvard Business School. New York: McGraw-Hill Book Company, 1954.

Towl, A. R.: Study Administration by Cases. Boston, Mass.: Graduate School of Business Administration, Harvard University, 1969.

Wernette, J.: The theory of the case method. Michigan Business Review, January, 1965.

Zeigler, E. F.: The case method of instruction as applied to the preparation of athletic administrators and coaches. Proceedings, National College Physical Education Association for Men. Minneapolis, MN.: The Association, 1968, 143-152.

CHAPTER 5
EXAMINATIONS AND GRADES

Examinations usually create difficult times for both students and teachers. At examination time one is tested, evaluated, or measured in some way. It is when the student is expected to prove that he or she has achieved a certain level of mastery over a course.

But what is being tested? We are, many say, testing the student's knowledge. A pupil is said to have knowledge if (s)he can memorize or learn certain facts, figures, and/or statements, and then record them on papge (usually) for someone to grade. Teachers lecture while students take notes. These notebook pages are often swallowed whole and regurgitated at exam time. The teacher, who knows what is wanted, sets the examination-- true-false, multiple-choice, matching, short answer, essay quesquestions, or some other type. A relatively few get "A's." Quite a few get "B's." Many pass. Some fail. What does it all mean?

A number of us have begun gradually to set up different criteria, in addition to those mentioned above. We believe there is more to the process of true learning than mere memorization of often isolated data. Our examinations give the students a chance to work some of the facts into a meaningful pattern. Data and facts are important, of course, and they are necessary bases for critical thinking. But where do we strike a happy balance? If the ultimate aim of education is a person capable of intelligent self-direction in society as well as in his or her chosen field of work, how can we test the achievement of this aim to a reasonable extent?

Admittedly, in a case method examination it is difficult for the instructor to explain why a paper is "superior, satisfactory, or unsatisfactory." Actually, the grading is quite subjective, and there is room for some disagreement among instructors as to the classification of grading possible. We lean toward the classification quoted above, but some might wish to grade papers excellent, good, fair, and poor. We are often forced to follow the A, B, C system with pluses and minuses right down to F, but the extent to which this latter approach is possible or desirable with a case method examination is debatable.

We must remember, of course, that our students have typically been trained by the traditional system. This means that we must be a bit patient as instructors when students attempt written case analyses and examinations. Here the objective is to develop examinations which will show us whether students have truly developed the ability to direct themselves capably in managerial situations involving a complexity of facts, half-facts, and opinions. It is no easy task for either the student or the instructor.

There is room for considerable variation in the actual make-up of the examination, although it should consist of the analysis of one or more cases. Within college and university circles we are usually expected to prepare examinations that will take a student two or three hours to complete. It should be possible to carry out a three-hour examination in an administration of physical education and athetics course. One plan is to hand out a written announcement outlining the purposes of the examination approximately two weeks in advance. Students can be given the opportunity to raise questions concerning this proposal during regular classtime. For example, three cases can be included. The first case can be given to the students the day before the actual examination. Students can then spend the evening analyzing the case in small groups, or in any way they see fit. This first case can then be allotted one and one-half hours of the student's time during the exam. A second case can be given out when this amount of time has elapsed, and it can be arranged so that the students will have one hour to read and write up the second case. This leaves only thirty minutes for a short case problem to be read and analyzed very briefly. With this short case the plan is to force the student to make a rapid analysis to show how his/her former way of thinking had, perhaps, changed through the course experience.

This type of examination should be graded only by the instructor who has taught the course--no marking by graduate assistants! This seems only fair, especially if class size is large and the number of opportunities for such analysis and scrutiny is limited. The individual cases should be graded one at a time, until the work of all the students has been covered. The identity of students can be kept unknown by having each student use his/her identification number at the college or university.

Considering the grading process more specifically--and undoubtedly both teacher and student should understand it as fully as possible--we would like to offer for consideration a grading plan that has been developed over the years. It is presented below in the form of a grading guide that can serve to decrease the subjectivity of such an experience to a considerable degree. The reader will observe that it relates largely to the format which is recommended for a written case analysis, asking both general and specific questions for the examiner to respond to as a C (acceptable), plus (+), minus (-), or ? (uncertain) mark is made in the space on the right of the grading sheet. The following, then, is a recommended grading guide for instructors who must grade case analyses:

Grading Guide for Case Analysis	(C or + or - or ?)
1. Statement of main problem and sub-problems?	_____
2. Knowledge base carry-forward?	_____
3. Personality analysis of individuals and relationships?	_____
4. Offers alternative solutions?	_____
5. Considers pro's and con's of each alternative solution?	_____
6. Presents a preferred solution (including pro's and con's)?	_____
7. Includes "currently useful generalizations" (from which future "knowledge base carry-forwards" may be drawn)?	_____
Specific questions to be answered as follows:	
8. Weighs final recommendation carefully?	_____
9. Doesn't re-hash too much of actual case?	_____
10. Is the tone of the analysis constructive?	_____

11. Weighs opinions carefully? _____

12. Avoids phraseology with "no meaning"? _____

13. Doesn't stereotype people? _____

14. Avoids "either-or" thinking? _____

15. Doesn't invoke "immutable principles"? _____

16. Continually presses for rapid action? _____

17. Qualifies everything too much? _____

18. Always reasons as "the boss"? _____

19. Has considered "the whole case"? _____

20. Avoids authoritarian solutions? _____

21. Tells how to improve the administrative process for the future? _____

The first time we tried this type of examination with students specializing in physical education and sport, good students reacted in the way various sources had indicated they would. They were concerned with the problem of communication and the achievement of a common basis of understanding. Those who seemed to be the better students took a more carefully defined clinical approach to the administrative problems involved in a particular case. They understood that no one can hope to learn all the facts in a given situation, and they realized that a person responds not to the facts, but to the facts as he or she sees them.

They believed that the attitude of the administrator was most important in determining the behavior of the various staff members. They stressed the point that action can be taken too fast in the light of possible reactions on the part of the subordinates concerned. They refrained from recommending hard and fast principles of administrative action. Instead they sugguested adoption of basic assumptions that had to stand the test of verification in specific situations.

One of these "basic assumptions," for example, might be that all staff members, as well as managers and supervisors, have good ideas on decisions and policies. They assumed also that staff members want to work for the achievement of the institution's purpose without being driven. They realized that people's behavior is governed by many different factors--that one factor might govern their action today, a different one tomorrow. They understood that staff members will not always be affected by logical thinking; hence, any given action on the part of a staff member might be taken in the light of the assumed favor or disfavor of the group.

Before considering some of the deficiencies of the poor student's approach, an example is offered of one student's solution of a case entitled Meadowbrook High School (A). This is a situation where a new department head discovers that the equipment on hand is of poor quality, orders some excellent new supplies at the lowest possible prices, and is surprised when the order arrives that the material is inferior and certain items are missing. This analysis was written by a third-year student in a _final_ examination. His class had discussed relatively few cases during the year. The following, then, was his case analysis, presumably the best in a class of twelve students:

Meadowbrook High School (A)

The Main Issue:

The main issue in this situation, I think, is that there has been no established administrative policy to guide the procedures to be followed when new equipment was to be purchased. Apparently, the Board of Education had just bought all equipment from Mr. Dobson, a local dealer. They do not appear to have given any consideration to the relative cost of equipment, quality, and service provided. When Bob Reston attempts to obtain good equipment, there is confusion and misunderstanding. First of all, they agree to allow him to have a free hand. Then they changed their minds and invoked the three-pronged policy regarding the purchase of new physical education and athletics equipment. I think, therefore, that the basic problem in this situation is the lack of standardized procedure.

Sub-issues:

(a) The service rendered by Mr. Dobson is a problem which Bob faces. Apparently, Mr. Dobson isn't too concerned with the service which he gives to the school. On two occasions he sent goods of inferior quality with part of the order missing.

(b) A second sub-issue is the relationship existing between the school board, Mr. Dobson, and the vice-principal. Mr. Ross, the business administrator, is a good friend of Mr. Dobson's, also.

Analysis of Individuals and Relationships:

(a) Bob Reston: Bob was a fairly experienced physical education teacher. He had been teaching at least three years. He seems to have been very interested in doing a good job. We see this from the care he took in regard to the ordering of equipment. When the first inferior order arrived from Dobson, Bob should have told the principal then and there and not have let it go. Of course, this may simply have been an indication of the fact that Bob did not realize the local situation in regard to buying. He should have found out.

When given a free hand in the purchase of equipment, Bob might have been wise to question this arrangement. Some control should have been kept by the school administration, and such control typically resides with the business administrator.

Bob made a mistake also when he examined Mr. Dobson's equipment in the Board Room instead of the gymnasium. All tenders should have been treated equally. Finally, Bob should have seen the principal when Dobson again sent a faulty order (because of the line-staff relationship existing within the system).

(b) Mr. Dobson: Dobson was very friendly with people on the Board of Education and the vice-principal. The fact that he delivered inferior orders certainly appears to be evidence of his lack of business integrity--unless someone else put the order together and delivered it without his inspection). He also used what influence he had to bring business his way. It was reported that "he spoke to various members of the Board and tried to put pressure on a manufacturer." All indications did point toward the accuracy of this statement as well as Dobson's actions themselves.

(c) Mr. Lord: Lord tried to help Bob by at least allowing him to attend the Board of Education meeting. Whether Bob should have gone or not is a good question. Possibly Lord himself, who was the buffer between Bob and the Board, should have taken his suggestion forward. On the other hand, it was obvious that Bob would have been able to explain the situation more accurately and capably.

After Mr. Lord took Bob to the Board meeting, no more is heard of the principal in the case. Bob believes that he is not really interested in physical education and athletics. Although we cannot be certain that this is true, it does give us some inkling of Mr. Lord's attitude.

(d) Mr. Ross: The Board's business administrator makes us suspicious, and we can't help but wonder about his integrity. The fact that he allowed Dobson to show his sporting goods in the Board Room, instead of the gymnasium where the others' goods were displayed, seems to bear this statement out. Once again there is a rumor that he receives a "kickback" from Dobson, but we don't know this to be true. However, it does give one an idea of the impression that is being created.

Alternative Solutions:

(a) Alternative #1: If Bob discovers that there are other serious problems in addition to the one presented here, he could ask to be relieved from the administrative aspect of his position. The only argument for such a solution is that Bob at least would not have to face similar struggles there in the future. But this is not a solution to the problem. The next department head would have to face the same problem-- and Bob would have to go on using Dobson's inferior quality equipment in his work as teacher/coach (knowing full well also that "top" dollar was being paid for sub-standard equipment).

(b) Alternative #2: Bob could enlist Ms. Giles' help as women's department head. Between the two of them they could gradually gather "hard" evidence if it were available. With such documented material, they could then work out a plan of action that would result in charges being made against the guilty parties at an appropriate time and place. Such an approach would be difficult and tricky to execute. In the final analysis, if the various suspicions and charges proved to be true, it is possible that certain people would be fired and others would be exposed for what they evidently were. This course of action could be followed, but the whole effort could easily backfire on the two physical education and athletics department heads.

(c) Alternative #3: Bob and Ms. Giles might approach the principal together and once more tell him of the situation.

They could ask him to request that the Board drew up a definite standard procedure to be followed in connection with the purchasing of equipment in the future--and urge him to see to it that this procedure, if adopted, would be followed at all times in all instances. At the same time they could inform the principal again that more inadequate supplies had been received from Mr. Dobson. If the Board is responsible for the procedure to be followed, Bob Reston can do no more than report inferior equipment to this superior. Further action is not up to Bob.

The advantages to this solution are that Mr. Lord, from what we are told of him, is an efficient and helpful individual. We are told that he wants a "big, happy family." When he learns of the dissatisfaction which is present, he will probably help Bob and Ms. Giles. If he is an efficient administrator, he will realize that the system used at present is not producing the best results. He may try to correct the situation gradually.

(d) Alternative #4: Bob could resign from the staff altogether on the assumption that this specific problem is only "the tip of the iceberg." This has the advantage that he would be completely out of the messy situation. On the other hand, this would still not really be a solution to the overall problem. At this point this problem doesn't seem to warrant such a drastic action. He would just be running away from what he had decided was a hopeless fight. Running away might not do own character any good in the long run.

Recommended Solution:

That Alternative #3 be followed in the hope that a definite policy for the purchase of equipment would eventually result. The Board has already introduced a scheme that has merit. Allowing Bob to purchase anything up to fifty dollars with the principal's consent seemed sensible. With any order from fifty dollars to two hundred dollars the further confirmation of the business administrator was recommended. Over and above this, three written tenders had to be submitted by dealers in sporting goods. Perhaps this three-fold plan could be incorporated in any statement offering further clarification to the matter.

In addition to what was stated above in Alternative #3-- the recommended solution--another advantage of this alternative is that the Board will presumably have to take some action if Mr. Lord himself speaks to them about the continuation of the problem. If Mr. Lord told them that the two department heads were very upset about the inferior equipment, the Board would almost be forced to consider some solution. Further, having just recommended that the school purchase better football equipment to prevent injuries, the Board appears to want to protect itself from public criticism. It would not help the Board's position to have the public know that the school system was paying exorbitant prices for inferior equipment.

An additional advantage to this alternative is that it might have long range results for standardization of purchasing procedure. Meadowbrook High School hasn't been in operation too long, and is definitely having some difficulty with certain policies and procedures regarding the purchase of supplies. This solution offers the possibility of a long range policy that could well have implications for the entire school system.

The possible disadvantage of this alternative is that some members of the Board are very friendly with Mr. Dobson. Furthermore, for some reason, Mr. Ross, the business administrator, hasn't been very cooperative with Bob to this point. Nevertheless, Bob seemingly cannot go too far wrong by taking this long range approach (#3) and allowing the situation to "iron itself out" gradually. However, Bob should be firm about not accepting any orders with missing or inferior equipment.

****

The above, was, of course, an example of an analysis by a very good student. Poor students, on the other hand, approached their case analyses in quite a different way. They tended to see things as either "black" or "white." Many of them accepted all opinions offered in the case as fact, while others completely discounted any statements or opinions as unverifiable. When some students found that they were making little or no headway in the analysis of a case, they "reasoned" that the case did not offer them enough information to gain insight from which they could arrive at a solution.

From the standpoint of the "science of meanings," most students' language and logic showed deficiencies. The words and the phrases that they used in their answers carried no real meaning. The instructor had difficulty in telling what thoughts they really intended to convey. They tended to say things like "the whole answer to the problem lies in the fact that the department head didn't establish good communications," or "that coach needs to lie on a couch and tell his troubles to a psychiatrist." One student seemed possessed with the idea that a departmental administrator has only two choices: either he or she gets efficiency, or the manager keeps his staff members happy.

Poor students often tend to operate on the basis that there are set principles of action for administrators to follow. (This was pointed out many years ago by Fuller in Andrews, ed., 1953, pp. 128-130, and it seems to be just as true today as it was then.) This approach on the part of students is quite easily understood at the present time because of what has been called the "failure of leadership" during the past decade. People seem to be wondering where all the leaders have gone, so to speak, not appreciating that changing times are bringing a new order with them. Earlier, of course, there was an endless array of courses with names like "principles of physical education," or "principles of educational administration." A number of administrators today are still the products of some of these "principles" courses. However, as we are seeing all around us today, complex departments cannot be administered merely through the implementation of a set of principles. Often the logic of some of these principles may be indisputable, but the staff members themselves are simply not ready emotionally to accept a carefully reasoned decision based on this or that principle. Further, it is most difficult to inculcate <u>principles</u> of good human relations into a society which has built up production to enormous heights but has often ignored the human element.

Some of the statements of a considerable portion of a specific class are very revealing. For example, "If he refuses to cooperate, fire him!" "Leaders resent it when their subordinates think of ideas before they do, so make it seem as if they are ideas and plans that they thought of themselves." "If you can't get along with him, or can't seem to get your own way, try flattery." "Put her in a job where she can do the least amount of harm." "Unmarried women teachers are usually emotionally unstable." "An administrator must be given the necessary authority to go along with his or her assigned responsibilities." "Teachers will resent an efficient colleague automatically." "If sympathy doesn't work, discharge him." "What we need is a new chart of organization!" How many more could you, the reader, add to the list?

Most students will come to examinations in a course such as this prepared to think, feel, and act in habitual ways. Only those students who have truly comprehended the lessons to be learned by the case plan of instruction have learned a new behavior pattern. Since examinations involve greater pressure, poor students revert to their basic ways of thinking because they have not mastered this new and different approach--it has

not been "internalized" adequately as part of their lifestyle.
They concentrate on one small area of the total problem. They
rarely show a new understanding of the administrative process
developed by careful analysis of the problem in the case based
on the objectives of the case method. They grasp for a solution and, because they are confused, resort to an authoritarian approach.

They see that a definite problem exists; hence it must be
solved immediately. They fail to see the many alternatives that
are available--for better or worse. "Either the coach should be
dismissed, or the recalcitrants put on probation." They tend
to "play God" and arbitrate in heavy tones. But what does the
second-string quarterback think? Who cares!

Some will qualify their statements to such a degree that
their proposed solutions are meaningless. Others develop
"should" complexes. "The coach should realize that he has been
too strict with the boys." "The boys should understand that
winning the Ohio State game means everything." "The athletic
director should be able to see that the coach is under great
pressure." Maybe all of these people should understand this
or that, but the reason we have cases to analyze is that they
don't!

Finally, we have tried to offer a number of insights here
that can be useful to both students and instructors. Actually,
these are but a few of the problems that you will face as you
confront a basically subjective task in as objective a manner as
is humanly possible under the prevailing circumstances.

References

Andrews, K. R., ed.: The Case Method of Teaching Human
     Relations and Administration. Cambridge, Mass.:
     Harvard University Press, 1953.

Schnelle, K. E.: Case Analysis and Business Problem Solving.
     New York: McGraw-Hill Book Company, Inc., 1967.

Towl, A. R.: To Study Administration by Cases. Boston,
     Mass.: Harvard University, Graduate School of Business
     Administration, 1969.

CHAPTER 6
WRITING A CASE

One of the most interesting experiences for student and instructor alike arises when the student writes a case for the first time. Most students will tackle such a problem with unusual enthusiasm. They seem to feel that it represents a challenge to their intellect, testing their power of observation as well as their ability to tell a story in a factual manner. Naturally, the best cases are written by experienced case writers. It is highly interesting, however, to witness the case that most students will put into the preparation of a case which they have observed or experienced. In this chapter we will confine ourselves to comments about the reporting and writing of a case, the assumption being that the chapter entitled "Examinations and Grades" (Chapter 5) provides the necessary informotion for the analysis of any case that has been written.

Generally a student should not report a case in which he or she is one of the leading characters, although this is not a fixed rule. It is true, however, that when students have been directly involved in a situation, they have the facts well in mind. Nevertheless, certain prejudices may well be evident in the reports, although students really seem to try to present both sides of the picture (despite any embarrassment they may feel). Of course, the instructor should emphasize that all "identifying marks" (names, places, dates, etc.) should be altered.

We recall the day when a young teacher/coach handed a case to us for the first time. He said, "I'm afraid you're not going to be very proud of me as one of your graduates. I play the 'leading role' in this case, and I think I made several bad errors in judgment during this past year." As a matter of fact, we were indeed quite proud of this person from several standpoints--including the fact that he felt the need to make such a statement.

Depending upon the length of the course, students should be given the chance to write (and analyze?) their own case at least once during the term. Not only will it give them an opportunity to write, which is usually sorely needed, but it also develops their powers of insight and analysis. This is true just in the preparation of the case, but the experience is intensified if they then follow through with analyses. When all the facts, half-facts, and opinions of a case are down on paper for the first time, the student has the chance to rewrite and polish his or her effort. Then, perhaps for the first time, he or she will be able to gain perspective about a problem which was reasoned through often in a hazy fashion.

By writing at least one case, the student is provided with an opportunity to compete with the others in the class. If the instructor should wish to reproduce the best cases for possible discussion by the class--a possibility but a tricky one for obvious reasons--it is wise to ask any such student involved for his or her permission privately. If the student shows any sign of embarrassment at such a request, such reproduction should be deferred until a later date, and then permission should be obtained (and preferably in writing) even though identifying characteristics have been removed. For example, a young man submitted a case in which his father was the leading character. Although he "did his best to defend Dad," it was quite obvious to the instructor that some members of the class would sharply criticize the actions of his father. For this reason, even though his work represented a very good case, it was not reproduced. One last thought--if the student is asked to write up a second case later in the course, the instructor will usually notice a marked improvement in the general level of the cases that are submitted.

A person who can write good cases would probably be a good reporter for a newspaper. (Some good advice along these lines may be obtained from Andrews, ed., 1953, pp. 215-224.) This point was brought home to us when we prepared a particular case a number of years ago. We have not included it in any text because of the national publicity it received at the time, although it would probably be considered "ancient history" now what with all the recent disclosures about seemingly improper activities in U. S. intercollegiate athletics. When the story broke in the newspaper of a large city, we decided that this particular problem situation would make an excellent case for discussion. We read the story first in Time and later a detailed account in Sports Illustrated. So we decided to follow through and obtain as many facts as possible. We wrote to several friends with first-hand experience in the area of the case, asking them a series of specific questions based on the information already in hand. We obtained copies of all available newspapers in the region and devoted several evenings to clipping and then digesting various articles. After all this work, including the responses from friends who were close to the situation, we came to the conclusion that Sports Illustrated had included all the essential material for a sound case study (not a research case). The story had in essence been written by a fine reporter.

Students may wonder whether a case they would like to report will be useful. One of the best advance tests of the usefulness of any case is the interest the student himself has in the problem. Also, we often hear about what might be called a "springboard case," in which the central issue holds great meaning for most of the class. Such problems engender lively discussions of many of the related problems which impinge on the main problem. When such a case appears--as becomes evident from the interest shown if and when the case is discussed in class--the instructor would be wise to seek permission to include the case with others for discussion in ensuing terms.

In writing a case, it is important to do everything possible to disguise it so that it will not be recognizable to others. Of course, a case must be factual, but we would never wish to embarrass anyone in this way--and, of course, there is always the possibility of charges of libel and slander. Business school and other case writers secure releases from the organizations and individuals involved before using a case for class discussion. In writing this text we realized that to secure written releases for many of the cases would be virtually impossible, since educators generally are not too familiar with the case plan of instruction, and especially the manner in which cases are collected. We discussed the liability possibility with two different attorneys, after explaining to them that all names and places, etc. in the cases had been changed. They asked if some statements included might be considered libelous. According to Webster's Collegiate Dictionary, a libel is "any statement or representation, published without just cause or excuse, or by pictures, effigies, or other signs, tending to expose another to public hatred, contempt, or ridicule." We explained that this would certainly not be the intent of a case writer, since effort is made to disguise all the persons concerned and, furthermore, half-facts and opinions usually be recognized as such. One lawyer suggested that so long as cases were factual, there would be no need to worry. He pointed out that anyone would be foolish to take a carefully disguised case to court because of the notoriety which a trial would bring to the complainant. Ideally, of course, this technique of teaching should be developed to a point where written releases might be obtained from the institution and/or leading personalities concerned.

Although some potential cases set up certain pitfalls in which an unwary student might get caught, and others give only little concrete evidence other than the statements of the complainants, the large majority can be readily analyzed in a systematic fashion. The following are some suggestions for the preparation of case material:

Suggestions for the Preparation of Case Material

1. A good reporter should be able to write a good case. Put on your "Sherlock Holmes hat" while collecting data.

2. Make every effort to develop a broad perspective on the case problem you are observing.

3. Don't invent any facts or figures; report what you saw and heard--nothing more.

4. Change names and places consistently throughout the write-up of the case to avoid embarrassment to all concerned--not to mention any possible charges of libel.

5. If you (as the case writer) are interested in the case, others will probably find it interesting too.

6. It is useful to include some cases in the discussion of which the students are apt to fall into a "booby trap." This presents students with an opportunity to work their way out in order to get at the truth of the matter.

7. If a case seems too complicated, but yet you find it highly interesting, it may be possible to set it up as a so-called series case (see Eastern State University A-J in the latter part of this volume).

8. If you encounter a case problem that seems to offer very little evidence that will help in the immediate solution of the situation, write it up anyhow in the best possible manner. This will provide students an opportunity to use their imaginations as they listen carefully to what the various complainants have to say.

9. Make every effort to make a case write-up as factual as possible by including conversations, letters, and memoranda.

10. Be as explicit as you can possibly be. "The athletic director told the case writer on November 7, 198-, that he thought Coach Foster had lost the respect of his team members."

11. Don't worry if some facts seem to be missing as you tell the narrative; no one ever knows everything about a situation.

12. If you can, give some ideas about the thinking of the case participants, but do leave out "inactive" facts.

13. Tell your story interestingly and accurately. It will probably be a useful case that will lend itself to systematic analysis.

14. The end of a case write-up must be arbitrary. Don't drag it out; leave room for discussion and recommended solutions.

15. The focus in writing cases about physical education and athletics might be in any one of a seemingly endless listing of problem areas and personalities. The reader could well review the listing of administrative areas or aspects presented at the beginning of Chapter 2 (see p. 15). Keep in mind that the major focus here is on decision-making and human relations.

References

Andrews, K. R., ed.: The Case Method of Teaching Human Relations and Administration. Cambridge, Mass.: Harvard University Press, 1953.

Arnold, S.: Preparation of case studies: the problem of abundance. The American Political Science Review, XLV, 2, 1951.

Leenders, M. R., and Erskine, J. A.: Case Research: The Case Writing Process, second ed. London, Ontario: School of Business Administration, The University of Western Ontario, 1978.

PART 3

CASE PROBLEMS IN PHYSICAL EDUCATION AND ATHLETICS ADMINISTRATION

Editorial Note

A chart follows immediately that explains the possible areas of discussion in the various administrative cases included in this text. In the table of contents, the reader will find a listing of the cases also with their appropriate page numbers. With each case there is a suggestion as to what may be the main problem area involved in the specific case at hand. The chart is an amplification of this showing how many different problem areas seem to exist in each case. Although some may say that these aids represent unwarranted "directiveness," we have risked this criticism because it seemed likely that such guidance might be necessary.

The cases and quotations included have been selected because it was felt that they would encourage a stimulating class discussion. Conceivably, these class discussions might cover all (or most) of the so-called administrative or managerial problem areas indicated.

A word of warning may be necessary. Do not assume that any written or spoken word is correct or incorrect. Many times the people involved in the various cases have used terminology that the allied professions are trying to eliminate (individually or collectively). You will have to guard at all times against taking people at their word. On the other hand, some case participants will make doubtful or incorrect statements unwittingly. Whether statements are right or wrong, desirable or undesirable, you will have to determine their accuracy and pertinence in order to discuss the cases intelligently.

Problem Areas	Glenhill High (1)	Oakwood High A (2)	Oakwood High B (3)	Eastern High (4)	Rand High (5)	Marlton High (6)	Nortown High (7)	Sutter Elem. (8)	Jensen Jr. High (9)	Rawlins High (10)	Eastern State A (11)	Eastern State B (12)	Eastern State C (13)	Eastern State D (14)	Eastern State E (15)	Eastern State F (16)	Eastern State G (17)	Eastern State H (18)	Eastern State I (19)	Eastern State J (20)
Aims and Objectives	●	●	●		●	●		●	●		●					●			●	●
Personnel (Internal Relations)	●	●		●	●	●		●	●	●	●	●	●	●	●	●	●	●	●	●
Policies and Procedures	●	●	●	●	●	●	●	●	●	●	●	●	●	●	●	●	●	●	●	●
External Relations	●	●	●	●		●		●	●	●	●		●	●		●	●	●		
Professional Preparation	●		●		●		●				●	●	●				●	●		
Professional Ethics				●		●					●	●			●					
Class Discipline				●			●	●		●										
Student Teaching							●													
Supervision							●													
Legal Liability	●		●	●						●	●									
Instructional Physical Education			●	●						●	●			●						
Competitive Athletics	●	●				●			●								●			●
Special Physical Education																				
Finance and Budget	●		●	●				●												
Facilities and Equipment	●		●	●	●		●			●	●			●	●	●	●	●	●	●
Evaluation								●	●			●								●
Elementary Physical Education								●											●	
Middle School Physical Educ.									●	●										
High School Physical Education	●	●	●	●	●	●	●													
College and Univ. Phys. Educ.	●		●	●	●				●		●	●	●	●	●	●	●	●	●	●

Suggestions for the Analysis of a Case

There is no fixed model, no infallible approach, or no standard pattern for the analysis of a case. The tone of the analysis is important, because it is advisable that the student avoid solutions that are primarily authoritarian.

It is always essential to develop as complete a mastery of the facts as possible. It is true, however, that any case is characterized by facts, half-facts, and opinions. For this reason it is especially important that a case be read critically, and that one's opinions are weighed very carefully. Which are the facts and are therefore pertinent? Which are irrelevant and must be discarded?

Try to determine for yourself what you regard as the main problem. Try to ascertain the exact question at issue, keeping in mind that it may be clear or obscured. Learning how to ask the right questions is basic to the art of administration.

Once you have determined what you believe to be the main issue, figure out what the sub-issues or sub-questions that need answers are. Formulating the best possible answer to these sub-questions or sub-issues helps you to get to the heart of the analysis. (Note: This seems to be a better way at first; the listing of pro and con arguments is usually much more helpful later when alternative courses of action are considered.)

In case analysis seek to avoid the use of basic principles of administrative as determinants of action to be taken. Avoid phrases that give no real meaning to the analysis of the problem. The "either-or" approach rarely works in management, and often ties in with stereotyped thinking about human relations.

As you proceed with the analysis, possible alternative courses of action will be discovered--often as many as ten or more (including variations). The plausible alternatives should be drawn out from the many, and then they can be "broken down" similarly into sub-questions. The most plausible alternatives may be "tested" in advance by listing the pro's and con's and by forecasting possible results if such-and-such were implemented as a solution.

The following are some approaches to avoid or "traps not to be caught in":

1. Don't memorize facts or conclusions from other cases.
2. Don't always press for some immediate action to be taken.
3. Consider the "whole case."
4. Don't always reason as the person who is the boss.
5. Avoid solutions that are primarily authoritarian.
6. Don't be afraid to use your imagination.
7. Don't make recommendations meaningless by over-qualification.
8. Don't regard each case as a wholly individual and isolated administrative situation.
9. Don't develop a case of "shoulditis"--"he should do this; she should do that; they should do this, etc."
10. Don't talk just to hear yourself talk; master the facts and analyze the case critically and methodically first.[1]

Finally, remember that the objective of this method of analysis is to help you develop power by providing you the opportunity to think in a constructive, orderly manner when facing new situations. When you finally do propose a solution, try to make recommendations that will improve the management process for the future. Through this type of analysis you will tend to develop your powers of discrimination and generalization. Before leaving a case, we should ask ourselves, "What currently useful generalizations may be drawn from this case?" Take these away with you, but keep in mind that they cannot be used automatically when confronted with other case problems.

---

[1] Some of these suggestions were taken from M. P. McNair and H. L. Hansen, Problems in Marketing. New York: McGraw-Hill Book Company, Inc., 1949, pp. 22-25. Professor Zeigler introduced the case method approach to the teaching of human relations and administration to the field of physical education and sport in 1959 (see Zeigler, E. F., Administration of Physical Education and Athletics: The Case Method Approach. Englewood Cliffs, N. J.: Prentice-Hall, Inc., 1959).

1. GLEDHILL HIGH SCHOOL

"Work Load"
(As reported by a department head)

Mr. Robert Turnbull, the principal of Gledhill High School, felt that extracurricular activities were fine in their proper place. This is not meant to imply that he didn't like to see his school's teams win. Once when he felt that a basketball official had ruled unfairly against the Gledhill team in the closing minutes of a game, he rushed out onto the floor to tell the official in no uncertain terms what he thought of him. After several technical fouls were called against the Gledhill team, he was finally led off the floor by the embarrassed coach.

Staff members generally recognized Mr. Turnbull as an unpredictable individual. When staff members wanted to see him about a problem, they would take care to determine just what sort of mood he was in on that particular day. One staff member recalls an incident in which Mr. Turnbull just about frightened some relatively innocent freshman "almost to death" for a minor infraction of the rules of the school. On the next day he dealt with a "hard-rock" delinquent youngster as if he were his "fair-haired" boy.

Mr. Turnbull prided himself on the fact that his high school had a high academic standing. First and foremost, he was what might be called an "academic man." He was due to retire shortly after a long career in teaching and educational administration.

Staff members were quick to admit that he had a number of good sides to his personality. When he hired a teacher for a particular job, that person soon learned that his job was "his baby." Mr. Turnbull was not the sort of person to interfere with the running of a department on the slightest provocation.

Following the War, Gledhill High School had an enrollment of approximately 1,000 students. What was considered to be an extracurricular program included only senior football, senior and junior basketball, senior tennis, and intramural basketball. Two physical education teachers and one other teacher, who coached basketball, were the only staff members available for the boys' athletic program. Both of these physical education teachers had not majored in the subject during

college and they were anxious, because of their age, to "retire" to the teaching of other subjects in the curriculum.

Shortly thereafter, the boys' athletic program expanded
to include senior and junior football, senior and junior basketball, volleyball, gymnastics, hockey, senior and junior track
and field, and tennis--in addition to intramural volleyball and
basketball, and also an annual school golf tournament. It was
at this time that two new physical educator/coaches took over
the department from the two "retiring" teachers.

George Thomas was named head of the boys' physical education department, and he was to be assisted by Frank Lloyd.
George was a big, friendly individual with a lot of drive and a
desire to develop an outstanding program. He was soon highly regarded by the physical education supervisor in the state
education department. The other teacher/coaches in the district respected him and his work as well. At one point he was
elected president of the state physical education branch of the
national professional association.

As the athletic program grew, it became increasingly apparent to George that he and Frank would need some help with
their many coaching duties. In addition to a full work load of
academic and physical education classes, George was coaching
senior football, senior hockey, senior and junior track and
field--and the gymnastics team. He also took responsibility for
the supervision of all intramural athletics. Frank Lloyd, his
assistant, coached junior football, junior basketball, volleyball,
and tennis. When he could, he helped George with intramural
athletics. Mr. Mahler, a history teacher, continued to coach
senior basketball, as he had done before George and Frank
were hired.

After discussing the matter at great length with Frank,
George decided to catch Mr. Turnbull in a good mood and tell
him that more help was needed. He explained to Mr. Turnbull
what was happening. He mentioned also that although two new
teachers had been hired that year, neither of these men was
qualified or willing to help with the extracurricular program.
Mr. Turnbull listened, but made no promises. George expressed the opinion to Frank after this interview that Turnbull still
felt that athletics were largely the domain of the physical education department, and that was the way it was going to stay.

George Thomas's philosophy of sport and physical education was such that it included an opportunity most boys to
take part in some phase of the varsity and intramural program.
He was quite concerned that students should have the chance

to learn leisure skills. With this end in view, George went to Mr. Turnbull later in the year and suggested that he use some of the money in his budget for the purchase of badminton rackets and golf clubs. Mr. Turnbull merely laughed. He explained that he felt any extra money should be used to develop further those interscholastic sports already in the program. He suggested that vertical rather than horizontal expansion of Gledhill's athletic effort would help produce more conference winners in the various senior sports.

Matters continued about the same for the next two years. Although interested in their work, George and Frank were becoming discouraged. One day, George figured out that he had spent 500 hours on extracurricular work during the past academic year. At the next monthly meeting of the coaches in the district, he mentioned this fact and found that many of the other coaches were facing similar situations. After a lengthy discussion, a committee was formed to make a survey. When they had the facts, the executive officers of the coaches' association asked to present their problem at one of the regular meetings of the high school principals in the city. When the principals saw the chart that the coaches had prepared, a great many questions were asked. They tried to show that mistakes had been made in the computations. When the executive officers finally left the meeting, the coaches felt that the principals had almost called them liars.

At the beginning of the next academic year, Mr. Turnbull hired three new male teachers, but not one of them was assigned any extracurricular duties. George, with his usual heavy work load, became discouraged. His wife began to complain because he had one team practice before school started in the morning, and another after school closed in the afternoon. About this time, a principal from a nearby school approached Mr. Turnbull to say that he would like to offer George a position in his school. Also, although Mr. Turnbull didn't know about it, George had received another attractive offer from a large insurance firm with headquarters in the city. Both George and his wife were impressed with the potentialities of this latter offer. Mr. Turnbull talked to George about the offer of the department headship at the other high school where the salary would be somewhat higher.

Just about this time, the physical educator/coaches in George's school district became aware of the fact that the teacher/coaches in Windham (a city of about 150,000, 120 miles away) were receiving extra compensation for handling extracurricular duties. They discussed this at their monthly meeting.

The Teachers' Association had considered this problem recently and had expressed general disapproval of this practice. On the other hand, the physical educator/coaches knew that they could not be forced to assume any duties beyond their regular classes in the daily curriculum.

During the fall, George had an outstanding senior football team. The team was doing very well, but the pressure upon George was great. Things were beginning to get on his nerves, and his usual genial disposition was beginning to disappear. Some of the boys on the team were temperamental and hard to handle. To make matters worse, George began to develop a series of boils. His physician was not sure of the cause, but he did point out that the stress and strain of George's work might be a factor.

The senior football team finally won the district championship. George was completely exhausted, both mentally and physically. His academic classwork began to suffer. Then Mr. Turnbull informed George proudly that Gledhill's team had been invited to represent their region in the state tournament that Saturday. George was happy and proud too, but he wondered if he could stand the strain of another such week as the last. His boils had been getting worse.

George's team did well in the tournament. The winner was determined by committee vote later in the day. Gledhill did not win, but they had given a fine account of themselves. They were an outstanding defensive team, but they didn't have any exceptional breakaway runners on the offense. All in all, it was a rough weekend for George. He had the complete responsibility of the group, including bus loads of cheering students. George had to be everywhere at once even after the game was over.

Next Monday morning, Mr. Turnbull called George to his office. George still hadn't recovered from the hectic weekend. Mr. Turnbull commended him on the team's performance. Then he said that George had been doing so well with his guidance and counselling work that he had decided to give him more responsibility in this area. He made no mention of any plan to lighten George's work load in any way. George "blew his top" at that point. As a result Mr. Turnbull became quite upset and somewhat belligerent. When he saw that George was adamant in his refusal to accept any more assignments, Mr. Turnbull calmed down. Both people appeared quite upset by the interview.

There was a good deal of tension during the next few months, especially when George told Mr. Turnbull that he was going to drop senior hockey from the athletic program immediately. He stated that he simply could not stand the pace, and that his health was being affected.

In February at the annual variety show, George met many of the students' parents. Several of the fathers sais that they were sorry that it had not been possible to have a varsity hockey team that year. Moreover, during the preparation for the show, George had told the other teachers that he would not be able to arrange for the usual gymnastics demonstration. He felt quite embarrassed about the entire evening.

As he was getting ready to go home, he overheard a conversation between Mr. Turnbull and an influential lawyer in the city. The lawyer, Mr. Garde, was quite upset that interscholastic hockey had been dropped. His son, Ray, was an outstanding player and felt very badly about missing a chance to play on a school team in his favorite sport. Mr. Turnbull appeared quite embarrassed and tried to pass over the matter. Mr. Garde pressed his point, however, by remarking that Gledhill was the only school in the district conference without a hockey team.

Suggested Questions for Discussion

1. How would you characterize Mr. Turnbull?

2. Does it bother you to have sport termed "extracurricular?"

3. Do you think George should have discussed the develop-
   ·ing program sooner with Mr. Turnbull?

4. What do you think of Mr. Turnbull's opinion that the responsibility of an athletic program is largely the task of the members of the physical education department?

5. If you were George, would you argue with Mr. Turnbull's position that so-called vertical expansion of athletics was a better policy than horizontal development?

6. What mistakes, if any, did the coaches' executive committee make in their method of presenting their case to the principals? Why do you imagine that the principals didn't seem to believe them?

7. Should George have made a point of letting Mr. Turnbull know that he was thinking seriously of taking the other school offer in order to pressure him for more help? Should George have told Mr. Turnbull about the offer from the insurance firm?

8. Do you think that both George and Frank should have gone to see Mr. Turnbull and pointed out that they were thinking seriously of dropping all extracurricular activities because their contracts would allow them to take such action?

9. Should George have refused to take his team to the state tournament because of his health? Should he have insisted on responsibility for the team only?

10. Why do you suppose that Mr. Turnbull asked George to assume further responsibility without lightening his load in some other way?

11. Was George right in "blowing his top?"

12. Should George have submitted his resignation after the argumentative interview with Mr. Turnbull?

13. Should George have decided to drop senior hockey competition?

14. Do you think parental criticism (e.g., Mr. Garde's) would have any influence on Mr. Turnbull's opinion concerning this issue?

2. OAKWOOD HIGH SCHOOL (A)

"Interdepartmental Cooperation"
(As reported by the athletic director)

As in most large high schools, the administration at Oakwood is organized with the principal at the head of a line relationship pattern. The various departments are supervised by department heads, who are responsible for the management and supervision of matters pertaining to their own departments, subject to the principal's approval on all matters affecting total school policy. Most departments are able to work in a cooperative and yet independent manner insofar as the curricular activities are concerned. When it comes to the matter of those activities traditionally conceived as extracurricular (co-curricular?), difficulties quite often arise over the use of facilities and personnel.

No matter how large or small a school may be, there seems to be a certain "core" (not clique) of students upon whom the success of these extracurricular activities depends. Teachers look to these people (the "doers") as their source of personnel.

The varsity basketball team at Oakwood High was potentially the strongest in many years. Many felt that Oakwood stood a good chance to win the state championship. Pre-season training and practice schedules were arranged with this end in view. Two trips to pre-season tournaments were scheduled by the coach and the athletic director. The athletic director, Mr. Carlson, agreed with Mr. Leonard, the coach, that this tournament experience against good competition would pay off in later season results. When Leonard asked Carlson if the team might have new "dress" warm-up suits to build moral, Mr. Carlson agreed and arranged for their purchase.

The major project of Oakwood's music department each year is the production of a "Varsity Show," which includes a wide variety of acts ranging from slapstick and drama to fine musical numbers, all involving groups of various sizes. This project was organized by Miss Smythe, the head of the music department. It is looked upon as the "school effort" of the year, a project in which all departments must cooperate to assure success.

One of the acts in the show which is always a "howling success" is a boys' kick-line. Although this number falls in the slapstick category, the young men usually put a lot of effort into it. They became quite adept at the various steps, and the audience seems to appreciate their skill as well as the comedy of the situation. Roger Jackson and Jim Blake, two of the outstanding performers on the basketball team, were chosen by Miss Smythe for the line. They were both tall, and their long "skinny" legs and fine coordination made them "naturals" for this act. Roger and Jim were flattered by their selection, as it gave them a different type of opportunity to earn the praise of their school friends. Mr. Carlson, the athletic director, was pleased about their selection, also. He reasoned that it gave some tangible evidence of the right type of cooperation between the athletic department and the music department.

Mr. Leonard, the team coach, took a different point of view. He could see that the necessary rehearsals were going to conflict with his practice sessions. The late hours that the players would have to keep on the three nights of the performance would interfere with the training routine that he had planned for the team. To make matters worse, the Varsity Show was scheduled to take place just one week before the regional tournament.

Actually, the regular basketball schedule was arranged so that it would be completed two weeks prior to the regional tournament. The coach had figured that this would leave sufficient time to rest injuries, to recover from "staleness," and to drill on certain details of team play for the tournament. He had also made tentative arrangements to take his team to a neighboring city for a preparatory game as a final tune-up for the tournament. As it happened, the tune-up game was planned for the same week as the Varsity Show.

A third member of the basketball team, Ray Saunders, was an accomplished piano player. Earlier, Miss Smythe had asked him to accompany the boys' chorus in one of the acts. Because he was on the second team, Mr. Leonard had told Ray that he was free to take part if he was interested. When Ray had participated in the last year's show, a number of the other boys had kidded him and behind his back referred to him as a "sissy" and a "mamma's boy." He was sensitive to this criticism and had asked to be excused from the show. He said that he feared his position on the team would be jeopardized by missing practices to rehearse for the show. To Miss Smythe, it became apparent that this was another non-cooperative gesture by the athletic department. She decided that matters had gone far enough, and she spoke to Mr. Regan, principal of Oakwood High. She wanted support for her viewpoint. Mr. Regan decided to call a meeting of all the teachers concerned to discuss the problem.

Mr. Carlson asked Mr. Leonard to come to his office to talk over the matter before the general meeting. He hoped he that they could reach an agreement between themselves.

Mr. Leonard had considered the problem very carefully. He reasoned that there were many other boys in the school who could perform as well in the kick-line as his star basketball players. Why not use some of the football players not engaged in a winter activity? If his basketball players didn't get involved in the show, his practice schedule could go on uninterrupted, as well as his pre-tournament game. Mr. Leonard did not think that any great value could be attached to the "cooperative" view, although he had made a concession by offering the services of Ray Saunders, the talented instrumentalist from the second team. In conclusion, he reasoned that he would be indirectly helping the show by playing his tune-up game in a neighboring city, thereby leaving the student body free to attend the performance of the show that might.

Mr. Carlson, as athletic director, was quite concerned about this matter of cooperation with other departments. He felt that keeping the basketball players out of the Varsity Show would tend to split the school into factions and work to the detriment of all. He reasoned that no department is strong enough to stand by itself. He stated that Mr. Leonard's attitude would put the athletic department in a bad light--perhaps even in the minds of many athletes.

Mr. Carlson added that, although he was anxious to see the team do well in the forthcoming tournaments, he feared that Mr. Leonard's approach would make the team members seem a group of "pampered darlings" with special privileges.

Finally, however, Mr. Carlson agreed to back the coach on all but one point--the playing of the tune-up game the same night as one of the performances. To him, this was an open display of indifference to a total school project.

Suggested Questions for Discussion

1. How far should cooperation go between departments in a high school?

2. How far should the interests or the desires of Roger and Jim be allowed to enter into the final decision?

3. Should anyone tell Miss Smythe the real reason why Ray Saunders didn't want to take part his year? If so, why?

4. What do you think of Miss Smythe's action in going to the principal, Mr. Regan?

5. What do you think of Mr. Leonard's stand in his preliminary meeting with Mr. Carlson, the Athletic Director?

6. Is Mr. Carlson being disloyal to Mr. Leonard if he refuses to back him in the general meeting on any or all points?

7. Should either Mr. Leonard or Mr. Carlson speak to Miss Smythe before the general meeting?

8. Should Mr. Leonard present his arguments to Mr. Regan before the joint meeting, inasmuch as Miss Smythe has already spoken to Mr. Regan about the matter?

3. OAKWOOD HIGH SCHOOL (B)

"Excuses from Required Program"
(As reported by a woman physical educator)

Mr. Robert Cramden was a successful young business man, who lived on a large farm about ten miles from Newport, a city of about 125,000. He was manager of the local branch of a large business machine corporation, a position which he had held successfully for ten years. Bob was interested in athletics and often served on a volunteer basis as a timekeeper at the University football games. On other occasions, he could be seen as a swimming or track official. He seemed to get a great deal of satisfaction from these public appearances. In addition, he always had the inside story (or thought he did) as to why the local team or a certain individual won or lost. He really liked this association with athletes and coaches. Sometimes during the year, for example, he would wander into the physical education office to pass the time of day. He often did a little needling, and he seemed to enjoy it when he got a lively discussion on athletics going. Earlier, Bob had been a physical training instructor in the armed forces, although he had not majored in P.E. during his university days. One day he offered a fine pair of instructor's trousers to the physical education department head at the University because, as he said, "they'll never fit me again around the middle again!"

Bob had a daughter, Carol, who was twelve years old and a fairly proficient swimmer for her age. She swam for the local Y.M.-Y.W.C.A. team, and Bob was always present at the home swimming meets, and usually drove a car full of team members to away meets whenever he could make it. Carol was in the ninth grade at Oakwood High School.

In March, Ms. Maxine Lanning, one of the two women physical educator/coaches at Oakwood, received a short, terse note from Mr. Cramden. He demanded that his child be excused from physical education. He stated in the note that no tumbling should be done without appropriate harnesses. Until such time, he wanted his child withdrawn from "any and all tumbling routines, and any other nonsensical physical contortions from which she may wish to be excused."

Ms. Lanning was annoyed by the note and the way it was worded. She had been teaching the girls some very simple routines, including a forward roll and a backward roll. The class was under her supervision at all times, and she herself served as spotter when any of the girls seemed to be having difficulty. No girl was forced to try any skill of which she was afraid. Of course, Ms. Lanning knew also that the physical education program was a compulsory subject in the ninth grade, and that a student could be excused only by a written excuse from a medical doctor.

Ms. Lanning learned from Carol that the child had told her father of an injury to another girl in the class. In a note to Mr. Cramden, she mentioned the injury, how it occurred, and that it was very slight. She said also that advanced routines were attempted only on a voluntary basis. She mentioned further that for such very simple routines if was not customary to use a harness. In conclusion, she pointed out a medical certificate was necessary for any student to be excused from participation in physical education at any given time.

Mr. Regan, the principal, had been shown Bob Cramden's original note and also the reply. He told Ms. Lanning that Carol should continue with her physical education classes. Also, if she heard anything more from Cramden, he should be referred to the principal.

In the meantime, Bob Cramden had gone to see one of the members of the Board of Education, Mr. Bovard. Bovard listened sympathetically to the story about the injury and the supposed need for harnesses. Mr. Cramden told him that he was experienced in such affairs, and that he simply did not trust his daughter in the hands of such a "green" woman teacher. Mr. Bovard reminded Mr. Cramden that the subject was a compulsory one right through the tenth grade. He said that Ms. Lanning had been well recommended to the Board. Then he suggested that this matter was rightfully a subject to discuss frankly with Mr. Regan and Ms. Lanning.

Having gone this far, and evidently not wishing to back down on his original stand, Mr. Cramden appeared unnanounced at Oakwood High School on March 26th. He went to the principal's office and repeated his demand that his daughter be excused from this sort of "nonsensical physical contortions" unless harnesses were used at all times. Mr. Regan was polite but adamant. He sent word to Ms. Lanning that Carol's father was in the office to talk over the matter. As she walked to the principal's office, Ms. Lanning wondered what to say.

Suggested Questions for Discussion

1. What is your initial impression of Mr. Cramden?

2. Should Ms. Lanning have been annoyed at receiving such a note?

3. Did Ms. Lanning follow the correct procedure in this situation by sending a note in reply?

4. Should Mr. Bovard have been present at any meeting that was held?

5. Suppose that Ms. Lanning had been in the middle of a class when Mr. Cramden arrived unnanounced, what should she have done then?

6. If you were Ms. Lanning, how would you organized an argument against a man such as Cramden? Are there several approaches that might be used?

4. EASTERN HIGH SCHOOL

"Beginning Teacher's Problems"
(As narrated by a new teacher, Bill Ladkin)

In September I walked into Eastern High as a greenhorn.
My only previous teaching experience consisted of some student
teaching and a few weeks of supply teaching when the regular
teacher at another school had fallen ill. Lorne White talked
over the situation at Eastern with me; you could call him the
"acting head" of the boys' physical education department--a
designation that I will explain shortly. Lorne had been a successful teacher and coach for a number of years. His football
teams had done exceptionally well.

In addition to a full teaching load of physical education,
as well as some health instruction, English (for which I had no
special preparation), and geography, I was expected to take
over certain extracurricular activities (for which we received
no extra remuneration). These included being backfield coach
of varsity football, varsity volleyball coach, varsity basketball
coach, supervisor of intramural volleyball, and chairman of the
publicity committee for the school variety show. I was also
asked to supervise some of the school dances, and I volunteered to gradually develop varsity wrestling. Wrestling had been
my best sport in college.

Unfortunately, my evidently youthful appearance was
such as to discourage respect. I looked more like a high
school student than some of the students themselves. The fact
that I had a close-cropped haircut and usually wore sport
clothes may have something to do with the students' attitude
toward me. In college I had won the conference wrestling
championship in one of the lighter weights, and earned a varsity letter as a defensive back in football in my senior year.
My academic average was good that year too, and I was very
pleased when my classmates elected me president of our student professional group.

At Eastern I soon learned indirectly that the normal line-
staff relationship existed only on the surface in the physical
education department. Somehow the actual authority for the
department was not really in the hands of the nominal department head, Mr. Laithwaite. He was about 60 years old, taught
no physical education classes, coached no sports, never entered the gymnasium, and never even checked equipment. As far
as I could see, his sole duty as head of the department, apart

from signing requisitions, was to collect his salary. At first when questions arose, I went directly to Mr. Laithwaite. He gave me only vague, off-hand answers, or simply said that he did not know. Gradually I turned for any help to Lorne White, who, by reason of his long service, certainly seemed to be the "acting" head of the department.

Having graduated from a reasonably well-equipped university, I was somewhat appalled by the physical situation at Eastern High. The building was old--an "architect's nightmare." The gymnasium was short and narrow, poorly lighted, and badly ventilated. Since its seating capacity was about 200 at most, the spectators' legs often protruded annoyingly into the playing area. Many of the onlookers at contests sat in a balcony that constantly creaked and groaned, seemingly ready to collapse at any moment.

During games the air became quite close in the gymnasium. To open windows we were supplied with a battered length of steel pipe improperly designed to manipulate window handles twelve feet overhead. At each end of the gym, it was necessary for safety's sake to hand mats on the walls under the baskets because the distance from the baseline to the wall was only eighteen inches.

The boys and the girls used the gymnasium for regularly scheduled classes on alternate weeks. A similar system of alternate days was used for extracurricular activities. The girls had the "facilities" on Monday and Wednesday afternoons; and the boys, on Tuesday and Thursday. Friday afternoons were split between the two groups. The group that did not have the gymnasium could use a small, low-ceilinged "spare room." The only activities possible in this room were games of low organization, wrestling, boxing, and some gymnastics. High bar work was not possible because of the lack of room overhead. One day, the box horse collapsed. Two weeks later, the low bar "succumbed to old age" while a student was on it. Luckily, he was uninjured.

The dressing rooms were archiac. There were no lockers, and pupils merely hung their clothes on hooks along the walls. This resulted in a great deal of petty thievery. To avoid the taking of soiled gymnasium clothes and running shoes into classrooms, we were forced to dismiss classes a bit early from a forty-minute period so that students could store their equipment in their hall lockers. This resulted in noise in the halls and complaints from other teachers that their classes were being disrupted. At a teachers' meeting early in the fall term, I heard that three different teachers had complained. This didn't help the relationship among departments.

Shower facilities were poor and inconvenient. The shower room was equipped with five nozzles controlled by a master valve in the nearby physical education office. To take a shower, the students had to walk down a narrow corridor past two urinals and one flush toilet. Because luncheon trash facilities were inadequate, the urinals often became plugged with discarded paper bags. The resultant overflow caused puddles through which the fellows had to tip-toe on their way to the showers. When I asked Lorne White about the possibility of improved facilities, he pointed out that Eastern High was in the center of a city that was expanding rapidly. He did not believe that anything could be done to the building until such time as it might be condemned.

On one occasion, when the state high school supervisor was being shown through the school, the group came to the spare room. The supervisor's comment, after being introduced to me, was, "Quite satisfactory for apparatus work, isn't it?" Before I could reply, he had started to leave. I called after him, "Yes, but you can't use a high bar here, and it will never take the place of a decent gymnasium!"

As a coach, some of my problems arose mainly because I was inexperienced, and because my looks belied my age and position. One night, after attending a teachers' meeting, I came a bit late to the practice football field. The varsity squad was going through its warm-up calisthenics, which I usually led. As I came through the gate on the opposite side of the field--a facility that was used by teams from another high school too--a raucous voice hailed me from somewhere within the ranks, "Where the hell have you been, you little _____!" Of course, this was followed by a great wave of laughter at my expense. The field was very muddy and I was not dressed to walk through such a mess, so I simply ignored the shout and went into the dressing room to change into my football clothes. I knew who had made the remark, but by the time I got out on the field the opportune moment for a reprimand has passed. I took the boy aside later and spoke to him about the incident, but he just shrugged it off. I wondered if this lack of respect might have been caused by the fact that the head football coach, Lorne White, encouraged the boy to call him by his first name. Naturally, they all had started right away to call me by my first name also.

When the basketball season rolled around, I took the reins as head coach of the basketball team. Most of the boys who played football played basketball as well. The previous coach had been a very mild person. While I had been a student teacher, I had thought of him as a bit slipshod in his ways. He had encouraged first-name calling too, and it had been my impression that he had been "manipulated" by the team (rather than controlling it in the right way). The members of the team had played together as a unit for three years. Although many of the individual team members were quite good basketball players, the team had won only three out of twelve games in the past season.

After the first few practices, I observed that the best players were all members of the football team. They treated me with a combination of good-natured condescension and a "hail-fellow-well-met" attitude. The center, John, was big, well-coordinated boy with an indifferent, joking manner. He did not seem to mind losing. When things went against him, he tended to treat it as a joke. I think he was protecting his feelings by pretending not to care.

Tom, the boy who had made the remark on the football field, was the ringleader of this clique. He had a very sarcastic tongue, a cocky attitude, and a show-off manner that tended to disrupt practices. He was an excellent performer, but thought practices were merely fun, and a joke was good only if you laughed at someone.

Art, the boy later elected captain, was of a different ethnic origin than the large majority of the students. One night after practice, he confided to me that he never went to dances. He said this in a sort of "sour-grapes" manner. He was quieter than the others, although he would join in and approve of any horseplay that the others might initiate.

A fourth player, Joe, was what might be called a "follower." He could be led one way or another. Like the rest of the clique, he was very resentful when criticism was offered. One day at football practice, he had walked away swearing after I had told him that he hadn't been trying his hardest.

I was concerned that this clique existed on the team. I wondered how it got started. I discovered that these four boys were what might be called the "tail end" of a series of fine athletes that had attended Eastern High. They had been on the squads of teams that had won football championships year in and year out and occasional basketball championships.

I wondered how this winning streak might have affected their attitudes, especially since Eastern had slipped down a notch from this position of athletic supremacy.

With these four boys forming the nucleus of the team, the basketball season started with a game in a nearby town. On the bus going to the game, the varsity players made the illogical request that they would like to go downtown while the junior varsity game was being played. I refused adamantly. Upon our arrival at the host school, the varsity players quickly brought their equipment into the dressing room and promptly disappeared. With one minute left in the junior varsity game, they finally showed up at the gymnasium. I had sent the manager after them, and he had found them eating in a downtown restaurant. I was angry and spoke to them about eating just before a game. During my "lecture," which was given in the dressing room, Art (the captain) got up and went to the lavatory. We lost the game.

Two weeks later, I learned from Lorne White that some of the players had started on informal "jam session" after practice one afternoon during the past week. They had gone to the band room, which was accidentally left open, and caused $180 worth of damage to equipment there.

We lost three subsequent games, all of which were played chiefly by this clique. Fortunately for our record, these were not all league games. It was quite disturbing, because there was no doubt that these four fellows had superior ability in comparison to the other members of the varsity team. What really upset me was that in two games Tom had been ejected for talking back to the referee and for unsportsmanlike conduct. In one game, he cost us six points on technical fouls. In addition, practices were difficult to run because he was constantly engaged in horseplay, bouncing the ball into the hoop from the ceiling, or throwing fake football cross-body blocks.

One night in a fast-break drill, he acted particularly stupid. I blurted out, "You can stop showing off now, little boy, everyone knows you're here." After this criticism I heard him say, "O.K., let's run it once more and get it right this time." The practice was over too soon after my reprimand to ascertain whether it really had any effect. Several days later I spoke to him in the shower and asked him when he was going to get down to business. He replied half-jokingly, "Oh, you're always picking on me. Besides, a guy's gotta have a little fun."

I must admit that I seriously considered that perhaps the time had come to cut Tom and maybe one other clique member from the team to see if it would improve matters. I reasoned that they had nothing else to lean on except basketball, however, so I hoped that perhaps I could help them along somehow through allowing them to share in a good team experience. Of course, I had to consider also that they were my best players.

After we lost our fourth game, I informed the team that I would now use a two-platoon system, and each unit would play equal amounts of time. I split up the regular starting team between the two units. We won the next game by twenty points. After the game, I was met by a "wall of silence" when I walked into the dressing room. Backs were turned on me; questions were answered in monosyllables, and some players just walked away from me. I decided to stick to the newly inaugurated system for the next game, and we won that game too.

The next context we lost to a team that used a zone defense. This seemed to baffle my players completely, and they made all the mistakes typical of a green team playing against a zone for the first time. I gave them instructions during the time-outs, but there wasn't much improvement. At half-time in the dressing room, I spoke to the captain about the technique of shooting long shots in an effort to break up the effectiveness of the defense we had encountered. Art only cursed in reply.

The following game against the second-place team in the conference was really important. Obviously, a two-platoon system wouldn't work. We simply did not have ten good players, and some of our personnel would really be outclassed by the opposition. So I played what had earlier been the first team, and we won with Art scoring twenty points as he played most of the game. When I replaced him in the fourth quarter when the games was obviously ours, he walked to the bench muttering and shaking his head. But after the game his attitude had improved greatly.

The team continued to play well--much better than I had expected. On the morning of the day we were to play in Southport, a nearby town, we learned that Eastern had just missed being invited to the state invitational tournament. The second-place team, whom we have beaten the night Art scored twenty points, received an invitation. We beat Southport that night.

After the game, I went back to the lunchroom where our team dressed to make a final check for any stray pieces of equipment. Of course, I never thought to look at the ceiling. You can imagine my surprise when I learned the next day that members of my team had punched nineteen holes through a new ceiling by standing on the tables and using a couple of broom handles. The matter was to be reported to the Southport School Board. I gave the entire square a stiff "dressing down" after this display of vandalism.

Now that the season was over, I began to recall some of the other troubles of the season. I remembered the dispute with John, my center, on the question of the players' transportation to the games. He didn't like the school policy of taking players on trips only in authorized cars or buses. He wanted to ride in a private car. When I refused, he countered that the private car was fully insured. If he were to pay the driver, he felt that it would be just the same as a taxi. I couldn't seem to get it through his head that the school could be sued if an accident occurred while he was travelling in a car with an unlicensed chauffeur. Finally, by speaking very harshly, I had managed to get him to drop the subject.

Joe, the fourth boy described earlier, did improve somewhat in his attitude. However, I recalled that in one game we had to play without our second-string center, I had asked Joe to sit beside me and stand by. John, our regular center, already had four personal fouls against him at that point. Joe was a forward, but in the emergency I wanted him to be ready to substitute for John if he fouled out. About two minutes later I heard him shout, "Come on John, foul out!" I turned to him quickly and asked him which team he wanted to win. He answered, "I just want to get in there." I was so angry that I yelled back at him, "Don't be so damned selfish." The next time he yelled it was to cheer for John who had just scored a goal.

On the whole, I was quite discouraged about the season. One week after our last tame, I went to see a district play-off game that involved some of our earlier opponents. At the half-time, Lorne White came over to me and said that the four boys on my team (the clique) were half-drunk down at the other end of the gym. The next day Lorne told the principal, who then decided to contact their parents.

Three days later, the following article appeared in the local newspaper:

131

WIN COSTLY FOR EASTERN QUINTET

Exuberance over their team's victory over Southport's Varsity Mustangs will cost a group of Eastern High School basketball players at least $35.00 each because of a decision made last night by the Southport High School Board.

The total sum involved is about $175, or $35 for each of the starting five players on the team. This should be sufficient to repair the nineteen holes punched in the ceiling of the boy's lunch room in the Southport school following the basketball game.

Deciding against permitting the boys to repair the damage themselves, the board agreed the work will be done by contractor, and the bill then forwarded to the principal of Eastern High School. From there it is assumed the students responsible will be assessed the cost. None of the boys was identified.

In a way I was pleased that the names of the boys hadn't been listed in the newspaper. The Southport School Board would have been surprised to learn that the damage was done before the victory. As I thought about the entire season and the many problems we had encountered, I wondered whether I had acted as wisely as I might have done. I wasn't very enthusiastic about coaching basketball in the coming year.

Suggested Questions for Discussion

1. What do you think of the work load assigned to Bill? Do you think he should have volunteered to take over wrestling?

2. Do you feel that Bill's appearance might have encouraged disrespect?

3. How might the "acting" department head situation affect Bill's reaction to his new position?

4. What attitude should Bill have taken toward the poor facilities for physical education and sport at Eastern High School?

5. What should Bill have done when someone shouted at him in such a manner as he reported to football practice?

6. What should Bill have done, if anything, when he realized that a clique existed on the basketball team?

7. What do you think of Bill's analyses of the four players in the clique?

8. What should Bill have done about the boys' request to go downtown during the junior varsity game?

9. When Bill learned about the episode with the band instruments, should he have said anything to the boys or taken any action?

10. Why do you suppose there was so much horseplay during practice? Should Bill have cut Tom from the squad?

11. What do you think about the idea of splitting up the first team in order to try a two-platoon system? Even after they won the game, why do you suppose the players were antagonistic to Bill?

12. Why do you imagine the boys punched the holes in the ceiling at Southport before the game? Should any action have been taken as soon as Bill learned about the incident?

13. What do you think of Bill's remark to Joe, when Joe wanted John to foul out of the game?

14. Do you think the basketball experience helped the personalities of the four boys in the clique?

15. What can we learn about Bill from reading his self-written case?

16. What should have been done about the four boys appearing at the play-off game (presumably) half-drunk?

17. Had Bill acted wisely most of the time? Should he feel discouraged? Should Bill try to get another position at a different high school with a "better class" of boys and newer facilities?

5. RAND HIGH SCHOOL

"New Department Head"
(As reported by a department head)

On April 16th, Mr. Cox called Mr. Ludlow, who has been appointed principal of Rand High School two years before, about the available position as head of the boy's physical education department. Mr. Ludlow expressed interest in Mr. Cox's application and made an appointment to discuss the matter on April 20th. As Mr. Cox thought about the time for the meeting, he reasoned that Mr. Ludlow would have sufficient time to inquire about his qualifications for the position, as they were both working in Newport, a city of about 125,000. At their first meeting, it was immediately apparent to Mr. Cox that Mr. Ludlow had not made any detailed inquiry about him. Mr. Ludlow did mention that he had read about Mr. Cox on the sports page of the Newport Record.

In this first interview, Mr. Cox was assured that he would have a "free hand" to experiment with the physical education program--if he became head. Mr. Ludlow mentioned also that Mr. Cox would be permitted to teach another subject in the curriculum, a point that was interesting to Mr. Cox because of his relatively strong background in the liberal arts and sciences. As Mr. Cox thought about the new situation, he felt that here might be a chance to get out of the "rut" that he had been in for the past fourteen years. During this time, he had taught physical education in two situations with many overly heavy work loads. As a possible deterrent to the acceptance of this position, Mr. Cox realized that these fourteen years might have left him with a little less of his original zeal and initiative for physical education/coaching work. In early May, Mr. Cox was notified that he was the first choice for the position. He accepted.

Soon after, Mr. Cox made two requests of his new principal. First, he asked for the opportunity to visit Rand High to observe the program. Second, as there was another position open on the department staff, he asked if he might be permitted to speak to possible applicants at a forthcoming convention. Mr. Ludlow thought that a visit by Mr. Cox was a fine idea, and he asked the acting department head to arrange for this tour. He was taken for a "breathless round" of the school. Many door keys did not seem readily available and, when doors were finally opened, the rooms were dingy and ill-kept. At this time, it was not possible for him to observe the existing class routine. Further, it was then necessary for Mr.

Cox to return for two days during the summer to re-trace his steps.

Mr. Ludlow did not agree to the second request. He did not see the need for Mr. Cox to be involved in the appointment of the second teacher in the boys' physical education department. He explained that he had advertised in various newspapers, and that the applications received gave promise that a good candidate would be among them. Mr. Cox asked if Mr. Ludlow would have the other new teacher contact him after the appointment had been made. When the second teacher signed his contract in the office of the superintendent, Mr. Cox was only two blocks away. Four months later, Mr. Cox and the newly appointed teacher finally met after an exchange of several letters and a motor trip by each one. In the meantime, Mr. Cox had discovered that a truly fine prospect with two years' experience had been interested in this second position. This person had not applied because of "the lack of a personal touch" that Mr. Cox felt he could have given to the search for a co-worker.

When Mr. Cox reported to his new position in the latter part of August, the first problem was the purchase of new equipment and the repairing of the equipment on hand. This had to be done within the specifications of grants obtained from the Board of Education. Certain items for extracurricular activities were within the budget of the Student Athletic Association. Mr. Ludlow gave Cox the figures available for gymnasium equipment and repair. Since these amounts had to be shared with the girls' physical education department, Mr. Cox spoke to Ms. Larson, head of this department. She said, "This is the first time in my eight years here that I have heard those figures." The buying she had done had been minimal, but she had no idea how those items had fitted into the total budget picture.

Mr. Cox learned that a sizeable amount of the money granted by the Board had been turned back quite regularly. He noticed that some of the equipment on hand was of good quality, while other material did not seem to be up to standard (and a bit was in terrible condition). Ms. Larson appeared to appreciate the honest approach that Cox had made to her about the matter. Cox asked her to let him know if the requirements of her department amounted to less than half of the total budgetary allotment. His plan was to build up the stock on hand for both departments with any surplus that became available. However, as Mr. Cox related it, "Her years of going to the 'boss' for every little item had become established as a behavior pattern, which will tend to keep the departments from full cooperation."

The procedure to be followed in purchasing equipment for the extracurricular activities was more complex. Mr. Cox was referred to Mr. Root, the vice-principal, who had charge of Student Affairs, and therefore he was responsible for the Student Athletic Association. When Cox approached Root about the purchase of some needed athletic equipment, he was told that Rand was not a "rich" school. Having been thus warned, Cox proceeded with caution in buying any items. Mr. Root had mentioned further that Mr. Cox should "call on the experience of Mr. Lawson, the equipment manager." Cox learned that Mr. Lawson had formerly been head of the boys' physical education department. In the five months Cox had been in his new position, he had asked a number of times if he could see an "accounting of the Association's balance." Root seemed hesitant to comply with this request, and always said offhandedly that "things are going well."

Another staff member was treasurer of the Athletic Association, whose main responsibility was accepting the receipts from admissions charged at the various athletic contests. When cash was needed, the treasurer simply gave Cox and Larson the money requested--if they were small amounts. Orders for any substantial list of items were initialled by Cox and co-signed by Root. Already, two incidents had occurred with sporting equipment suppliers. One store owner, who keeps "notoriously bad books," was certain that Rand High owed him $300 (but had no proof). The other supplier had recently presented two invoices for small purchases that still had not been paid. Mr. Cox had stated that these matters had been embarrassing to him.

There appeared to be no direct connection between the equipment manager and the boys' or girls' physical education departments (see Figure 1). Mr. Cox and Mr. Lawson, the equipment manager, had discussed buying certain items of equipment for several sports. However, unbeknownst to each other, they had both finally purchased the needed equipment without consulting the other. Up to now, this was the first time that such a problem had developed. Mr. Cox always told Mr. Lawson what he had bought, but Mr. Lawson had not reciprocated. So Cox usually had to learn incidentally from the suppliers themselves.

In drawing the organizational diagram for this case, Mr. Cox listed the Athletic Association initially with dotted lines. He reported that "heretofore students elected to office in the

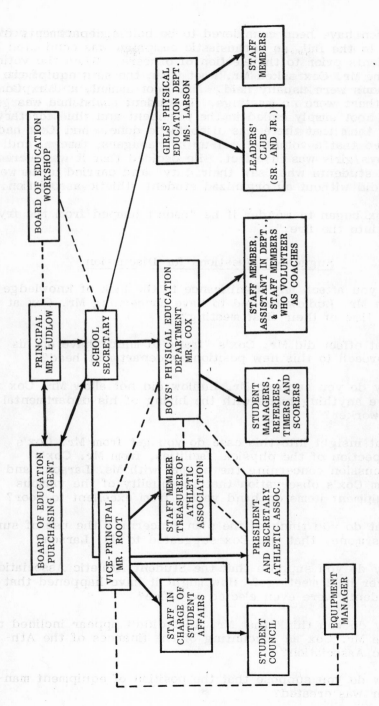

Figure 1. Organizational Diagram Related to the Rand High School Case.

Association have been considered to be holding honorary positions." In the fall, an enthusiastic campaign was conducted by the students prior to the election of officers. When the voting was over, Mr. Cox asked Mr. Root when the meetings of the Associations were usually held. Mr. Root smiled, and explained that there were no meetings. If student assistance was needed, Root simply called in the president and the secretary and told them that there was a job to be done. Mr. Cox had discovered that a volunteer set-up of managers, timers, and water boys/girls was in effect. He decided that it was a credit to the students who "saw their duty" and carried on as well as they did without an organized student athletic association.

Cox began to wonder if he "hadn't jumped from the frying pan into the fire."

Suggested Questions for Discussion

1. Do you attach any significance to the lack of knowledge that Mr. Ludlow seemed to have concerning Mr. Cox at the time of their first meeting?

2. What effect did Mr. Cox's "frame of mind" have on his approach to this new position as department head?

3. Why do you suppose Mr. Ludlow did not allow Mr. Cox to have anything to do with the hiring of his departmental co-worker?

4. What insight into this case do you get from Mr. Cox's inspection of the physical facilities, from Mr. Cox's discussion concerning the budget with Ms. Larson, and from Cox's observation that the quality of the various equipment items on hand varied from excellent to poor?

5. What do you think of the plan concerning the use of surplus money that Mr. Cox suggested to Ms. Larson?

6. Why do you suppose that the Student Athletic Association never held meetings? How might it have happened that students were even elected to office?

7. Why do you think that Mr. Root didn't appear inclined to give Mr. Cox an accounting of the finances of the Athletic Association?

8. How do you suppose that the position of equipment manager was created?

9. Why do you suppose the "two incidents" with the sporting goods suppliers had developed?

10. What significance do you attach to the fact that Mr. Lawson did not tell Mr. Cox what equipment he had purchased?

11. Why was Cox disturbed about the fact that the student officers were called in and told when there was work to be done?

12. What, if anything, should Cox do about the "volunteer set-up" that had developed with the various student assistants in connection with athletics primarily (either intramurals or interscholastics)?

6. MARLTON HIGH SCHOOL

"A Male Coach for a Girls' Team"
(As reported by a student)

Marlton High School had about 500 students and a staff
of 11 teachers. The school had one small gymnasium in which
it was impossible to hold more than one class at a time. There
was no other room in which any type of physical activity could
be carried on successfully. The auditorium was already being
used as a regular classroom. As a result of these conditions,
physical education was forced to take a back seat to what are
typically called "academic courses." The community of Marlton
was extremely sports-conscious, however, and there was considerable interest in school athletics.

One year, the situation arose in which no woman teacher
on the staff had the knowledge or the experience to coach the
girls' basketball team. Because of the lack of facilities, a
qualified physical education teacher was not employed for the
girls. Instead, the teacher with the lightest work load was to
be given the responsibility for the program. Question: Who
should coach the girls' basketball team?

Mr. Barton, the principal, liked to win. It was all or
nothing with him. One year, the school's top track and field
athletes went to the regional meet but did not win. The next
year, even though Marlton won its district meet, no one was
allowed to enter the regional meet. Thus, the person chosen
to coach the basketball team would most definitely feel a certain amount of pressure to win.

The woman assigned to take charge of the girls' physical
education program was conscientious and willing to learn the
game. She had never played basketball herself and didn't
understand many of the terms and skills. Two young women
in the school had attended a leadership training camp during
the summer, and both expressed their willingness to help. Ten
girls from the previous year's team were back, so she would
have an experienced team on hand. The principal decided,
however, to appoint Mr. Allan as coach. Mr. Allan was a
history teacher who taught a few boys' physical education
classes. Because of the line-staff relationship in the school--
with the principal as the "supreme commander"--the basketball
coach for girls was really responsible to the principal and not
to the woman in charge of girls' physical education.

Mr. Allan did not want the assignment. He had refused to help coach the backfield of the boys' football team on the grounds that he had too large a work load already. He had no idea of the girls' game of basketball either, and would have to learn a lot. As a result, he was none too pleased with the assignment--but felt constrained to accept because he had already rejected any work with the football team.

One thing that Allan had to learn was that girls were a lot different to manage than boys. One girl went home crying during the first week when he yelled at her. He really was "turned off" at their shrill talk and giggles. He didn't seem to understand their greater excitability and lesser endurance powers. And, what made matters worse, he was newly married and his wife didn't like him coaching the girls--and spending the extra time away from home.

As it turned out, representatives of the other schools in the league were taken aback at the thought of a man coaching a girls' basketball team. At the coaches' meeting there was a heated discussion, but no attempt to change things was made. Immediately, Marlton got the reputation for being a rough team. It was the team to beat, the team to get. The games became rough shambles, and with such "battling" there was no pretense of friendly competition. As a result, there was great emotional stress on the players. No friendships were made between Marlton team members and members of the other teams. Also, it was quite obvious that members of the other teams remained friendly to each other. At lunches after the games, members of the Marlton team huddled together in a group alone.

The coach himself had many difficulties too. He couldn't very well take the team into the dressing room at half-time. He couldn't understand what he considered to be the girls' lack of interest in the games. He was constantly being ridiculed by the other male teachers. The women coaches couldn't make up their minds whether to welcome him or reject him. Above all, his wife was against the idea of him coaching girls.

Despite these difficulties, Marlton managed to win the district championship. There were few if any congratulations from representatives of the other teams involved. Mr. Barton was pleased, and the team was sent to the regional championships where it was eliminated in the first game. Mr. Allan wondered what to do about the coming year. Also, many of his team members were graduating in June.

Suggested Questions for Discussion

1. In your opinion, would the woman teacher with interest but no knowledge of the game be better for the team than a Mr. Allan with knowledge but very little interest?

2. Should use have been made of the student leaders?

3. What are the advantages and disadvantages of a man coaching a girls' team?

4. What would be the community's reaction to the situation?

5. What is the significance of Allan refusing to coach the backfield in football, but accepting the basketball assignment?

6. Should Allan's personal life have had any influence of his acceptance or rejection of the assignment?

7. Could Mr. Allan have coached and still maintained friendly relations with other coaches in the league?

8. Is there any significance to the fact that the principal didn't seem to care whether other coaches in the league were upset about Allan's appointment?

9. Is there any way to control emotional stress on the part of the players? Was the district championship worth it?

10. What should Allan do now that the season is over--if anything?

7. NORTOWN HIGH SCHOOL

"Student Teaching"
(As reported by a student teacher)

Nortown High School is a Class C high school and is used by Eastern State University as a training school for student teachers. Nortown is located about five miles from the university campus and holds classes from grade nine to grade twelve. The students at Nortown might be considered typical high school students, although some student teachers have stated that they are a "tougher group" than the average--whatever that might mean. The parents of most of the students are either farmers, factory workers, or white-collar workers.

In rather direct contrast to Nortown, the university has another training school, University High, situated on the campus. University High is also a Class C school, but the students are screened more closely before admission. Thus, to a considerable extent, University High gets the "cream of the crop," as far as social and economic standings go. Most of the university faculty send their children there, as well as the families in the higher income brackets.

Nortown and "U" High are both in the same athletic conference, and there is a strong rivalry. The fact that University High uses the University's fine new athletic facilities adds greatly to this keen competitive feeling.

The teachers at these two training schools are considered to be on the staff of the University. They must have a Master's degree to be hired initially, because they act as critics to the student teachers under them. Most of the high schools' staff members have a common goal--advance to the university level as a professor.

All university students majoring in education are required to teach one semester at each training school in their senior year, one semester in his/her major field, and the other in the minor field.

John Mancato was a senior student majoring in physical education. His first assignment was to teach seventh-grade physical education at Nortown. John had won varsity letters in both football and baseball at Eastern, and he expected that this background would help him with his student teaching. His minor subjects were English and business administration, but he dreaded the thought of having to teach either.

John's first day at Nortown was unfortunate. He had just been introduced to Mr. Blane, his critic teacher, when Blane began to criticize John's attire. Mr. Blane advised him to get used to the idea of wearing a suit, shirt, and tie every day. John was offended, but he found out later that previous student teachers had made Blane very sensitive about this matter. Mr. Blane was athletic director, as well as head football and track coach.

For the first few days, John just took the shower check in order to get acquainted with the students in the class that he was to take over. The class consisted of sixty boys, and the gymnasium was much too small for a varied program. Mr. Blane ran the class by himself for the first three days. It soon became evident to John that the boys had no concept of discipline. Blane imposed no penalties for misbehavior and remained composed at all times. John felt that he was almost pleading with the boys instead of putting his foot down. John concluded that he was going to have a difficult time when he started to teach.

When John did take over the class, things were rough at first. He found out that Mr. Blane was insistent about a student teacher's using lesson plans and units. John was unhappy about the extra time that he had to spend on these lesson plans, but he could see that well-planned activities were essential to a successful physical education and sport program.

As time went on, John felt that he was getting along fine with both his class and Mr. Blane, although the five-mile daily bus ride each way from the University and back was quite a chore. John disagreed with Mr. Blane over various teaching methods employed, but he never did express his feelings openly. What Mr. Blane wanted done, John did. He was not allowed to try any of his own ideas. The shirt and tie regulation was a big nuisance. It really did seem pointless, because he changed into his gym suit immediately after he entered the school and never even ate lunch there.

One of Mr. Blane's ideas was that the teacher should be dressed in exactly the same outfit that the class was required to wear (shorts and a white T-shirt). Blane felt that this put the instructor on the same level with the students. It was a major task to get the students to wear this uniform, and a number of the boys argued that they couldn't afford it.

Finally, there was just one week to go. Up to this time, John and Mr. Blane had only one "critic" meeting. Mr. Blane was always very formal with John, and he did not once have a

"heart-to-heart" talk with him about his teaching techniques.
John felt that he was doing a good job but would have welcom-
ed an encouraging word from his mentor. John prepared the
final exam that had both theoretical and practical components;
administered it; and then corrected the papers submitted for
the theory part. Then he gave Mr. Blane some suggested
grades for the entire group. Later he discovered that quite
radical changes had been made in many instances by Blane--
even though John had taught every class after the first three
days. John was very disappointed about this, but he decided
not to make an issue out of it.

Just before the second semester started, John awaited
his assignment uneasily, since he expected that he would be
teaching one of his minor subjects at University High. Much
to his surprise, he was assigned to teach ninth grade physical
education. He approached this situation with confidence, feeling that he would do very well at "U" High after surviving a
semester at Nortown. His critic teacher at the University
school was Mr. Wolk, who was head of boys' physical education
and also athletic director and head football coach. Mr. Wolk
had his affairs carefully organized. He had been at University High for twenty years.

The conditions at University High were excellent, and
John was very pleased. There were only twenty boys in his
class, and they were all in correct uniform. They addressed
him politely, many commenting about his play as an athlete at
Eastern. There was no discipline problem whatsoever. Mr.
Wolk knew these boys from the first day they entered. What
he said, they did. If a boy made trouble a few times, he knew
that Wolk had the power to challenge further enrollment at University High. There wasn't even any trouble with dirty uni-
forms, as this meant a certain number of demerits.

Mr. Wolk had his good points and his bad points. He
had a critic meeting every week. He had an informal talk with
John and the other student teachers about their progress and
the various teaching techniques that might be employed. He
always offered valuable constructive criticism. He didn't even
require that student teachers wear shirts and ties!

Classes were relatively easy to handle. Wolk never mentioned lesson plans or units. He had everything in his mind.
When it was time for the class to start a new unit, Mr. Wolk
took it for the first day. After he had affairs established
properly, John followed with the subsequent classes by imi-
tating the pattern established. John found himself taking

things almost too easy. He enjoyed this experience, but he wondered if this were the ideal type of experience for a student teacher to have. When it came time for the final exam, Mr. Wolk simply referred John to his files. All John had to do was check over the exam and record the scores.

When the year was over, John wondered which situation had been the most beneficial. He also wondered whether he had been provided with a sufficient number of student teaching experiences. There had been no opportunity to get involved with coaching, and somehow he had escaped teaching in a classroom environment.

Suggested Questions for Discussion

1. How many different types of situations should student teachers have?

2. Could anything be done to improve the "bitter rivalry" between the two high schools?

3. Why do you imagine that John dreaded having an assignment in English or business education?

4. How should student teachers or teachers dress? How should students dress for that matter?

5. What did you think of Blane's approach and teaching methodology?

6. What do you think of the idea of daily lesson plans and units?

7. How should Blane have handled the set of grades turned in by John?

8. How would you characterize the difference between the discipline problem at Nortown and that at University High?

9. How did John's second-semester experience strike you?

10. What comparison would you make between the two experiences? What other suggestions and/or recommendations would you make?

8. SUTTER ELEMENTARY SCHOOL

"Class Discipline"
(As reported by a physical education teacher)

Sutter Elementary School, with an enrollment of over 1,200 students, was one of the largest elementary schools in Metropole. The school was located in an underprivileged neighborhood, which had been deteriorating for a number of years. Each year, Sutter had a large turnover of teaching personnel.

Typically a great deal of a teacher's effort at Sutter was directed toward trying to maintain a semblance of discipline. The teaching of any subject-matter was very difficult, some teachers actually considering it a secondary objective. A certain percentage of the students were usually quite uncooperative, although some teachers did much better with class control than others.

Principal Boggs was sixty years old. He had been at Sutter for more than fifteen years, and this year he was going to retire. It was generally recognized (by the men) that he was more sociable toward the women teachers and seemed to get along better with them. Some of the teachers, including some of the women, mentioned that Boggs talked to them as if they were children.

It was said that a certain amount of the poor school discipline was caused by Mr. Boggs' very lenient attitude toward students who caused problems. Often when a student was sent to the office for misconduct, Mr. Boggs evidently acted as if he didn't believe the teacher's statement concerning the incident. He would often send students back to class without taking any action other than a few fatherly words. He most definitely wanted to avoid any unpleasantness with them or with their parents.

The physical education department at Sutter consisted of four men, two whites and two blacks. Every other elementary staff in the city had at least one women physical education teacher. Floyd Miller, a black, was the director of physical education. He was thirty years old and possessed a Master's degree and five years of elementary teaching experience. Floyd had been sent to Sutter by the district supervisor to straighten out the "awful mess" in the department. When he arrived in 19--, there were two women physical education teachers, one of whom had a habit of drinking during working

147

hours. Both of them had resigned at the end of the year. Floyd was an ambitious person and hoped to become an assistant principal before long.

In September of the following academic year, the year in which the principal presumably was going to retire, John Brooks was hired to take the place of one of the women physical education teachers in the physical education department. He was thirty years old, and had one year of teaching experience at another elementary school in the city. John had asked for a transfer from the other school because the facilities had been very old and completely inadequate. However, he did not know he was to be assigned to Sutter until the beginning of September.

One of the other male physical education teachers had been on the staff for two years, while the other was a young man who had just graduated from college--this was his first job!

During the first few weeks of school, Mr. Miller mentioned to his staff that Mr. Boggs had not agreed with his administration on many occasions. In one instance, Mr. Boggs objected to the fact that Mr. Miller had disciplined a disorderly class by having them sit for an entire period on the gymnasium floor. Mr. Boggs had said that if he would offer an interesting program, the classes would not be disorderly.

During the third week of school, Mr. Boggs called John Brooks to his office for a get-acquainted talk. He had a standard story that he told to all of his new physical education teachers about a former P.E. teacher who had used force to maintain discipline. It was obvious that he didn't agree with this approach, but he didn't suggest any alternative methods.

During the next six months of school, John had a great deal of trouble maintaining class discipline, as did the rest of the physical education staff. He did manage, however, to achieve a certain amount of teaching success. One class was unusually difficult, so that one day John made the entire class stand for thirty minutes while he tried to establish order. The next day, one of the parents complained by telephone to Mr. Boggs.

Mr. Boggs called both Brooks and Miller in for a conference. He was upset about the matter, and said that such punishment was too much of a physical hardship on the children. He pointed out that he personally would find it very difficult to stand that long.

148

John explained the situation as best he could, but Mr. Miller did not give him any support. Mr. Miller did ask if it would be permissible to have them sit on such an occasion. Mr. Boggs agreed to this suggestion. Mr. Boggs concluded the meeting by advising John to consult with either Mr. Miller or himself for advice in all future disciplinary problems before taking any such drastic action.

The difficulties with discipline continued. When John encountered a really troublesome case, he sent him to the main office. This would occur about once a day on the average. After a couple of weeks, Mr. Miller came down to the gymnasium and told John that the assistant principal wanted John to take care of his own disciplinary problems.

Suggested Questions for Discussion

1. Does the situation at Sutter sound like an unusual situation?

2. If a principal is seen as being lenient, does this mean that school discipline is going to be bad?

3. If there is a preponderance of one racial or ethnic group as opposed to another in a school, does this mean it will be that much difficult for a teacher of that racial or ethnic minority to be effective in that school?

4. Should girls be taught by teachers of the opposite sex, or should boys be faced with the same situation, at the elementary school level? The high school level?

5. Do you think John was right in using the "class standing" technique as a means of discipling an unruly group?

6. How would you discipline one or more youngsters?

7. Should Miller have given John more support in Boggs' office?

8. What is accomplished by sending an unruly boy or girl to the principal's office?

9. Do you believe in corporal punishment for unruly youngsters?

10. Why do children from so-called underprivileged homes seem more difficult to discipline?

11. Now what should John do?

9. JENSEN JUNIOR HIGH SCHOOL

"Intramural Athletics"
(As reported by Roberta Martin)

Two years after it was built, Jensen Junior High was
overcrowded with an enrollment of 2,100 students. To accommodate this number of students, another junior high was to be
constructed within a year and a half. At present, however,
the seventh and eighth graders were attending schol on half-
day sessions, while the ninth grade students went to school
for the entire day. About ninety per cent of the students
commuted by bus.

Because of difficulties in scheduling, only the eighth and
ninth graders were offered regular physical education. Intramural activities were conducted in both the girls' and boys'
departments. Inter-school basketball and track were offered
to all grades, while inter-school baseball was available to ninth-
grade boys only. There were two men and two women on the
physical education staff. Three other faculty members helped
the regular male physical education staff members with the athletic coaching for which they received extra compensation.
Two other women teachers were prepared to help with athletic
teams that were planned to start as soon as possible for the
girls.

The gymnasium was regulation size, but it was necessary
to divide it with a folding door. The outdoor facilities were
barely adequate with the rising interest in inter-school competition for the girls.

The working relationship between the girls' department
head, Ms. Martin, and the boys' department head, Mr. Wilson
had been extremely good. Prior to the basketball season, Ms.
Martin and Mr. Wilson had a meeting to decide what times each
would need after school for varsity teams and intramural athletics. This was to be the first year that the young women
would have an inter-school team as well, not to mention that
there was considerable interest in the intramural program for
girls on the part of the women teachers. Since both halves of
the gym were needed to run a practice successfully for the
men's team especially, or to accommodate the large number of
girls taking part in intramural basketball, it was decided that
Ms. Martin would use the entire gym twice a week. The three
boys' basketball teams would practice the other three days.
Ms. Martin would have liked to have had the use of the facilities three afternoons a week, but there was more emphasis on

basketball for the boys--and they had started the inter-school program as soon as the school opened. It really was difficult to find practice time for three different boys' teams. As a matter of fact, intramural basketball for the boys couldn't be scheduled until the varsity season was over. This meant that a good deal of the enthusiasm had been dissipated.

During the spring, Mr. Wilson decided that something had to be dropped. There simply were not enough facilities to offer a program for all the students. Since intramural basketball involved approximately 300 boys and girls, he decided that the facilities should be used for this group during the season. As a result the forty-five boys on the three varsity basketball squads and the fifteen girls on their relatively new squad would be faced with the elimination of their specialized program. A memorandum went out to the rest of the faculty in which both boys' and girls' varsity basketball would be eliminated because of lack of facilities. A meeting was called so that all interested parties could discuss the matter and possibly present a further recommendation to the principal.

The meeting was attended by the principal, the two assistant principals, the five teachers (three men and two women) engaged part-time to assist with the coaching, and the two men and the two women of the physical education staff. Mr. Benson, a classroom teacher who coached the seventh-grade basketball team, was strongly opposed to Wilson's recommendation. If "something had to go," he felt it should be the intramural program, as he believed there was little value to it. Ms. Thompson, the coach of the relatively new girls' basketball team, was upset because this effort had just gotten off to a good start the previous year. Generally, the feeling was expressed that the boys and girls who participated in varsity sports achieved a much greater satisfaction and a finer educational experience. Several pointed to their own earlier experiences as varsity athletes.

Ms. Martin tried to point out to Benson and Thompson that the first responsibility was to the larger number of students. She used the analogy of the physical education triangle, or pyramid, to explain her point. She stressed that the base of the triangle is formed by all the students learning basic skills and knowledges in required physical education classes. The middle section consists of intramural athletics, where the majority of the students should have an opportunity for a competitive experience at their level of ability. She agreed that the more highly skilled should have the chance to compete at their level too, but in this case it seemed impossible. If something had to be eliminated, she said that they, as educators, had a responsibility to work from the bottom of the triangle to the top.

Then Mr. Wilson spoke and said that it was an extremely difficult recommendation for him personally to have to make. He stated that he believed strongly in varsity sports, and that he himself had competed in varsity basketball in college. He reasoned that perhaps the needs of the highly skilled boys and girls could possibly be met through intramural competition. They would become leaders on the various teams and, since they were only at the junior high level, they weren't really that highly skilled yet (comparatively speaking). They had no elementary school physical education program behind them, and actually almost all had a backlog of skills to make up before they could really compete on even terms with all of the other junior high schools in the area.

Principal Glanz stated that he wanted to let those faculty members concerned with this problem make their own decision. He could see both sides of the question--but he couldn't see an answer. The two assistant principals nodded their heads. Mr. Glanz concluded his remarks by mentioning that he had already received a telephone call from Mr. Jackson, the coach of the nearby high school basketball team. Mr. Jackson was very upset that Jensen was considering the dropping of varsity basketball. He said that he was having a hard enough time as it was developing a good high school varsity basketball program. He was also afraid that his position would be in jeopardy because of this proposed move in a community where interest in basketball was very high.

Mr. Haggerty, the other male physical education teacher, pointed out that inter-school competition for boys and girls at this level was subject to a certain amount of criticism anyhow. It tended to be overemphasized, and a number of educational groups had expressed opposition to such overemphasis.

Mr. Wilson, who was chairing the meeting, took the lead suggested by Principal Glanz. He suggested that all present think over the discussion and the various points that had been made. He stated that he would distribute ballots to each person present within two days. He could see that there was going to be bitterness over the issue--no matter how the proposed ballot came out. This had been a "happy family," and "keeping peace" was important for the future. Finally, he asked all of those present to think of possible solutions to the problem whereby all interests would be satisfied.

Suggested Questions for Discussion

1. What influence should the construction of a second junior high school have on this problem, if any?

2. Should required physical education be made available to the seventh-grade students also?

3. Should faculty members receive extra compensation for coaching duties?

4. Was it fair that the girls be restricted to two afternoons a week in the use of the gymnasium?

5. Should the principal and the two assistant principals be involved in the final decision?

6. What do you think of Ms. Martin's argument as opposed to that of Mr. Benson?

7. Are inter-school athletics desirable prior to the high school level?

8. If so, what sports should be considered? For boys? For girls?

9. Should something like this really be decided by majority opinion?

10. Can you think of a solution to this problem whereby all interests would be fulfilled?

10. RAWLINS HIGH SCHOOL

"Legal Liability"
(As reported by a high school teacher)

Ms. Bolling was in her first year of teaching girls' physical education at Rawlins High School. She had just graduated from Middle State University, where she was both a good student and a good athlete with interest and ability in a number of sports. Although not a large person, she was energetic and had a personality that commanded the respect of the students.

From the time she started at Rawlins, it soon became evident that in a short while there would be an interesting and varied program for the girls. Previously the program was only minimally taxing and had consisted of only a few games.

A few girls, as might be expected, were not overly impressed by Fran Bolling. They did not seem to be fond of physical activity, and they certainly were averse to required physical education classes where they felt they were being overworked. As a result, their participation was usually as passive as possible.

Ms. Bolling, cognizant of the fact that this was her first position, made a special effort to treat all the girls fairly. What one had to do, all of them had to do. Because she showed no partiality, her treatment of students earned here the respect of the students to the extent that soon some of the teachers began to send their discipline problems to her.

Irene Skowron was sent to Ms. Bolling by the study hall monitor because of her misbehavior. Since she arrived very early in the class period, Ms. Bolling told her to dress for gym (which she hated) and join the other girls on the playing field.

This particular playing field had been created by dumping fill in a low area behind the school. In situations like this, occasionally below-surface currents cause a sinking of the surface at various points. This possibility was recognized and careful checks were made periodically. When a trouble spot did develop, it was blocked off and repaired as soon as possible.

When Irene arrived at the play area, she was chosen for a team by one of the captains. After playing quite conscientiously for a while, she began to "showboat" and make a travesty

of the game. Ms. Bolling soon noticed this, so she replaced
her immediately with the intention of further disciplining her.

Just then Ms. Bolling's attention was diverted by another
problem with one of the other games that was taking place. As
she was looking after this matter, a scream was heard from one
part of the field. Irene had wandered off and stepped into a
hole. As she lay there crying loudly, it appeared that she was
badly hurt.

First aid was administered, and she was taken to the
hospital for treatment. After an x-ray was taken, the diagnosis was that Irene's fibula was fractured just above the ankle.

Upon receiving this news. Mr. and Mrs. Skowron consulted their attorney, who agreed that a suit citing neglect should
be brought against the teacher. The school board furnished
Ms. Bolling with a lawyer. During the trial, the prosecution
tried to show that it was the neglect of the instructor that
caused the incident. It was stated that the teacher had a responsibility to see that the entire playing area was free of conditions where a student could be injured. It was stated that
this area could almost be called an "attractive nuisance." Further, the point was made very strongly that Irene should not
have been in that class at that time.

The attorney for the defense argued that the injury had
been incurred when Irene went into an area that was clearly
forbidden to students. He argued also that Irene's presence
in that class, when she was scheduled to be in a study hall,
was not unusual either. It was customary at Rawlins to ask
other teachers to assist on occasion with discipline problems.

Ms. Bolling was really worried. If she were found
negligent, she could be declared liable for a large money
settlement. Further, she did not know to what extent the
school board would stand behind her. It was understood that
the school board had insurance to protect itself, but a teacher's negligence is a different matter.

No matter how the jury decided in this case, Ms. Bolling
was afraid that her contract might not be renewed. There had
been a great deal of unfavorable publicity over this incident.
Even if they were to renew her, she reasoned that it might be
better to get another start elsewhere.

Suggested Questions for Discussion

1. How should you treat students in a class who have an evident dislike for the activity?

2. What can a teacher/coach do to show clearly to students that he/she is attempting to be as impartial as possible with the students?

3. Do you think that problem students should be sent to other teachers for possible disciplining by them?

4. Do you think that problem students should be sent from study hall to the gymnasium or playing field?

5. What steps should be taken by a teacher to alert students about the presence of a dangerous area? What should the school authorities do?

6. Do you blame the Skowrons or the attorney for taking the matter to court?

7. In this instance, would you (if you were Ms. Bolling) rather have a trial by judge or a trial by jury?

8. Do you feel that Ms. Bolling was indeed negligent?

9. Do you feel that the school authorities themselves are largely to blame?

10. As a juror, how would you decide?

11. If Ms. Bolling were exonerated, should she expect another contract? Should she accept it? If she is adjudged negligent, what should she do?

Editorial Note
(The Series Case)

In an effort to improve the quality (i.e., "strengthen, deepen, intensify, heighten," etc.) of our case discussions, we have introduced here for the first time in our field what may be called a series case or a case series. Eastern State University is a fictional name, of course, for a "real, live" university where this series of cases occurred as described (or at least as we understand it to have happened). All names have been carefully changed as well, and you, the reader, will appreciate that our intentions here are purely educational. Case A, you will discover, is the longest of the ten cases, and it should serve as the "foundation case" for the other nine. For this reason we urge you to study and discuss Case A most carefully--for perhaps two or three periods so that all concerned will be thoroughly familiar with the facts, the half-facts, and the opinions. Then we suggest that you develop a series of "currently useful generalizations" based on Case A. This will provide you with a "Knowledge Carry-Forward" component that should be most helpful as you use it in connection with the other nine case discussions of Eastern State University. We urge you to continue to build on the listing of currently useful generalizations, perhaps even subdividing into categories. You will be agreeably surprised at the "quality and quantity" of the listing at the end.

(For further reading on "Current Trends and Future Developments" in case writing and analysis, we urge you to read Chapter Twelve of Case Research: The Case Writing Process, 2nd ed., Michiel R. Leenders and Erskine, James A., eds. London, Canada: School of Business Administration, The University of Western Ontario, 1978.)

EASTERN STATE UNIVERSITY (A)[1]

"Required Physical Education"
(As reported by Dr. Friedrich)

Eastern State University, at this time a relatively small, semi-public university, had retained a two-year requirement in physical education after World War II. Dr. Clark (M.D., Ph.D.), age 42, was chosen as the new president. He showed great interest in all of the affairs of the Department of Physical Education, a fact that was attributed by some to his earlier experience as a college athlete.

Upon the retirement of the director of physical education, Mr. Jonas (age 38, with college experience but no degree) was appointed director of athletics. This was a newly created position, as intercollegiate athletics was previously under the Department of Physical Education. Upon the recommendation of the retiring director, a man with an outstanding reputation and an impeccable character, Mr. Robins (age 36, M.A.) was appointed head of the Department of Physical Education (from which intercollegiate athletics had been separated). Mr. Robins had completed a successful career as an army officer, where he had administered a large program of sport and physical training, prior to re-entry into the physical education field.

At this time there were no indoor physical education and sport facilities on campus. The students used the local high schools and the Y.M.C.A. through a rental arrangement. A beautiful new physical education and athletics building was planned, however, and was scheduled for completion in two years.

A general meeting was called by the president who felt that a requirement in physical education at the college level was unwise. There was a great deal of discussion about the subject. Miss Harcourt (age 36, B.P.H.E.), the Director of Women's Physical Education, was very upset by the stand that the president took. Soon after, she resigned in protest, because she considered him to be a "most unreasonable man." To

---

[1] This is the first of a series of ten case problems about Eastern State University. Appendix B, a newspaper article about Eastern State, appeared in 19__. You are urged not to read Appendix B until all discussions about Eastern State are over!

explain her action she wrote a strong letter and sent copies to various influential people connected with the university, including the Board of Trustees. It was rumored that Mr. Robins had worked with her in composing the letter, although this was never proved. Miss Harcourt was said to be well-to-do financially. Because of her outstanding war record and obvious ability, she soon located a top position in her field and has been very successful.

About this time, certain frictions were developing between Mr. Jonas, who served as head football coach as well, and Mr. Robins. It became generally known around campus that Mr. Jonas and President Clark were quite friendly, both on and off the campus. It also became apparent that Mr. Robins and Dr. Clark were not in agreement on a number of matters concerning the work of the Department of Physical Education. Their personalities seemed to clash on a number of topics related to the program of physical education especially. As a result, the Department was not operating at a truly effective level.

One of the staff members, Mr. Lawrence (age 23, B.S.), was completing graduate study at the Master's level in one of the recognized universities. He was to return to Eastern State to take a post on the physical education staff, where he would teach physical education classes and assist in the coaching of football and basketball. At the suggestion of Mr. Jonas and Dr. Clark, Mr. Lawrence found a person who would soon be qualified to take over the position as head of the Department of Physical Education that was held by Mr. Robins.

Mr. Friedrich (age 28, M.A.) was offered a position as assistant professor with the understanding that he would soon be made a full professor and the department head. Mr. Friedrich was employed in physical education and athletics at a prestigious Eastern university. Realizing that this situation looked promising for the future, Mr. Friedrich sought advice from one of his graduate school professors where he was completing a doctoral program on a part-time basis. He was advised to ask Eastern State to hold the post open for one year. His professor reasoned that he would have his doctorate by that time, and that the problem with Mr. Robins might be resolved. This suggestion was received favorably, and Mr. Friedrich accepted the appointment to begin in July of the year that the new building was scheduled to be opened.

Upon Mr. Friedrich's arrival, however, Mr. Robins was still on the job - and gave no indication that he was leaving. While at summer school, Mr. Robins had learned second-hand from Dr. Scott, the same graduate professor from whom Mr. Friedrich had sought advice confidentially, that Mr. Friedrich was being hired to take his place. Thus, there was considerable strain in the relationship between Robins and Friedrich upon the latter's arrival. They treated each other fairly, however, and managed to carry on with a satisfactory relationship. Because Friedrich served as line coach in football under Jonas, it must be admitted that Robins was typically playing a "lone hand" during that year.

In January of his first academic year on campus, Mr. Friedrich - after considerable deliberation and discussion - wrote the following letter to President Clark:

Jan. 25, 19--

Dear Dr. Clark,

I want to thank you for the time that you have spent discussing my situation and our department during the past few months. This past weekend, Mrs. Friedrich and I did practically nothing else but try to clarify our thinking about my position at Eastern State. When I learned that I wouldn't be able to see you until possibly Friday, I decided to write you this note in advance. I hope you will understand my reason for writing instead of waiting to talk the entire matter over with you personally. I sincerely hope that you will be kind enough to take the matter up from this point and correct anything which you think that I have misstated.

I would like to say that the key factor in my decision to come to Eastern State was the telephone conversation which we had after I had called George (Jonas) about the other opportunity I was presented with when still at H_____ immediately after I had accepted the position here at Eastern. At that time I understood you to say that if I came you would grant me a full professorship. You stated also that I could be looking for someone to take Mr. Robins' place by the end of the present academic year.

Knowing that he would not be here after this year, I have made every effort to keep the entire situation peaceful. I'm sure you realize what a problem this has been. The entire situation is one that cannot by the farthest stretch of the imagination be called professional. There are many problems which have come up that I never dreamed of, even after I had been here several months. I believe that I can help enormously a condition which, at the moment, can only be described as sad.

Again in December, when you confirmed my earlier understanding about Mr. Robins, I continued to try to win friends for both the Department and the Division of Intercollegiate Athletics. I felt that moving to a new building with a more harmonious "regime" would help to soothe troubled waters. With many of the important matters now coming up for next year, and Mr. Robins not giving the slightest indication of leaving, and your avoidance of the matter in our last talk, I cannot help but wonder if he will indeed be gone.

If I do not succeed to this promised position. it would appear true that I have made a very grave mistake in coming to Eastern State. Giving up my previous position was a difficult decision to make, but I was confident that it was the right move. To date I have been completely happy about the move, confident that the promised position would materialize. I am very enthusiastic about the unusual opportunity for service to my field here.

I would appreciate it very much if you would clarify this matter for me, so that I can put my mind at ease. If we are to obtain further qualified help, we must start now. I sincerely hope that I will have the opportunity to be of service to Eastern State in a way that I feel qualified to do.

Cordially yours,

E. C. Friedrich

In early February, certain pressures were brought to bear on Mr. Robins to encourage him to resign. It was rumored that he was guilty of some personal misconduct, but this was never brought out into the open. About this time too the new physical education building was finally completed. There were a number of vexing problems along the way mostly caused

162

by inadequate planning and knowledge by those concerned in the construction of such facilities. In April, Mr. Robins did resign as of June 30, but he was to be retained at full pay six additional months to complete some research which had been underway.

LINE-STAFF RELATIONSHIP AT EASTERN STATE UNIVERSITY

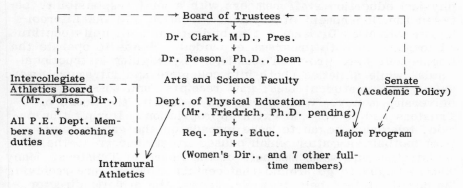

With Robins on the way out, Dr. Clark discussed his plan to reduce the physical education requirement to one year with Mr. Friedrich. Friedrich agreed that this amount of time for physical education should be sufficient at the university level. (Just about this time Friedrich completed his doctoral program, an accomplishment that had been part of the original agreement.) After obtaining the approval of other staff members, Dr. Friedrich recommended the one-year plan to the Faculty of Arts and Science, and it was subsequently approved by the Senate of the University.

Because the physical education staff felt that physical education was a very important subject for freshmen, a great deal of time was spent in planning for the new one-year program to be inaugurated.

The staff decided that students could gain exemption from the various six-week sessions by passing proficiency tests in swimming; body mechanics and fitness; combatives (wrestling) for men and dance for women; and leisure skills. The program appeared to be accepted as quite satisfactory. All staff members (including Dr. Friedrich) taught at least one section of this course. Students continued physical education and sport activities in increasing numbers in their leisure during the remaining years at the University either in intramural

163

athletics, intercollegiate athletics, or voluntary physical recreation.

A physical education major program had been instituted at Eastern State two and one-half years before the new building opened. Seven years later it had the largest enrollment of any major program in the Arts and Science Faculty. With an increasing enrollment on the campus a need arose for more physical education staff members with a joint responsibility between the Department of Physical Education and the Intercollegiate Athletics Division. The budgets of both units continued to grow as both programs expanded. Funds to operate the Department were provided completely by regular instructional funds, while athletics (both intercollegiate and intramural) were supported by student fees, gate receipts, and some regular university money. When there was a deficit, the Board of Trustees had to vote an extra appropriation. During this period, television began to make inroads on the gate receipts from football, a matter which caused great concern to the administration and some members of the Board of Trustees. Many rumors began to go around that certain athletes were receiving "under-the-table" help from Mr. Jonas, the athletic director. This rumor appeared to cause great embarrassment to the administration. Dr. Clark told a member of the physical education staff one day that Mr. Jonas was to be asked to resign on the following day. This "resignation" did not take place, however, as Mr. Jonas threatened to call a press conference and bring to light from just what sources money had been obtained.

About this time, which was four years after Friedrich's arrival, the Dean of Arts and Science became ill suddenly and retired. Dr. Reason (age 48, Ph.D. in English) was appointed in his place. Dr. Reason had been the commanding officer of the R.O.T.C. Unit at Eastern State during World War II. He voiced opposition to the idea of any physical education requirement at the university level. His predecessor had generally discussed departmental budgets with department heads before the budgets were finally approved by the Advisory Committee composed of the President, the Vice-President, the Business Officer and the Dean of Arts and Science. The previous year before Reason arrived on the scene, the various department heads (of which there were twenty-one) had voiced considerable oppositions to salary recommendations in general. But shortly after Dr. Reason became dean, it was announced that the Advisory Committee (to the President) had decided to abandon such discussions. A number of department heads expressed dissatisfaction with this decision. Even Dr. Friedrich, as a young department head, was very concerned about this development. He went so far as to compose a letter to Reason, but for reasons of diplomacy at that particular time the letter (which went as follows) was not sent:

Dear Dean Reason:

   Thank you very much for your letter containing information about our budget for next year. I know that all members of the department will be pleased to learn about their salary increases. We have appreciated the fact that for the past few years annual increments have been possible.

   I know how many meetings you must have during the course of the academic year. Because time was so short, I presume that you didn't have time to go over the budgets with department heads before they went to the Board. I thought this was a very fine practice, and would appreciate the reinstatement of this practice in the future if you deem it advisable and feasible.

   I do sincerely, appreciate the increase which I have been given. I am sorry, however, that it was not possible to follow the 15% recommendation suggested by the Faculty Council [a group of department heads formed to give them an avenue of approach to the President]. I mention this because I feel that the differential between senior and junior staff members is not large enough. I do appreciate how difficult these matters must be.

   Thank you again for this information. I sincerely hope that our department may continue to develop because of your increased support.

                              Cordially yours,

                              E. C. Friedrich

   The Faculty Council, a group ultimately responsible to all faculty members of the Arts and Science Division, had met only once or twice about inconsequential matters. It met at the call of the Dean and was not convened in the second and third years of Reason's term of office.

   During the spring just after his appointment, Dr. Reason had said to Dr. Friedrich in a private meeting, "We don't like empire builders around here." On another occasion two years later, Dr. Reason had told his secretary, "It isn't that I dislike Dr. Friedrich; it's just that I don't like the place of his subject in the curriculum."

At about the same time, the following telephone conversation occurred between Dr. Reason and Dr. Friedrich:

"Edward, this is John."

"Yes, Dr. Reason, how are you?"

"I'm very busy, Edward, but there are two matters which I must call to your attention. The first has to do with a report from Mr. Wallis [the Business Officer] that young men are wandering around the basement of the gymnasium with their navels exposed when they go from the locker room to the special exercise room. Because our business offices are located on the lower floor [temporarily], this has been embarrassing to some of the ladies in the office."

"I will speak to the locker room supervisor right away, Dr. Reason, to see if the men can be checked at the locker room door before leaving."

"The second matter has to do with one of your women staff members who was seen in her gymnasium costume holding hands and standing extremely close with a young man in a corner of the hall. President Clark reported this to me, and it has got to be stopped."

"I think I can explain this, Dean Reason. She became engaged recently to a graduate student. I will speak to her about this."

"It's not only this behavior that bothers me, but these gymnasium costumes that the women are wearing are not appropriate outside of the gymnasium proper."

"I'll discuss this with the staff and give them your thought on the matter. I'll bet that they . . ."

"This is not a matter to discuss with them. The commanding officer [President Clark] has spoken, and it's our duty to obey."

"Dr. Reason, I have never been in the army.
I'm not in the army now, and I don't believe I'll ever
join in the future."

"Call my secretary and make an appointment to
see me tomorrow morning" (Dean Reason hung up).

Friedrich made the appointment for 11:00 a.m. the next morning and called a staff meeting for 10:30 a.m. A quick agreement was reached as to the approach to take in these two matters. To Dr. Friedrich's surprise, Dean Reason was very
amiable. He congratulated Friedrich for causing him to lose
his temper and hang up the telephone. Dr. Friedrich said that
the staff was agreed on both matters, and that they would do
their best to prevent the occurrence of similar incidents.

At this point the Women's Director of Physical Education
and Athletics resigned for a variety of reasons. She was not
happy with her particular situation as a person, nor was she
pleased with the situation in general from a professional standpoint. She became terribly annoyed several times at meetings
of the Athletic Directorate, when Dr. Clark seemed to be guiding the thinking too strongly of this group composed of students, faculty members, alumni, administration members, and
some members of the Board of Trustees. Also, one of her
parents was seriously ill, and she wished to be nearer to her
home. Lastly, some of her students had called a meeting to
present her with a set of presumed grievances. Her letter of
resignation read as follows:

Dear Dean Reason:

Please accept my resignation from the Department of Physical Education, and from Athletics, as
of June 30, 19--. Before leaving Eastern State, I
should like to say that the working relationship with
Dr. Friedrich has been entirely satisfactory. He
realizes that the staff has opinions, ideas, and
ideals and gives them ample opportunity to express,
explain, and justify them. He does his best to im-
plement suggestions approved by the staff as a
whole. A sincere interest in the students and the
course is of primary concern, and I think the attitudes and atmosphere within the Department of
Physical Education are good.

Miss T. Washburn
Women's Director

During this spring, the Faculty of Arts and Science appointed a committee to consider the work load of first-year students at the university. Dr. Friedrich was called in to explain the physical education program (the one-year requirement). Prior to the meeting, the physical education staff met to consider the best approach for Friedrich to take in the forthcoming session. It was decided to submit a list of objectives for the required program, as well as a summary of the time length of the requirement (if such was in existence) at representative colleges throughout the country. The following is the list of objectives for the required program (latest revision):

OBJECTIVES OF PHYSICAL EDUCATION 10

1. To develop physical recreational competence and to provide enjoyment.

   a. Achieved by instruction and participation in leisure carry-over recreational activities such as tennis, golf, squash rackets, badminton, volleyball, etc.

2. To develop an understanding of, and interest in, the attainment of physical fitness.

   a. Achieved by the following program activities:

      i. Activities of a vigorous nature to bring the physically "illiterate" individual to a state of reasonable strength and motor ability.

      ii. Combative, self-defense activities (e.g., wrestling, judo, etc.) are included under this heading to increase strength and agility, as well as to enable the individual to defend himself.

      iii. Several forms of dance activity are included to assist in the development of movement skill and aesthetic appreciation.

      iv. Correction of remediable physical defects upon the diagnosis of a physician and the prescription of exercises to be carried out under the supervision of an exercise specialist.

3. To develop the ability to swim (a physical recreational skill).

    a. Achieved through participation in an instructional class until the person is able to pass a beginner's test. Water safety experiences are provided so that the person learns elementary methods of saving himself/herself and the provision of assistance to others in emergency situations.

4. To develop desirable attitudes toward the field of physical education and sport (including health and recreation education) and to foster an understanding and appreciation of its place in later life.

    a. Achieved by the evaluation of the individual's "personal fitness and health profile"; the development of knowledge, competencies, and skills relative to personal and community health; and the active involvement of students in an adequately planned program which stresses the various benefits to be derived.

5. To foster the development of a desirable personality (including such traits as cooperation, leadership, integrity, perseverance, etc.) and to promote general social proficiency.

    a. Achieved by participation in team, dual, and individual sports.

At the meeting the matter was discussed fully, and no recommendation was made to abolish the requirement. One member of the committee remarked to Dr. Friedrich as the session was breaking up that it was difficult to argue his department down on a point because it was always so well prepared. The chairman of the committee, a personal friend of Dr. Friedrich, told him later that some of the committee members were against the requirement. However, the committee as a whole decided that required physical education was at least as important as several other courses demanded of all students in the first year.

The following academic year in the spring, which was actually Friedrich's sixth year at Eastern State, he was invited to give an address at a state education convention (to the physical education section). His talk was on the topic of "administrative problem areas in physical education and sport." Present at the talk was a large group of high school and college physical education personnel. It was well received, but didn't cause any stir whatsoever at that time. This convention was held in the state capitol, a large city with three competing newspapers. Representatives of each newspaper asked for a copy of the talk. (Additionally, the local newspaper representative from the city in which Eastern State was located had a asked for a copy in advance. Further, because he knew that this was a fairly important presentation, Friedrich had asked several staff members to read the paper in advance, and no one made any special mention of the problems to be discussed. There were fifteen different problems to be presented with brief emphasis on each.).

That same evening Dr. Friedrich attended a conference banquet, and three or four colleagues mentioned that they enjoyed his afternoon presentation. Friedrich left town immediately after the banquet to attend a national convention in another state. The following morning, therefore, he attended a meeting at the national convention, and in the middle of this session a colleague entered the room and told him there was a telegram for him at the hotel's main desk. Dr. Friedrich went right out to claim the telegram; to his surprise it was from Dean Reason back home at Eastern State. It read as follows:

PLEASE BE DISCREET IN YOUR PUBLIC UTTERANCES AND SEE ME MONDAY MORNING AT NINE.

Unable to figure out what the difficulty was, Friedrich called home immediately. It seems that representatives of the press had the day before - a quiet Easter Monday with relatively little news - seized on certain statements out of some of the administrative problem areas that Friedrich had discussed at the state convention. In each of the major newspapers (and there were three of them), one of the problems he had discussed was featured prominently on the first page. As a result these statements made headlines right across the country. The newspaper in Dr. Friedrich's city, where Eastern State was located, stressed his criticism of the state director's policy - the civil servant whose political appointment put him in charge of the state's educational policy. This man had expressed a policy which removed gymnasia from a list of essential facilities for high schools throughout the state. And, unfortunately, it was an election year. What made the matter still more delicate was that the newspapers in the convention city each in some fashion had stressed the point made by

Friedrich concerning under-the-table aid to athletes. Then the hometown paper, which the day before had featured Friedrich's criticism of the Director's policy regarding funds for gymnasia construction, decided to do a follow-up story about the aid to athletes question that had been featured in the newspapers of the convention city. It evidently appeared to Dean Reason and others that Dr. Friedrich had given several addresses, and this was why the telegram had been sent to the hotel where the national convention was being held. All in all, it developed into quite an embarrassing situation even though those who heard the talk though nothing of it, so to speak.

After Dr. Friedrich received the telegram at the national convention, he sent the following letter immediately to Dean Reason, air mail, special delivery:

April 12, 19--

Dear Dr. Reason,

After seeing the headline in the Daily Journal, I wondered whether it might be advisable to con- tinue travelling westward. I can well appreciate your concern about ill-chosen headlines.

I have asked the State Convention Committee to mail the original copy of my talk for your pe- rusal. Before giving this paper, I asked three col- leagues to read it carefully for criticism. No one felt that it wasn't well-organized and factual in every regard.

Naturally, we are very concerned with public relations in our field. Four high schools are plan- ned in Parkhurst without gymnasia. In my opinion, this is a tragedy and we must speak out against it - if we would be true to our principles.

In like manner, our universities are faced continually with the problem of underhanded help to athletes. One of our students was just recently of- fered fifteen hundred dollars if he would transfer to King State University next year. This must not continue.

My talk covered problems in our total field. There were fifteen problem areas discussed, and the above two points were simply mentioned in passing under certain of the fifteen sub-headings. I'm sorry if it is considered wrong for me to state my principles on these matters to my associates.

Our National Association through its executive stated recently that we are usually talking and writing to each other, rather than the public. It is recommended that we do indeed make our views known at every opportunity. Quite inadvertently, I followed the Association's recommendation, and the "roof fell in." The headlines were unfortunate, to be sure, but the thoughts and beliefs stated under those headlines should be the concern of all.

I do hope that this letter helps to clarify the situation. Kindest personal regards and all best wishes.

Very sincerely yours,

E. C. Friedrich

P.S.   I am enclosing an extra copy of this letter for President Clark, if you wish him to have one.

On Monday morning at 9:00 A.M., Dr. Friedrich appeared to discuss the matter of the newspapers' releases with Dean Reason. The Dean appeared quite calm about the incident. He stated that he didn't see how Dr. Friedrich "could give so many public talks, write so many articles, and still do his job adequately." He stated further that he planned to recommend to the total Faculty of Arts and Sciences that the physical education major program be reviewed by a group of the faculty members. Further, he said that he planned to recommend to the Faculty additionally that the one-year physical education requirement be dropped. He emphasized several times that there was absolutely no connection between these two recommendations and the "unfortunate publicity."

President Clark also asked Dr. Friedrich to see him about the newspaper publicity. Very quitely, he explained to Dr. Friedrich that this publicity might well cost the University a further grant of $160,000 from the State Department of Education. President Clark had called the State Director personally to explain that this address did not represent the opinion of the University. Dr. Friedrich again expressed his regret for

the unfortunate aspect of the publicity. The extra grant
eventually came to the University.

Just before Dr. Friedrich had attended the two conven-
tions (state and national), he had written two letters to a local
"Letters to the Editor" column, answering sharp criticism of
physical education in the schools. The second letter appeared
in the newspaper shortly after Friedrich's return. Dean Reason sent the following letter to Friedrich shortly thereafter:

Personal and Confidential

April 20, 19- -

Dr. E. C. Friedrich, Head
Department of Physical Education

Dear Edward,

I have been informed that you are the author
of several letters which have appeared in the local
newspaper over the signature of "University Professor." Of these, the only one that I have seen
is that which appeared last night (April 19). From
the address and the internal evidence, I assume
that my informant was correct.

I should like to point out that I strenuously
object to the use of a university rank as the signature for what is a personal expression. I might as
well admit that after our interview on Monday morning the appearance of the letter startled me. I felt
that you were not anxious to rush into print again.
It may be, of course, that your letter was mailed
to the editor before you started on your travels.

Yours sincerely,

John J. Reason, Dean

Dr. Friedrich called the Dean immediately and explained
that the letter had indeed been mailed before he left for the
convention. He stated that he had asked the editor to leave
out his name so that he might avoid personal publicity. He
mentioned also that he would not write the newspaper again.

From this time on, the President's Advisory Committee embarked upon a course of action designed to eliminate the physical education requirement. When a physical education staff member resigned, a replacement was not appointed even though recommendations were made.

In June, Dr. Rogers (a friend of Dr. Clark), the University Health Service physician who had joined the staff six years earlier, wrote a letter to Dean Reason stating that he didn't think any first-year student should be forced to take physical education. He expressed particular concern about the number of injuries that had occurred in wrestling (one of the areas required for men who could not demonstrate competency in self-defense). This stand was prompted possibly by the fact that Dr. Rogers was hired for only three hours a day, five days a week, and did not have time to care for all the health problems. Dr. Rogers had gone to Dean Reason once before with the complaint that the supervisor of the men's required program was demanding written excuses for absences when the student was obviously unable to take part. The practice of written excuses had started several years before Dr. Rogers had assumed office. In his letter to the Dean, Dr. Rogers raised several other minor objections to the required program. The Department of Physical Education on that earlier occasion had met after the Dean had read that letter to the entire Faculty of Arts and Science at a general meeting, and subsequently informed Reason that it was ready to accede to the recommendations concerning the necessity for written excuses and the other minor problems listed.

Dean Reason appeared determined to eliminate required physical education and asked the Faculty to refer the matter to its Educational Policy Committee. Meetings were to be held during the summer months, and Dr. Friedrich was invited to attend one of these sessions. Almost all of the faculty members at this meeting appeared to have no strong convictions on the problem. A number of these people were personal friends of Dr. Friedrich and made a point to tell him privately that they favored the one-year physical education requirement, with possible exemption from certain areas upon demonstration of proven competency. Dr. Reason did seem to be "spearheading" the idea of abolition at the meeting which Dr. Friedrich attended. Friedrich suggested that he would like to outline the case for retention of the present arrangement. He said he felt that he should then withdraw so that the matter might be discussed freely. Since he was not an official member of the committee, this suggestion was accepted.

After a number of meetings during the summer at which many of the members were often not present, Dean Reason informed Dr. Friedrich that the committee was prepared to recommend to the Faculty in the fall that physical education should be elective, except for non-swimmers and serious corrective cases needing remedial exercise. He suggested further that the elective program should be instituted immediately to solve the staff shortage problem for the fall. In view of the fact that no additional staff was to be made available, Dr. Friedrich had no choice seemingly but to concede that this would be the better approach until the Faculty and the University Senate could decide whether to accept the special committee's recommendation. A few days later Dr. Friedrich sent the following letter to all his staff members:

August 5, 19--

Dear _____,

Dr. Reason has just notified me that the Educational Policy Committee is recommending to the Faculty that Physical Education 10 be an elective subject henceforth, with the exception that non-swimmers should receive instruction, and that those requiring remedial corrective work should receive help, if possible, as recommended by Dr. Rogers and Dr. Mason (a specialist in Physical Medicine). It was stressed further that students should be encouraged to participate in leisure skills on a voluntary basis.

Naturally, the implementation of such a recommentation would change our entire approach to this work, and I guess we will have to decide as soon as possible after Labor Day just what we are going to do - and how much manpower it will take. The President's Advisory Committee has re-affirmed its decision not to replace Mr. Y [the staff member who had just resigned to take another position]. This leaves us $2\frac{1}{2}$ staff members short according to last year's overall work load relative to the work load formula for individuals that we are using. We will still have to offer beginning swimming at each hour left free for such election by Dean Reason. We could probably offer one other leisure skill at that hour.

175

I had suggested that Mr. O [another staff member who had resigned to take up medicine the year before Mr. Y] might be approached to administer intramural athletics for men during the next few years, but the Advisory Committee feels that we should be able to handle this within the Department. At any rate, we should know early in September what work load seems to be required. We can make any further recommendations at that time.

Dean Reason has suggested that we inaugurate the elective program immediately to help solve the staff shortage problem. He feels that the recommendation of the Educational Policy Committee will be approved at the fall meeting of the total Faculty of Arts and Science, and then subsequently by the University Senate.

Dr. Reason is still anxious to have our program for physical education majors reviewed. The feeling exists that we are working students too hard in the laboratory phase of the curriculum.

Please think about these various matters in the next few weeks. I'll be looking forward to seeing you in the early fall. Kindest personal regards and all best wishes.

As ever,

Ed

All staff members of the Department of Physical Education were present at the fall Faculty meeting of Eastern State where the Educational Policy Committee presented its recommendation concerning physical education. The chairman of the committee was asked from the floor to give some supporting rationale for the recommendation. He didn't appear able to do this and called for support from the other members of the committee. No one gave him much help, so Dean Reason (the chairman of the Faculty meeting) sought to speak on behalf of the committee. The membership of the Faculty then discussed the matter at considerable length. When it appeared almost certain that the recommendation would be defeated if a vote were taken, a member of the committee moved that the matter be laid over to the next meeting of the Faculty. This motion passed.

At the next meeting of the Faculty, the chairman of the committee again presented the recommendation, this time much more forcibly than previously. Someone suggested that there appeared to be great haste to "push this matter through" the Faculty. At this point Dr. Friedrich asked the chairman of the meeting (Dean Reason) for permission to read a brief statement by an eminent educator on the place of physical education in education. The permission was granted somewhat reluctantly, so Friedrich read a statement which challenged the field of physical education "to take its rightful place in general education, or else be cast aside as a branch in a swiftly flowing stream rounding a bend." In an obvious attempt to down play the importance of such a remark, Dean Reason inquired as to "what august educator" had made such a comment. When Dr. Friedrich answered "President Clark," and explained that it had been part of an address by Eastern State's president at a physical education convention only two years previously, the meeting of the Faculty was disturbed somewhat by laughter and attendant discussion between individuals.

Dean Reason called the meeting to order, and again there was considerable discussion of the matter. A science professor mentioned that he thought that the committee had made an excellent point when it recommended that first-year students needing remedial treatment be required to take corrective exercise. Dr. Friedrich pointed out that not one student had been recommended that fall by the University Health Service for such rehabilitative work,[2] although Dr. Rogers had known that this recommendation was supposed to take effect a month earlier at the time when all university students received thorough medical examinations. After more discussion, Dr. Reason put the motion of the committee to a vote. The voice vote was not decisive, so he decided to ask for a show of hands. The counting of raised hands evidently became confusing to him too, and he asked for a division of the house by a standing vote. The motion to eliminate the physical education requirement was defeated by one vote.

Matters appeared to quiet down. Dr. Friedrich was called in by Dean Reason to discuss certain questions on Reason's mind. In a seemingly friendly atmosphere, Dr. Reason pointed out to Friedrich that he felt that Friedrich had, to all intents and purposes, called him a liar at the Faculty meeting when he disagreed with Reason's explanation about the necessity for

---

[2] During the week immediately thereafter, Dr. Rogers called the Women's Director and blamed his secretary for forgetting to send the list of remedial cases.

temporarily inaugurating an "elective program" for this year only because of a staff shortage. Dr. Friedrich denied this and argued that he had said that Dean Reason "had unwittingly misinterpreted the facts a bit." The point was dropped. No guarantee was given by the Dean that there would be sufficient staff for the required program in the next year.

Several months later, the rumor spread around the campus that Dr. Friedrich was considering an offer to take a responsible position at one of the nation's top ten universities.

Suggested Questions for Discussion

1. Might it be expected that President Clark, a medical doctor, would have certain feelings about a program of required physical education including the opportunity for remedial corrective exercise?

2. Would President Clark's previous experience as an athlete influence his thinking about required physical education?

3. Why do you suppose that two separate departments were created upon the retirement of the original Director of Physical Education?

4. What do you think of Miss Harcourt's action in writing a "strong letter" after resigning? Do you attach any significance to the fact that Miss Harcourt located a fine position serving a national constituency soon thereafter, a post which she held until her retirement?

5. What is your reaction to the reported "friendliness" of Mr. Jonas and President Clark? Why do you suppose Mr. Robins had difficulty in getting along with both of these men?

6. What do you think of the method whereby Mr. Robins' successor was located?

7. Do you think it was wise to have Mr. Robins and Mr. Friedrich on the same staff at the same time?

8. Does Dr. Friedrich's letter to President Clark give you any insight into the situation?

9. Are there any implications from the fact that Dr. Friedrich served for two years as line coach in football under Mr. Jonas?

10. Why do you suppose that Mr. Robins left the university without writing a letter of protest, giving his story to the newspaper, or taking some other overt action as a form of protest?

11. Why do you think that Mr. Robins was allowed to stay on for six months at full salary to complete his research project?

12. What do you think of the physical education staff's plan for a one-year required program that would permit exemptions for proven proficiency in the various areas?

13. Do you attach any significance to the inauguration of a major program in physical education after President Clark assumed his post at the head of Eastern State University?

14. Later, why do you suppose that the plan to force Mr. Jonas to "resign" did not materialize?

15. Do you attach any significance to the letter that Dr. Friedrich wrote to Dean Reason, but did not send? Do you believe that Dean Reason was responsible for the deviation from the previous policy of allowing department heads to see their budgets again after the President's Advisory Committee had made its recommendations?

16. What significance do you attach to the fact that the Faculty Council had not met for two and one-half years?

17. Why do you suppose that Dean Reason made the statement about "empire builders" to Dr. Friedrich so soon after taking office?

18. What might be gleaned from the letter of resignation written by the Women's Director on May 17th?

19. What do you make of the telephone conversation between Dean Reason and Dr. Friedrich relative to the young men running around with "exposed navels," etc. What do you think of Dean Reason for more or less apologizing for losing his temper the next day?

20. Why do you imagine that the Faculty Council (of Arts and Science) had not decided to abolish the physical education requirement sooner?

21. How do you suppose that Dr. Friedrich learned about Dean Reason's remark to his secretary that "he didn't necessarily dislike Dr. Friedrich, just the place of his subject in the curriculum?"

22. What do you think of the "Objectives of Physical Education" as revised?

23. Is is possible that there was a connection with the decision of higher administration to re-open the matter of required physical education after Dr. Friedrich's convention talk?

24. What do you think of the telegram? Of Dr. Friedrich's reply?

25. Do you think that Dean Reason truly felt that Dr. Friedrich wasn't carrying out his campus duties satisfactorily when he made the remark that Dr. Friedrich should write and talk less for public consumption?

26. Why do you think that Dr. Rogers, the University physician, wrote the letter to Dean Reason without discussing the matter first with Dr. Friedrich?

27. Do you think the dpeartment was right in acceding to all the suggestions made by Dr. Rogers so readily?

28. What significance do you attach to the fact that the meetings of the Educational Policy Committee were held during the summer? To the fact that Dean Reason appeared to be guiding the discussion when Dr. Friedrich was invited to attend one session? To the fact that the chairman of the committee appeared unable to defend the committee's recommendation for elimination of the requirement at the fall meeting?

29. Why do you think that the Faculty voted to retain the requirement? Do you think that Friedrich's quotation from President Clark's earlier address swayed people in their thinking?

30. Do you feel anything truly significant is indicated by the fact that nine physical education department members (not all mentioned in the case description) had resigned from such a relatively small unit (commencing with Mr. Robins)?

31. Why do you suppose that Dr. Rogers, the University Physician, had sent no list of students needing remedial corrective exercise to the department until after the matter had come up in the meeting of the Faculty Council?

32. What do you think of Dr. Friedrich's answer to Dean Reason when the Dean said that he felt he was being called a liar?

33. Do you think that Dr. Friedrich should resign from his position?

EASTERN STATE UNIVERSITY (B)

"Personnel Relationships"
(As reported by the department head)

Ms. Taylor Washburn was an assistant professor in charge of women's physical education and athletics at Eastern State University. This program was one of several that came under the jurisdiction of the Department of Physical Education. She had an excellent background for her position. In addition to a B.A. degree with a major in history, she also held a B.S. degree in health and physical education. Additionally, she had completed the M.A. degree in health and physical education with distinction. She was thirty years old, and apparently had no intention of getting married.

Taylor's superior at Eastern State was the department head, E. C. Friedrich. He and Taylor got along together very well. No one seemed to be keeping any secrets from anyone else on the staff, and this applied especially to the relationship between Washburn and Friedrich. All staff policy was discussed openly and freely at regular meetings. It could be said that Washburn was not liked too well by the rest of the staff, because she fought hard for the rights and privileges of the program which she supervised. She often came out with strong statements at staff meetings, but Dr. Friedrich did not worry about this too much, because he knew that he could generally reach an acceptable compromise with Professor Washburn. Friedrich sensed also that Washburn was not especially popular with the students, but he reasoned that students did not have to like an instructor and coach so long as they respected her.

Washburn paid careful attention to the administrative details of her post. All who associated with her knew exactly where she stood on administrative matters. For example, the locker room supervisor thought highly of her, because she was thoughtful and yet businesslike in all her dealings. The other two women staff members who worked completely under her supervision did not get along with her very well. One occasionally complained in a minor way, while the other - a recent immigrant to the country with an outstanding background as an athlete, coach, and teacher in a north-central European country - became quietly emotional in discussions with Dr. Friedrich about some of her relationships with Professor Washburn. Of course, matters never appeared black and white to Dr. Friedrich, and Washburn seemed to be making a sincere effort to get along with these two teacher-coaches.

The administrative officers of the university thought highly of Washburn, although it must be admitted that they knew relatively little about the specifics of her work. She dressed well, attended meetings regularly, spoke meticulous English, and in their opinion was a fine representative of the physical education field.

Professor Washburn's father and mother were quite old, and their health was poor. They lived in a city about 400 miles away and were very attached to this locality. Taylor visited them whenever possible. She had mentioned several times to Dr. Friedrich the possibility of taking a post at the high school level in that city. She was an only child and felt a strong responsibility to her aging parents. By such a move, she reasoned that she would be able to help them over some of life's rough spots.

The State Director of Physical Education held Washburn in high regard, and always asked about her when Friedrich visited the state office.

The entire staff of the Department understood that the Ph.D. degree was considered necessary for a promotion to the rank of associate professor. Except for this qualification, Professor Washburn could have reasonably expected to receive this rank fairly soon. For this reason, she had made tentative plans to complete her doctorate. She and Friedrich had talked this over carefully on several occasions, while considering the best programs available.

Professor Washburn was not too happy about the dictatorial habits demonstrated by the university president at meetings. Dr. Friedrich felt exactly the same way. Policies decided upon democratically by the staff of the department often received rather harsh treatment when they were brought before the President's Advisory Committee (chaired by Dr. Clark). As the president was fairly young and likely to hold his office for a considerable time, Washburn wondered if the department was going to continue to progress. She and Friedrich had discussed this matter on occasion.

When Dr. Friedrich presented his budget for the forthcoming academic year, he said that he could not recommend a promotion to the rank of associate professior for Professor Washburn. Washburn understood that her lack of the advanced degree was Friedrich's reason. Friedrich did recommend, however, a sizeable salary increase, because he felt that Washburn was underpaid.

The next morning the dean directly over Friedrich called to say that the Advisory Committee was going to recommend the promotion in rank for Washburn. Friedrich did not like to hold a person back, but he said that he could not agree whole-heartedly. In other departments that were considered academic, a person needed the doctorate for promotion to the rank of assistant professor. In the professional schools - which physical education was considered to be - Friedrich felt that the doctorate should be required for promotion to the rank of associate professor. He made another statement to the effect that several other staff members also should be promoted if the matter of the Ph.D. degree was to be overlooked. Dean Griswold, who was later succeeded by Dean Reason, stated that President Clark felt that Washburn should have the promotion, and that was the way it would have to be. Dr. Friedrich didn't know what to do, because he knew that several other members of the departmental staff were going to feel that they had been passed by unfairly.

No sooner had the telephone conversation concluded than one of the outstanding senior women students entered Dr. Friedrich's office. She asked the department head if he would come with her to one of the classrooms on the same floor to discuss an important matter. When they arrived, Dr. Friedrich found sixteen students present. Madalyn Nearing, the student who had come to get Friedrich, explained that the group wanted to air some grievances about Professor Washburn. Professor Friedrich was dumbfounded. He didn't know whether he should listen to what they had to say. Finally, he stated that he would listen, but that he wanted to get both sides of the story. Friedrich wondered if he should have called Professor Washburn to the room, but he reasoned that such a meeting would be embarrassing to all concerned. The Head listened quickly as the students spoke. On several occasions he argued on behalf of Professor Washburn. On certain points he stated that he would look into the matter. Finally, Ms. Nearing presented Dr. Friedrich with a list of all the complaints. Friedrich promised to consider the matter carefully.

After Friedrich read over the list several times in the privacy of his office, he decided to discuss the matter immediately with Professor Washburn. He went to Washburn's office and said, "Taylor, I don't know what to think of something that just happened, but I think I should discuss it with you right away." Washburn looked at him quizzically and said, "What's up?" She could see that Friedrich was very upset. In a kindly way, Friedrich told her exactly what had happened and then showed her the list:

Women Physical Education Students' Complaints

Prof. Taylor Washburn:

1. Teaching incompetencies

    a. Washburn's organization of classes is poor.
    b. She cancels classes at will.
    c. She doesn't seem to care about students or their im-
       provement.
    d. Her grades are not computed objectively.
    e. Test papers are not grade adequately.
    f. She taught us gymnastics for one-half year, but now
       says that the grades for this work won't count in our
       final averages.
    g. She didn't cover the subject of community recreation,
       but now states that we be responsible for the course
       inadequacies on the final examination.
    h. In our course on Methods and Materials of Physical
       Education, all we got was information on materials.
    i. As an instructor, she has inadequacies but makes no
       apparent effort to improve her work.
    j. In the activity course that includes square dancing,
       the students report that they have learned nothing.
       Over half of the classes were cancelled. Now the
       students are being tested on last year's material. No
       theoretical examination was given - only a practical
       one.
    k. One morning, in place of teaching the regular class
       work, the group was read a fairy tale.

2. General Comments

    a. The reason there are only three women registered in
       the second year of the major program is that the
       junior and senior women are telling younger students
       to take a minor instead of a major in the department.
    b. Students have lost their confidence in Ms. Washburn's
       ability, administration, and leadership.
    c. She has shown extreme favoritism with one junior stu-
       dent. The work and personality of other students
       have been discussed.
    d. Ms. Washburn has interfered with the work of the
       other women instructors on a number of occasions
       during class. She has contradicted them in front of
       the group of students present.

Washburn read this indictment slowly, without saying a word, and then read it again. Both Washburn and Friedrich realized that the students had misinterpreted a number of the items. One question remained, as they both knew. Could Washburn continue in the face of this statement demonstrating the students' dislike and lack of confidence in her as a person? Both teachers sat quietly for a few moments. Then Taylor said, "Ed, maybe it's time for me to take that high school position near my folks." Friedrich replied, "Taylor, the world isn't going to come to an end. Let's have lunch. It's my turn to buy."

Suggested Questions for Discussion

1. Just because staff members and students did not seem to like Washburn, should Friedrich have looked more carefully into the matter sooner? How would he go about this (if your answer is in the affirmative)?

2. Everything considered, what opinion do you get of Washburn? Of Friedrich? Of President Clark? Of Dean Griswold? Of Madalyn Nearing?

3. Do you believe that Washburn's dislike of the President and her anxiety for the welfare of her parents had anything to do with her work and conduct?

4. When Friedrich learned that Washburn was going to be promoted despite the policy generally in effect, what should he have done?

5. Should Friedrich have left the room when he discovered what the impromptu meeting was about?

6. Should Friedrich have discussed the matter immediately with Washburn?

7. What should Washburn do?

8. Should Friedrich conduct a further investigation? If so, how should he carry out such a venture?

9. What should Friedrich do, knowing that the promotion to the rank of associate professor was to be approved the next day by the Board of Trustees?

EASTERN STATE UNIVERSITY (C)

"Office Management"
(As reported by the department head)

Eastern State University was a relatively small state university with an enrollment of about 5,000 students. The physical education major program consisted of about 70 students rather evenly divided in number among the four years of the course. The faculty members - seven full-time men and three full-time women - were considered as full-time departmental employees, although all of them were on loan to intercollegiate athletics and received a share of their salaries from the athletic budget. The director of athletics was not listed as a faculty member on the physical education staff. The department head received his salary completely from the departmental budget, although he did serve as coach of the swimming team.

The physical education department was responsible for the one-year program required for all first-year men and women students. The program of intramural athletics was under the department as well. All intercollegiate sports were governed by the athletic board of control, of which the director of athletics was an ex-officio member. At this time the entire program moved into a new multiple-purpose building called Bartram Hall.

Just as the physical education office was being moved from temporary quarters to Bartram Hall, the departmental secretary gave notice. The department head, Professor Friedrich, told the rest of the staff about Miss Collins' resignation and asked them whether they knew of anyone who might be interested in the position. The Dean's Office was notified, and a call was placed to the Dean of Men. A file of positions available was kept in the latter's office, and requests were typically received there from applicants for jobs on the campus. Unfortunately, no applicant was available at the moment. In fact, it appeared that it was going to be very difficult to fill the position because of the low starting salary offered. Professor Friedrich was concerned because he wanted to keep the office functioning without interruption. Further, he wanted to locate another young woman soon so that the departing secretary could break the new person in on the intricacies of the office procedure.

Professor Friedrich gave some thought to the qualifications that a new secretary should possess. Certainly she should be intelligent and personable. Age and maturity were rather important, because the individual would be meeting students over the counter all day long. Typing and shorthand ability had to be considered, because she would be taking dictation from department members, keeping important records, and typing stencils and dittoes. Then Friedrich thought of the low starting salary again with all of the deductions that were removed automatically at the source.

At lunch one day shortly thereafter, the Alumni Secretary, Mr. Rogers, mentioned that he had heard from a friend about an attractive and personable young woman who might be interested in the position. Her name was June Borden, and she had graduated several months ago from a nearby business school. An appointment for an interview was made. Miss Borden appeared right on time, and she made an excellent impression. She was an attractive, willowy blonde, exceptionally well-dressed. Her personality traits were excellent, and she appeared anxious to get the position - even after Professor Friedrich explained about the starting salary. It seemed that she was living with her parents and could afford to work for that amount of money. She was 19 years old, had graduated from high school the previous year, and had been continuing in the business school to improve her typing and shorthand. This last bit of information prompted Professor Friedrich to forget about the idea of asking an applicant to take some shorthand and type out a letter. He thanked her for coming for the interview and promised to notify her shortly about the decision.

After talking over the appointment with the dean and the department members who had met Miss Borden, Professor Friedrich called her and informed her that her application for the position had been accepted. It was generally agreed that it was simply not possible to locate an older person for the salary offered, and also that it might be advisable to hire a younger person and train her gradually for the position.

Miss Borden made a sincere effort to master the position. The previous secretary had been moody, but Miss Borden possessed an even disposition and treated all in a friendly manner. Her predecessor had not handled telephone conversations very well. She insisted on calling out for staff members by their first names and sometimes she would say, "I don't know where Jack is right now; he never tells me." Miss Borden, on the other hand, handled telephone conversations very efficiently.

The former secretary had shown a great affinity for members of the opposite sex and would leap from her desk to the counter to greet the young men who dropped in at the office for information. Miss Borden was friendly, answered questions to the best of her ability, and returned to the work at hand. The other secretary had pounded over mistakes in her typing, but Miss Borden was very careful about erasures and took pride in neat letters.

It was this latter point, however, that caused a great deal of difficulty. Professor Friedrich and the other staff m members soon learned why Miss Borden had stayed for a few extra months at the business school. She and the English language had never become fully acquainted. This deficiency had not been apparent in her conversation, but it was obvious in her letters. One day in closing a letter to a colleague, Professor Friedrich had devoted a few closing lines to describing a farm property that he had purchased recently. Later, when he started to sign the finished letter, he was startled to learn that he "had a lovely Greek running across the back of the property." Miss Borden's inadequate vocabulary and poor knowledge of English grammar was to prove an outstanding problem, although she was always willing to type letters over. However, letters going out from the department had to be read very carefully, and they could never be sent out over the secretary's signature. Presumably, it should be possible to hand a routine letter to a competent secretary and say, "Please answer this letter to Mr. Hensley and tell him that I can't attend the meeting on that day."

Another annoying problem developed. Miss Borden was very careful about filing letters and their replies - in the wrong folder. Professor Friedrich had hoped that Miss Borden would be able to help him with his own professional file. In a short time, he took a day off to straighten out his own filing system and relieved Miss Borden from this extra duty.

A further problem arose in connection with the collection of small fees from students. One such item was the matter of collecting three dollars each year from major students to help defray the expense of the variety of dittoed material which was given to them. Miss Borden left her desk drawers unlocked occasionally, and one morning noticed that seventy-two dollars was missing.

Miss Borden was very accommodating to staff and students alike, and students soon began to take advantage. Professor Friedrich sometimes found her typing short term papers and other items for students when other work was waiting to be done. To help her avoid doing these favors, it was suggested that she refer such requests to the department head. This problem had been relatively simple, but a similar problem was somewhat more difficult. One of the professors outlined his class lectures in great detail and continually asked Miss Borden to type out the class notes. In a way this was department business; in another way it wasn't. Professor Friedrich who by nature of his administrative post made great demands on her time, was a bit fearful about discouraging this practice of the other professor, because he didn't wish to hurt his colleague's feelings. It did not seem to be part of the job of a departmental secretary, however, so he mentioned a number of times over a period of two years what a great help a knowledge if typing was to a teacher. The other professor agreed and said that he wished he knew how to type. However, he never found time to take a course in typing.

A bulletin board in an office can be an asset or a cluttered-up affair that people rarely look at. Professor Friedrich tried to keep it organized and suggested that Miss Borden accept this as one of her responsibilities. Quite a large board was obtained, but even this was not large enough to hold all the items. Unfortunately, there was no additional wall space available for a second board. An effort was made to categorize the areas of the board according to positions available; timetables of the various years of the major program, the required program, and certain intramural fixtures; daily notices regarding class changes, etc.; current newspaper and magazine clippings; and newly published books. From time to time, the department head made an effort to tidy it up; Miss Borden would occasionally agree that it "had become a mess again" and leave it at that.

The closing of the office during the lunch period caused a slight problem. Professor Friedrich felt that the office should be locked when Miss Borden went to lunch. Unfortunately, the door at the far end of the office, where the athletic director had his office, would be open at times and locked at others, depending on the presence of the director. Miss Borden put up a small notice on the office door at the physical education end which stated that office hours were from 9-12 a.m. and from 1-5 p.m. Thus, people would understand if the doors were locked from 12 to 1. This was satisfactory, except that Miss Borden did not always find it convenient to eat from twelve to one. The cafeteria was crowded at noon; at other times she asked if she might start her lunch hour a bit late in order to keep an appointment downtown.

190

Coffee breaks often become a problem. Here they began at 10 a.m. sharp. All of the secretaries went over to the cafeteria, roughly a quarter of a mile away. What started out to be a fifteen-minute break had a way of lengthening into half an hour or more. About three o'clock in the afternoon, this practice was repeated. As a result, the switchboard operators often found it difficult to get an answer.

Fortunately, Miss Borden felt that most of the students were quite juvenile and did not have dates with any of them. The previous secretary had found many male students interesting and would show her likes or dislikes, depending on whether a minor courtship was developing or had just been broken.

From time to time, other secretaries resigned from other departments in Bartram Hall and were replaced. Miss Borden soon realized that new women were starting at the same salary level as she, even though she had received small raises each year. Professor Friedrich asked the dean about this, because it did not seem fair. He was told that the cost of living had been rising steadily, and it was therefore necessary to pay more to obtain new employees. The fact that Miss Borden's seniority was involved to a degree did not seem to disturb him. Another disconcerting element was that Miss Brown, the secretary for intercollegiate athletics, was making at least one thousand dollars more than any other secretary in the entire building. However, she had been working there for almost ten years.

Secretaries received one week of vacation for each year of service up to a maximum of three weeks. Miss Borden preferred to split her vacation in various ways, and always asked about this well in advance. Also, she was careful to ask if this arrangement would cause any hardship. As there was no summer school in physical education, these "split" vacations did not create a problem in themselves. However, the dean felt that much of the department's correspondence was unnecessary in the summer. On several occasions he borrowed Miss Borden for other duties during the summer. These absences, combined with Miss Borden's "split" vacations, occasionally caused some hardship to Professor Friedrich.

Car parking was a perennial problem. Although adequate space was provided behind the building, the athletic director insisted on parking in front of Bartram Hall near his office. Other staff members resented this and gave the parking attendant a great deal of difficulty because he could not control the parking habits of the director. Tickets were issued, but the

rules could not be well enforced because the university property was private. Miss Borden began to park her car out front
on every occasion when the attendant might be in some other
area of the campus. It was difficult to chastise her, since
other people were also flouting the regulations.

The physical education department purchased a ditto machine, and soon the other departments in the building started
to use the machine as their own. Although they provided their
own materials, repairs were paid for by physical education.

The secretary in intercollegiate athletics often complained
that she was too busy to work for various department members
that had to do with the functioning of intercollegeiate sport.
Some felt that she wasn't that busy and just didn't wish to be
bothered. These requests then came to Miss Borden, who did
her best to keep up with them. At times her day became rather hectic, especially preceding athletic weekends in the winter
season.

A file of Alexander Bibliography Cards was kept in the
physical education office, so that major students could check
to see if certain books needed for reference were available in
the main library. Many books not available there had been
purchased by individual staff members, who lent them to students on occasion. A system was devised whereby students
could sign out for these books through Miss Borden. This
system worked fairly well, until students became lazy and
borrowed books from staff members that were in the main
library. At the end of the academic year, Professor Friedrich
noticed that eleven books were missing from his personal library.
Miss Borden had no record of them. A similar system whereby
films and other audiovisual aids were lent to high school teachers and coaches was misused occasionally when staff members
borrowed these items and did not make notations in the book
provided. When Miss Borden was not in the office, certain
staff members would lend films and forget to notify her.

In a physical education office, decorum is often a delicate matter. Students should feel that the office is a friendly
place and that they are welcome, but the office is primarily a
place of business. It was often necessary for Professor Friedrich to come out of his own office and ask students and, at
times, certain staff members to keep their conversations down
to a "dull roar." Miss Borden never complained since she enjoyed these "sessions," but naturally she did not accomplish
much work at these times.

Miss Borden was helpful with a problem that her pre-decessor had tended to aggravate. This was the matter of the students' tendency to call staff members by their first names. She made an effort to refer always to staff members by their proper titles. This problem probably arises more often in physical education than in other fields.

At the beginning of her fifth academic year, Miss Borden's parents moved to another city. She found it necessary to rent an apartment and made an arrangement with one of the unmarried women staff members. She soon realized that her salary was not sufficient to cover rent, clothes, and the mainte-nance of her small car, as well as the many other necessary expenses. She spoke to Professor Friedrich, who agreed that her salary was low. He said he would speak to the dean about an increases, although he knew that this request would proba-bly not be looked upon favorably. The dean listened to the request, which was given to him in writing at the same time. He promised to discuss it with the Advisory Committee com-posed of the President, the Vice-President, and the Comp-troller, in addition to himself. Nothing more was heard from him.

In the spring, Miss Borden was told by a friend about an opening with a large airlines company. After a short train-ing period at the company's expense in a large city, she would return to the same community where Eastern State was located. The position involved taking air reservations over the telephone. The starting salary was significantly higher than Miss Borden was making currently, with regular increments up to a maxi-mum. Miss Borden asked Professor Friedrich whether he thought she should apply. His opinion was that she should certainly look into the opportunity to see if the proposition ap-pealed to her. One drawback to the job was that she would work from 7:00 A.M. to 3:00 P.M. one week and from 3:00 P.M. until 11:00 P.M. the next. In addition, she would have to work every other weekend. After several interviews, she was offered the position. She came to Professor Friedrich again and asked for his advice as to whether she should accept.

Professor Friedrich was now in a quandary. He realized that he only had to apply a little bit of pressure, and it was quite possible that Miss Borden would stay. There were some disadvantages to the new position, but the salary was certainly more attractive. He thought of all the good points in connec-tion with Miss Borden's work - her loyalty, her willingness to undertake just about any assignment, her even disposition, her pleasant way of dealing with people over the counter, and the many other attributes that become apparent when an individual has given five years of service to an organization. On the other hand, he recalled that she still had difficulty with grammar and spelling, and that her present position was indeed a dead-end job. He reasoned that it was her decision to make - and that he, as an administrator, could not afford to lose sight of the welfare of individuals, despite the fact that her resignation would leave quite a gap for some time to come.

With these thoughts running through his mind, Professor Friedrich told Miss Borden that he didn't wish to influence her unduly and that it was truly her decision. This did not satisfy her and she pressed for some further advice, as she insisted that she really did not know what to do. Rather than offering any direct suggestion either way, Friedrich recommended that they think it over some more. He promised to tell her what he thought would be best the next morning.

Suggested Questions for Discussion

1. What qualifications should a departmental secretary possess?

2. Do you think it is absolutely necessary to give an applicant some dictation before hiring her?

3. Would it have been wiser to have made a greater effort to locate an older, more experienced person?

4. When it was learned that Miss Borden had difficulty with spelling and grammar, should she have been asked to find another position?

5. What should have been done when it was discovered that a petty thief had stolen seventy-two dollars from Miss Borden's unlocked desk?

6. Should Professor Friedrich have made it clear to the other professor that the typing of his class notes was not the sort of work that Miss Borden should be doing?

7. Who should have been responsible for the maintenance of the bulletin board?

8. What arrangement should have been made for the lunch period when the office was left unstaffed?

9. What policy should be set about coffee breaks?

10. Should employees be allowed to have dates with students?

11. What do you think of a situation in which new employees receive the same salaries as older staff members?

12. Should employees be allowed to take their vacations one week at a time?

13. Should Professor Friedrich have insisted that Miss Borden comply with parking regulations?

14. What should have been done about the other secretary who refused, in a sense, to do work that was rightfully hers?

15. Should a formal system be devised whereby books and films are made available for loan?

16. How do you keep a physical education office from becoming a place for between-class social gatherings?

17. Should students ever call staff members by their first names?

18. Should Professor Friedrich have forced the issue with the dean about a raise for Miss Borden?

19. Should Professor Friedrich have refused to give Miss Borden any advice about her acceptance of the new position?

20. If he advised her, what should he have recommended?

"A Nice Swimming Pool, but . . ."
(As reported by Dr. Friedrich)

About eight months after the new physical education
building opened, Mr. Lawton, an assistant professor and the
assistant swimming coach, complained to Dr. Friedrich, the
partment head and head swimming coach, about a number of
problems he was encountering as aquatics supervisor. Dr.
Friedrich knew from first-hand experience that Lawton was not
exaggerating, so he agreed to speak right away about the matter to Mr. J. C. Jonas, the director of intercollegiate athletics,
who was the chairman of the Athletics Facilities Committee that
had been established. Subsequently, he wrote the following
letter to Mr. Jonas:

August 10, 19--

Mr. J. C. Jones
Chairman, Athletic Facilities Committee
Physical Education Building

Dear John:

According to our conversation, I would like to
raise again some problems concerning the Layton
Memorial Pool which have been troubling us. Our
failure to solve many of these problems reflects upon
the University in the eyes of the public and visiting
swimming teams. Our only concern is, of course,
that the pool be operated as efficiently and econom-
ically as possible.

Those items requiring further discussion are
listed below:

1. Water Level (Gutters):

Despite what we are told the State Department
of Health has to say about the closing of drains in
so-called "scum gutters," I would like to reiterate
that this area is no longer conceived as an expectoration receptacle. If the Department of Health does
not recognize this fact, at least we should make an
effort to educate them in this regard. Nowadays
there is no need for any water to be wasted in a

swimming pool <u>except</u> when the filters are backwashed. The water running over the top of our roll-away gutters can be safely re-circulated through the filtration system. Thus, in addition to the saving possible if the gutter drains were adapted this way, we would have the added advantage of a more functional pool from the standpoint of rough water. Now it is impossible to effectively trap the waves created by swimmers' wash unless the water is kept at a constant lip level. A low water level caused by the pool water going down the drain makes it more difficult for both instructional classes and the training of the competitive teams (men and women).

2. <u>Pool and Shower Room Signs</u>:

Certain signs seem necessary on some of the walls in the shower room, drying room, and pool. It is suggested that these signs be painted with block letters at logical points.

a. Either above or at the side of the receptacle for expectoration, it should state clearly, "Use This [with an arrow] for Expectoration."

b. One sign in large letters stating "Never Swim Alone" or "Swimming Alone Absolutely Forbidden" should be placed in a very conspicuous spot where all can see it.

c. In both the men's and women's drying rooms and showers, on the way to the pool, people should be confronted with a sign reading something like this: "Always Take a <u>Complete</u> Soap Shower Before Using the Pool." <u>Typically</u>, women are the worst offenders in this regard, but many men take a shower with their bathing suits on prior to entering the pool areas.

d. In the entry leading to the drying rooms and showers on both sides, another sign should read something like the following: "Persons Wearing Shoes Not Allowed on the Pool Deck." This rule is being broken every day by people who should know better. A large "unavoidable" foot bath on each side (men's and women's entrances) completely blocking entry would stop this practice.

3. Use of Swimming Suits:

At the moment any individual can wear any swim suit, whether clean or cut, into the pool without being challenged. Steps should be taken to correct this practice. Lint and other impurities from these suits may well become a sizeable and costly proposition in a very short time.

4. Soap Dispensers:

Inasmuch as cleanliness is so important in keeping down the bacteria count in the pool water, it is being suggested that soap dispensers be installed in the two shower room units. A type of lath-urn soap can be purchased relatively inexpensively for use and replacement. Bar soap is becoming increasingly expensive, and soon may have to be discontinued as a service. If such were to occur, the percentage of people taking full soap showers would decrease sharply.

5. Safety Precaution:

People are still slipping and falling on the very slippery floor in the locker room--on the stretch of floor immediately after people leave the drying room areas. In my opinion the University migh be held legally liable if someone were to hit his/her head on the terrazzo floor and suffer a concussion. The area is too great to cover it with a rubber mat. The condition of the floor could be improved somewhat from this standpoint by treating it regularly with a hydrochloric acid wash, or by applying paint mixed with carborundum to the area.

6. Safety Equipment:

The ring buoy hanging on the wall in the pool currently is about twice as large as necessary. If a drowning person were ever hit on the head with it, he/she would most certainly be stunned. Two smaller ones (with 25 ft. attached ropes) should be hung on the wall on each side of the pool about at the midpoint of the pool's length. A shepherd's crook could be placed on the wall behind the diving boards with appropriate wall brackets.

7. Bulletin Boards:

Two bulletin boards should be installed at each end of the pool at the point where swimmers enter the pool area.

8. Lighting Equipment:

It is recommended that lighting in the pool be controlled by three master switches--one switch for pool overhead lights, one for seating area lights, and one for the underwater lights. This recommendation is made for greater safety, and it would be much more practical for use during practices, classes, swim meets, and water pageants. To turn on the lights at present requires the flicking of approximately thirty switches!

9. Additional Lines:

As soon as possible, vertical lines (one foot wide) should be painted on both end walls in alignment with existent bottom lines. These lines should extend from the top lip of the pool downward at least four feet. At the moment when the pool is flush with the deck (the proper level), swimmers are experiencing difficulty in making turns during competition.

(Before the surfaces of a concrete pool are painted, the walls should be prepared by sanding or other method to remove all loose particles and elements to which any paint applied may not adhere. Sulphuric or muriatic acid should then be applied, after which it should be washed away with clear water in quantity, and the surface permitted to become completely dry.)

10. Other Items Needing Attention:

There are a number of other items needing attention when possible as follows: (1) a first aid kit should be readily available; (2) the fulcrum on the one meter board is not functioning properly; (3) the three meter board is hazardous because the platform that holds it sways excessively under use; (4) some electrical outlets at convenient points around the pool would be most helpful; (5) there are numerous rust stains at various points around the pool; (6) the ropes holding the plastic lane markers rot regularly and should be replaced with a more permanent line; (7) a number of ceiling and underwater lights need replacement; and (8) the pool itself needs better care from the standpoint of sanitation, clarity and temperature of water.

We would certainly appreciate your early attention to these items, many of which are urgent. Thank you for any possible assistance.

Very sincerely yours,

E. C. Friedrich, Ph.D.
Professor and Head

cc: Mr. John Longstaff, Supt.
Buildings and Grounds

Shortly after this letter was sent. Dr. Friedrich passed Mr. Jonas in the corridor of the Physical Education Building. Mr. Jonas, as part of the casual conversation, made reference to Friedrich's detailed letter, saying that he had to call a meeting with Mr. Longstaff, the superintendent of buildings and grounds, about the matter. Friedrich responded with a suggestion that perhaps the entire athletic facilities committee could meet with him as well. Jonas shifted the conversation to another topic at that point, so Friedrich was not certain whether he was agreeable to the idea of such a session. At any rate, it was still the vacation period, so Friedrich decided that he would not press Jonas about the matter for a month or so (even though attention to many of the items mentioned would have been very helpful as Eastern began its new academic year). Thus, when Mr. Lawton asked Dr. Friedrich in early September whether any progress had been made, Friedrich said, "Let's give him a week or two more to get something done."

As it happened, Mr. Jonas, who was also head football coach, became extremely busy with coaching and athletic administration duties in mid-August and early September. So whenever Dr. Friedrich mentioned the swimming pool situation to him, all he got was a response which indicated that Jonas would have to check up on the buildings and grounds people to see why not very much had happened. A few of the items --relatively minor ones--that were listed in the letter to Jonas were corrected, but they were so inconsequential that it was hardly worth mentioning. Finally, in November, Friedrich-- who periodically "received static" from Lawton on the topic-- said to Jonas one day in passing, "John, this pool situation is ridiculous. You haven't had much luck, so I think that I'm going to complain to the President. Mr. Jonas seemed concern- ed about Dr. Friedrich's intent, and promised to "get after" that s-- of - b---- right away."

However, nothing more happened, so on December 12 Friedrich sent the following letter to President Clark:

December 12, 19--

Dear Dr. Clark:

Based on our telephone conversation this morning, I am writing you about the Memorial Swim- ming Pool and some attendant problems. In asking for a solution to many of these problems, I hope that your Advisory Committee will appreciate my sincerity in asking for a high standard in connec- tion with our facilities. Unless we can come fairly close in this matter to acceptable standards. I feel that much of our work in the professional prepar- ation of teachers, coaches, and administrators is wasted. I would like to stress that I am not asking for control of the so-called athletic facilities. My only thought in this matter is to rectify a situation which has become an annoyance and frustration. Not only is there no chance for staff members and me to offer opinions in joint meetings regarding athletic facilities, but our professional opinions are also being ignored by the Building and Grounds Department. For your perusal I have enclosed a copy of a letter sent last August 10th.

Thank you for any possible assistance in this matter that has become even more urgent.

Very sincerely yours,

E. C. Friedrich
Professor and Head

Soon after this letter was received by President Clark, his secretary called and stated that Dr. Clark would make "some inquiries" about the matter. However, it was close to Christmas break at Eastern, and Friedrich did not expect any response until after the New Year. On January 11th Dr. Friedrich sent the following letter to President Clark:

January 11, 19--

Dear Dr. Clark:

On December 12 last I sent you a letter concerning the facility problem in the Physical Education Building. At the end of the first paragraph I stated that "our professional opinions are also be being ignored by the Building and Grounds Department." I wish to retract that statement and apologize for any embarrassment that it may have caused Mr. Longstaff.

Yesterday, quite accidentally, I met Mr. Longstaff in the hall of the Arts Building, and we had a long talk. Last August I went to Mr. Jonas to discuss the facilities problem. As a result of this discussion, I followed the talk up with a letter in which I outlined all the points upon which we had agreed. A copy of this letter was sent to Mr. Longstaff. Upon receiving the letter, Mr. Longstaff had in fact gone over it point-by-point with Mr. Jonas. Many of the recommendations, earlier agreed upon with me by Mr. Jonas, were negated by him at that time. I had not learned about that get-together until yesterday. Since that time I have been blaming Mr. Longstaff for carrying out certain suggestions in direct contradiction to a number of the recommendations expressed in my letter of August 10th.

I am sorry that it is necessary to write this letter, but I do wish to clear up this matter for Mr. Longstaff's sake. We followed up this chance meeting with a second session at poolside among Mr. Longstaff, his assistant Mr. Bow, Mr. Lawton and myself. We have worked out a common understanding as to how problems of this type can be reported in the future. I must state, however, that there was a fair amount of disagreement regarding

what could be done, what should be done, etc.
For example, Mr. Longstaff maintains that most of
the recommendations will have to be deferred (1) because of the money involved, (2) because the pool
would have to be emptied, and (3) because the
state authorities have to be convinced of a few
items.

In regard to the matter of the adequate functioning of our Athletic Facilities Committee, that
problem still needs to be resolved. Any assistance that you might provide in this regard will be
appreciated by all.

Very sincerely yours,

E. C. Friedrich
Professor and Head

cc: Comptroller Will Ross
Mr. John Longstaff, Supt.

As he signed this letter and dropped it into the campus
mail, Dr. Friedrich thought ruefully to himself about the ongoing problem. He asked himself the question: "Have I really
solved anything?"

Suggested Questions for Discussion

1. Why do you suppose that there seemed to be so many
   problems attendant to the opening of a new swimming pool?
   Is this an unusual number?

2. Do you agree with the issues raised both generally and
   specifically?

3. Was Dr. Friedrich wise to write such a detailed letter
   listing all of the concerns that both he and Mr. Lawton
   had?

4. Should Dr. Friedrich have acted sooner? Could he have
   handled the matter in a different way?

5. Why do you imagine Mr. Jonas handled the entire matter
   as he did?

6. Do you feel that Friedrich was justified in taking the matter directly to President Clark in December?

7. What should Friedrich do now, if anything?

EASTERN STATE UNIVERSITY (E)

"Faculty Selection"
(As reported by the department head)

At the end of his second year as department head, Professor Friedrich asked the administration of Eastern State to
allow him to add another male faculty member to the department.
Although the scope of the physical education program had been
increasing, the President's Advisory Committee informed Friedrich via Dean Reason that there was hesitation about granting
this request. Professor Friedrich discussed the situation with
Mr. Jonas, the athletic director, who would be using the new
appointee part-time as a coach in football and wrestling. Mr.
Jonas agreed to speak to the president to emphasize the need
for another man. One week later, the dean called Professor
Friedrich and told him to begin looking for a junior staff member.

Eastern State had a two-year requirement in physical
education for all students, in addition to voluntary programs
in intramural and intercollegiate athletics. A major program in
physical education had been started several years before Friedrich's arrival on the scene, and the first three (male) graduates completed their programs at the end of Friedrich's first
year on campus.

The new faculty member was to have responsibilities in
various phases of the physical education and athletic program.
The appointment was to be at the instructor level, with an
annual starting salary of $13,000. After a two-year probation-
ary period, teachers were generally promoted to the assistant
professor level if their work was satisfactory. This promotion
meant that the position was "permanent," although there was
no tenure at Eastern State in the generally accepted use of the
term.

The dean and the president were interested in a man
with a sound liberal arts and science background, as well as a
sound preparation in physical education and sport. They were
concerned also about the religious preferences of the applicant,
although they did not make an issue of this point openly.
Professor Friedrich did not fully understand their reasoning in
this last matter, except that Mr. Jonas, the athletic director,
and one other male faculty member were Catholic. The administration seemed to want to preserve a balance of Protestants
over Catholics on the staff.

Mr. Jonas, who was a keen judge of men, wished to obtain the best man possible under the circumstances. He was particularly concerned about the individual's ability to assist in varsity football and to coach another sport as well.

Dr. Friedrich agreed to a large extent with the others. He wanted to hire a man with a broad philosophy of physical education. At the same time, he was anxious to find a person who would fit harmoniously into the staff picture. There was some unrest between the athletics department and the physical education department, and Friedrich thought it important to engage someone who would not wish to overemphasize one aspect of the program.

Professor Friedrich wrote to the placement office of a long-established private college in New England, about 400 miles away from Eastern State. This institution had been one of the first to establish a professional preparation program for physical educators, and had the reputation of turning out well-qualified men in physical education and sport. Because so many professional courses were included in the four-year curriculum there, however, the liberal arts background of its graduates was typically weak. The placement office sent Friedrich the credentials of six graduating seniors. The credentials were carefully screened by Friedrich, Jonas, and other senior staff members. One man, Arthur Donaldson, seemed to be qualified. In addition, he would be available for an interview at Eastern within the next two weeks, as he was planning to visit his father in a city only 150 miles away. Since the dean was quite anxious to save on travel money, they decided to invite him for an interview at that time.

Mr. Donaldson was twenty-six years old and had served in the Air Force for two years. He was five feet eleven inches tall and weighed 190 lbs. He was Catholic and had been married after his first year in college. There were no children, and his wife was anxious to seek employment as a nurse wherever her husband worked. His major subject at college was physical education, and his minor, recreation. During college he had participated in a variety of so-called extracurricular activities, including football, basketball, wrestling, and tennis. During the summers he had been active at various camps as a waterfront director. His grades were above average, and he was anxious to start graduate work in the summers. Many references were included in his brochure, and they all added up to one conclusion - Arthur Donaldson had made an excellent record as a student and as an athlete in his college.

Mr. and Mrs. Donaldson came to Eastern State for the interview. They spent the afternoon looking around the campus and meeting members of the departmental staff and the university administration. All seemed favorably impressed with the couple. Art was a rugged, personable fellow with a strong jaw and just about the right amount of aggressiveness. He had had strong opinions about a number of the current problems in physical education, but he tried to be tactful. He was full of confidence and highly praised his college's undergraduate program in physical education. He spoke in glowing terms about his football coach, who had evidently been a real "slave-driver." The Donaldsons were an attractive, well-dressed, personable couple. The dean commented especially about Mrs. Donaldson's appearance and personality. The president didn't have much to say one way or the other.

The Donaldsons had dinner at the home of Professor and Mrs. Friedrich, and about 9:00 P.M. made a pre-arranged visit to the home of Mr. and Mrs. Jonas. Upon their return, they appeared impressed with the new home that Jonas had just built. The mentioned the names of several influential people in town that the Jonas's had said they could introduce them to if they came to town. Mrs. Friedrich mentioned to her husband later that this couple would find it difficult to live on an instructor's salary. In the morning, the Donaldsons took their leave after thanking all profusely for their kindness. A few days later, Professor Friedrich received the following letter from Mr. Donaldson:

Box 6, Springford College
Springford, CT

Dr. Edward Friedrich
Professor of Physical Education
Eastern State Univerity
Roxboro, Michigan

Dear Ed:

Thank you for your kindness during our visit of March 24th and 25th. I greatly appreciate the time and consideration you gave us.

We were deeply impressed by the University and all the fine people that we met. The physical education position that we discussed is definitely interesting to me, and I hope that I shall have the

good fortune to become a member of such a con-
genial staff.

Please give your wife our very best wishes.

Sincerely,

Arthur Donaldson

Jonas mentioned to Friedrich that he also received a letter.

The second candidate asked to come to Eastern State for
an interview was George Nelson. Friedrich had heard about
George from Professor Fears of the Eastern physical education
staff. Fears had a friend completing his degree at nearby
Greer State University. When this friend heard about the
available position, he had suggested to Fears that George
Nelson might be just the man for the position. George was just
completing his master's degree at Greer State and had been
serving as assistant wrestling coach. George had majored in
physical education at a small midwestern college that was known
in the athletic world for its outstanding wrestling teams. Fears
asked the head coach of wrestling about George and received a
fine recommendation. The coach pointed out that George was
an excellent student, a fact that was substantiated by the department head at Greer State. Upon Friedrich's request, Fears
asked Mr. and Mrs. Nelson to come to Eastern for an interview.

The Nelson interview followed the same pattern as that
with the Donaldsons. They were shown the campus and the
particular facilities that would be of most interest. Friedrich
liked Nelson instinctively, probably because he was personable,
quite, and yet calmly confident. Mrs. Nelson was not so at
attractive a person as Mrs. Donaldson. Mrs. Friedrich described her aptly as more of a "home-body" type. The dean
for some reason liked the Donaldsons better. Professor Friedrich arranged for the president to meet him and Mr. Nelson
at the cafeteria for coffee. Mr. Nelson talked easily with the
president and mentioned that he knew quite a few high school
wrestlers who might be interested in coming to Eastern if they
knew that he was going to coach wrestling. When Friedrich
talked to the president later, the point arose that Mr. Nelson
ought to have some plastic surgery performed on one of his
ears that had been "cauliflowered" by wrestling competition.
The president seemed to prefer Donaldson of the two and did

not bring up his earlier point about the prospective faculty member's religion.

Later in the afternoon, Friedrich had a long talk with Nelson about the position. Nelson was relatively inexperienced with football, a point which Jonas stressed later. In addition, Nelson felt that he couldn't afford to take the position under $15,000. He mentioned that this figure was the "going price" at which men with M.A.'s were leaving Greer State. If he couldn't get this salary, he indicated that it might be better for him to proceed with his doctorate at Greer.

The Friedrichs had the prospective candidate and his wife to their home for dinner, as they had done with the Donaldsons. Mr. Jonas did not appear to be interested in having the Nelsons visit his home, as the Donaldsons had done. The evening was spent in pleasant fashion. Before the Nelsons left in the morning, Professor Friedrich told Nelson that he would hear from him shortly after the third candidate had been interviewed.

Friedrich has met the third candidate at a national convention. This man, Roger Baldwin, was four or five years older than Donaldson or Nelson. Roger appears to have an excellent background and was extremely personable. He had his doctorate with a joint major in physical education and psychology from Rockwell State University in the Far West. At present, he was director of physical education and instructor of psychology at a small midwestern college. Friedrich asked Baldwin if he would be interested in a post at Eastern, and Baldwin said that he would be in the vicinity of Eastern State within the next two weeks and would be glad to pay a visit. He also mentioned that he was interested in an assistant professorship and a salary of at least $17,000.

Two weeks later Dr. Baldwin telephoned Dr. Friedrich from a nearby city and said that he could visit Eastern the next day if convenient. Arrangements were made and Friedrich met him at the railroad station. For some reason, although he was very anxious to like Baldwin because of his excellent qualifications, Friedrich was not so impressed with him out of the convention atmosphere. Baldwin was well-dressed, but his clothes were rather ill-fitting because he was overweight. Friedrich and Baldwin made a rather hasty trip around the campus and stopped briefly to meet a number of the staff members. Baldwin impressed Jonas with his knowledge of football and indicated his willingness to coach wrestling (although he had been away from it since college).

Baldwin was very interested that Eastern had made tentative plans to start graduate work in physical education. Friedrich felt that another man with a doctorate would give increased stature to his staff. He reasoned also that this man's background in psychology would be looked upon favorably by other departments on the campus. Baldwin had held a very responsible position in a private agency before taking his present position. Friedrich felt that this administrative background would be helpful at Eastern. Friedrich took Baldwin to meet the dean and then the president. Both were favorably impressed, as was the head of the psychology department at another meeting. Friedrich mentioned that perhaps he could make arrangements for Baldwin to teach one psychology course and thereby augment his salary a bit. Friedrich talked to the president later about Roger Baldwin, and the president mentioned that he didn't see how they could afford the services of Dr. Baldwin at the rank of instructor with a salary higher than the $13,000 figure mentioned earlier. Friedrich mentioned that Baldwin did require more money and a higher rank than that told Friedrich earlier. The president did not commit himself, but agreed to discuss it with the dean.

Professor Friedrich took Baldwin home for dinner. He took him out to see the horses that he raised. Although Baldwin had expressed an interest in horses, he continued to talk about the physical education and sport field and hardly looked at the animals that Friedrich was trying to show him. When they went into the house, Baldwin excused himself for a minute and came back with a bottle of rye whiskey that he had brought for a gift. He seemed anxious to have a drink before dinner, so Friedrich mixed a drink for him and explained rather apologetically that he and Mrs. Friedrich didn't drink. He suggested that Baldwin might as well take the remainder of the whiskey with him so that it wouldn't go to waste. Baldwin said that he hoped that the Friedrichs didn't mind the fact that he liked an occasional drink. They assured him that they certainly had no objections. Later in the evening, Baldwin had several more drinks.

Friedrich and Baldwin talked enthusiastically about physical education and sport during dinner and after. Baldwin described his various undertakings at great length. Professor and Mrs. Friedrich found his analysis of living conditions in his own state quite interesting. At one point in the conversation, Baldwin mentioned that a mutual friend had told him earlier that day that he (Baldwin) would be the best thing that ever happened to the Eastern physical education staff. Friedrich and his wife laughed about this later, because they thought that the remark was a little out of place, even if true. Dr.

Baldwin thanked Friedrich for his courtesy the next morning with a cheery goodbye. He said he would be looking forward to hearing from him when a decision had been made.

As Friedrich thought about the various applicants, he didn't know whom to recommed to the administration. He talked to the dean and the president, who said that it was up to him, Mr. Jonas, and the staff members to make a recommendation. They didn't commit themselves about the salary requirements that would be necessary for the applicants with the higher degrees. They did appear to have considerable concern about the need to conserve money, and the dean made the point that the Donaldsons were "certainly a fine couple."

Mr. Jonas seemed partial to Arthur Donaldson, although he was impressed with the qualifications of Dr. Baldwin. The fact that both of them could help with the coaching of football was important to him.

Staff members were divided in their opinions. Professor Fears was partial to Nelson, because both the head wrestling coach and the department head at Greer State had recommended him so highly. Another faculty member seemed concerned about the request by Baldwin that he be granted the rank of assistant professor.

Friedrich liked tham all, but he realized that the president and the dean wanted to conserve money. After meeting Donaldson, the president had said nothing more about the subject of religion. Friedrich agreed with the dean that the Donaldsons were a fine couple, but he was impressed with Nelson's outstanding wrestling background. He thought also about the fact that Baldwin had his doctorate completed, but he wondered how Baldwin's personality would "click" with the rest of the staff. Yet, he reasoned that it wasn't fair to judge a man only on the basis of one visit. He remembered the president's comment about Nelson's cauliflower ear. He considered further that Donaldson had no teaching and coaching experience at all and only a Bachelor's degree. Friedrich was truly puzzled. Whom should he recommend for the position?

Suggested Questions for Discussion

1. What do you think of an arrangement whereby a physical education faculty member is used part-time by athletics?

2. Why do you suppose that the president and the dean were concerned about the religious preference of the applicant?

3. When hiring a new faculty member, which quality should you consider most important, if any?

4. How much difference does it make whether an applicant graduated from a "recognized" college or university?

5. Does the possession of a sound liberal arts and science background make a great deal of difference?

6. Who do you think should be responsible for screening the various sets of credentials that are received when a position is available?

7. Should an applicant ever be hired without an interview even if money for travel is limited?

8. Which candidate appealed to you most? Which recommendation concerning any of the applicants would you regard most highly?

9. How much consideration should be given to Baldwin's extra qualification in psychology?

10. If Baldwin or Nelson were to be hired, how should Friedrich go about convincing higher administration to allow more money for salary purposes?

11. Do you feel that the president, the dean, or the athletic directed exerted too much influence on Friedrich about what the final decision should be?

12. How much consideration should be given to background and job experience?

13. How should the decision be made? Whom would you select?

EASTERN STATE UNIVERSITY (F)

"Athletic Training Rules"
(As reported by Ron Miles)

During a practice session in January, Mr. Lawton, the coach of the Eastern State swimming team, called the team members together for a brief meeting. Mr. Lawton was well-liked and respected generally by the team. He had the reputation among the swimmers of being a strict conditioner with a good knowledge of coaching techniques. Prior to becoming head coach, he had worked three years as an associate coach at the university with the department head who had been asked to take over another responsibility. In the physical education department, matters were decided by majority vote if general agreement concerning a policy could not be reached.

However, Mr. Lawton, as associate coach working with the head coach (the department head), had told him often that he was not in complete agreement with such a democratic approach. He felt that the administrator of a group of individuals might have to overrule them on occasion if he knew he was right, especially since he was responsible to higher-ups for the total operation. Mr. Lawton was short and slight. He had not been a competitive swimmer, although he understood the mechanics of swimming quite well. On occasion he had a sharp tongue and was regarded as quite a "kidder" or "needler." He was very helpful to the department head and was was an exceptionally loyal staff member--even though he often disagreed violently with majority opinion in faculty meetings.

When the swimmers gathered on this particular day, Mr. Lawton told them that after the last swimming meet he had observed one of them smoking, and that this constituted a violation of the training rules laid down by him in October. Rather than name the offender, he requested that the person involved make an appointment to see him. He stated further that the offender would not swim in the next meet; and if the person did not come to see him at all, he would not swim in any more meets that season.

This action by Lawton created quite a problem for the team members, because there were actually five of them who were smoking at the time. By a process of elimination, the team members came to the conclusion that Ron Miles, the team's outstanding middle distance swimmer, was the only person whom the coach could have seen smoking. Ron had shown great promise as a swimmer before he went to Eastern State. Since

213

his arrival Ron had not attained the quality of his previous efforts. This was probably because not so much emphasis was placed on intercollegiate swimming at Eastern State, and the schedule was shorter and with mediocre teams. Ron was a quiet lad with a mind of his own, but he was very enthusiastic about swimming, his only sport. As a matter of fact, without him the team would probably lose every meet this particular year. He did not wish to miss a meet, but at the same time he did not wish to give up smoking. The next day, Ron made an appointment to see the coach.

In the meantime, Coach Lawton discussed the matter with the athletic director and also with the head of the department. Even further, presumably because he was so concerned about the problem, Lawton presented it in a general sort of a way to members of a fourth-year class he taught as part of his work load in the professional program. Although he mentioned no names, students knew about whom he was talking, and a lively class discussion took place. In private conversation with the former head coach, both he and Lawton agreed that something should be done. No definite action was suggested by the department head.

Before he went to see Mr. Lawton, Ron got together with the other smoking members of the team. With some encouragement from Ron, and because of a rather strong feeling of guilt among them, they all decided to go with Ron when he kept the appointment. When five team members appeared, Coach Lawton was greatly surprised. He talked the problem over with them for two hours and finally asked what they thought he should do. They told him that he should not allow any of them to swim in the next meet. Mr. Lawton was not convinced of the wisdom of this suggestion, because he wouldn't have much of a team left to swim against the next opponent. However, he again emphasized the bad effects of smoking on an individual's performance and on the morale of the team. Finally, he said that he would let them swim, despite the infraction of the training rule. As the team members left his office, they promised that they would stop smoking until the season was over.

At practice that night, the coach told the other members of the squad what had happened--and that he had finally decided to let the offenders swim in view of their promise to stop smoking for the remainder of the season. Then he asked the team if they knew who the one swimmer was that he had seen smoking in the cafeteria. They said that they knew. After a moment's reflection Mr. Lawton said that he would like them to vote secretly whether that one person should swim in

the next meet. He said that he was asking them to do this because he wanted everything to be democratic. The squad
voted to let Ron swim. The feeling of the majority of the team
members was that Mr. Lawton had used poor judgement. (In
defense of Coach Lawton, it should be mentioned that the former head coach had told him that he had used the voting idea
three years before, when a valuable team member had missed
many practices for no apparent reason. At that time the team
members had voted in favor of suspending the offender for one
meet.)

One week later, Ron and another team member were seen
smoking by the coach in the school's cafeteria.

Suggested Questions for Discussion

1. Should a coach lay down strict training rules for a team
   at the university level? At the high school level?

2. Should Coach Lawton have suspended the offender immediately and then told the team about his action at the
   next practice?

3. What should Lawton have done when five young men
   appeared at his office?

4. What do you think of the coach discussing the matter with
   the athletic director and with the department head? With
   the senior class in a general way (anonymously)?

5. What do you think of the idea of asking the team members
   to take a vote in a matter of this nature?

6. Do you feel that the coach used bad judgment in this
   matter?

7. What should Lawton have done when he saw Ron and the
   other team member smoking in the cafeteria for the second
   time?

"Student Managers"
(As reported by a team member and the coach)

Jay Proctor reported to body-building workouts before the regular swimming season started. At that time the coach saw that Jay would have difficulty in making the team because of his lack of previous experience, his lack of coordination, and also because of his general physical condition. A good deal of kidding took place at these sessions among the returning lettermen and some of the newcomers. Jay liked to enter into the bantering back and forth, but he seemed to get upset when some pointed remarks were directed particularly to him. One day before the land drill, he mentioned to Coach Friedrich that he really had come out only for the experience, because he probably wasn't a good enough swimmer to make the varsity. Actually, he was probably going to have difficulty making the junior varsity team, but the practice was to cut no swimmer who was willing to train hard.

When the coach realized that last year's assistant manager would not be able to assume the post of manager, there was some discussion at practice as to who should be manager. Proctor announced that he would like to take over the responsibility, as this would give him an opportunity to take the away trips--which he probably wouldn't earn otherwise. Several of the returning lettermen pointedly suggested other possible candidates. But Coach Friedrich, anxious to secure the help that a manager would provide, missed the intent of their suggestions. When no one else appeared to be interested in the job, the coach announced that Proctor would be the manager.

Even then, certain team members suggested that perhaps last year's manager would be available after Christmas vacation. For a week it had been discussed with Proctor that perhaps it would be better for him to serve as an assistant manager for a year--if indeed last year's manager could serve again. Finally, the manager from the previous year told the coach that he just could not spare the time because of his questionable academic record. Proctor hadn't been too enthusiastic about this idea anyhow, but he had been willing to accept it.

This year's swimming team was a closely knit group containing a small clique. This clique was composed of students who were fraternity brothers and former teammates; some had worked together in the summer. The general atmosphere in the locker room and various exercise areas involved much kidding of a personal nature. The kidding sometimes went to extremes among members of the clique.

Coach Friedrich prepared an outline of the manager's typical duties and discussed it at some length with Proctor. Because the manager's post involved so many duties that the presence of an assistant manager was desirable, they agreed that Proctor could not handle everything. The coach offered to do those items that Proctor, because of his experience, did not appear capable to handle.

The first few weeks of practice slipped by, and Jay did very little work. Some squad members felt that he should be keeping accurate records of membership attendance. After the Christmas vacation, the team buckled down to harder workouts. Proctor did not appear to be improving on what could be termed a poor start. Managers usually take a lot of kidding, and Jay didn't get into the spirit of the idea at all. He missed practices with rather lame excuses and, when he did appear, he usually had to leave early. Actually, there wasn't too much for him to do during the practice sessions, and he certainly didn't look for things to do. He installed the lanes when he arrived on time, and he took them out when he was still present at the end of the sessions. He asked if he might continue to swim with the inexperienced swimmers for practice. This request was granted, because it was pointless for him to stand around for a certain length of time each day. On Thursdays, when time trials were taken, he was expected to help in several ways, mainly as a recorder. Several times when he didn't know a freshman's name, he called "Hey, kid," which didn't seem to go over so well with the freshmen.

Before the first meet, which was scheduled at home, he reported to the coach, and a division of duties was discussed. Everything would have been fine, except that he was late and almost all the details had already been handled by the coach and several other swimmers. He chatted with the visiting team members, while the coach and others hurried around making last-minute preparations. Finally the coach said, "Jay, I'm doing what you agreed to do and you're doing what I generally do." Jay readily saw the point and rushed to attend to the installation of the rope lanes, a task that another swimmer had begun.

Jay did a capable job of announcing (considering it was his first effort), but immediately after the last relay he said that he wanted to get away in a hurry because someone was waiting for him. He asked the swimmers to return their own suits and robes to the locker room attendant. They let him know in no uncertain terms that this was his job, but he left anyhow, telling them that they were being unreasonable. Several of the veteran swimmers were irked over this incident.

On the first Thursday in January, time trials for the first away meet was held. Proctor was timing the races and neglected to take split times. Barry Campbell, a veteran swimmer and a member of the clique, asked him, "Proctor, you lazy crumb, why aren't you taking split times? How in Hell are people supposed to learn pacing if you don't bother getting the splits? Here, give me the watch, and I'll do it!" Proctor retorted, "Here you are, Big Noise." Proctor appeared to relish his new name for Barry. He used it and other "endearing terms" whenever he saw him. Barry was small in stature, and Jay didn't hesitate to "hand it back" to him.

On the first trip away from home, the veteran swimmers did not care to travel in the same limousine with him. Finally, the coach asked Jay to travel with the first cab, because one swimmer was late. Coach Friedrich figured it would be better to wait himself with the second vehicle. Eastern State won the meet handily, and the team started home immediately. Proctor got carsick and seemed quite ill. This was a huge joke to most of the other swimmers in that limousine. The next week Jay informed Coach Friedrich that he would not be able to make the second trip away. In addition, he missed several more practices. One of the swimmers volunteered to assume Proctor's duties for the second away trip and did a fine job. Eastern State won their third straight meet, and team spirit was high.

On Monday, evidently after some discussion with other team veterans, the team captain, Jerry Thomas, spoke to Jay and suggested that he improve his efforts. Everyone respected Jerry, including Jay, and he said that he would try to do better.

On Tuesday afternoon, Jay came to the pool in a pair of grey flannel trousers. He got rather close to the edge of the pool and was "accidentally" splashed by Barry Campbell who was swimming by. The dripping manager ran around the deck of the pool in the general direction of Barry crying, "Come out and fight like a man, you coward!" Barry simply remained in the center of the pool. laughing so hard he could barely stay afloat. Jay became enraged, tore off his clothes, and jumped in after Barry, who evaded him with ridiculous ease. Jay floundered around for a few minutes, became discouraged, and went to the dressing room for a towel. He left his trousers behind, and another swimmer hid them on top of the 3-meter diving board. When Jay returned and couldn't find them, he was so furious that he was shaking all over. He attempted to start a fight with Barry, but all were laughing so uproariously that it simply couldn't materialize. Frustrated, Jay strode from the pool area, having lost the last vestige of any dignity.

Just at this moment, Coach Friedrich was passing through the locker room on his way to the regular workout that followed an initial warm-up period of thirty minutes. He greeted Jay, but got no reply. Upon entering the pool area, the coach found the swimmers in a state of uproar that was characterized by great hilarity.

The next afternoon before practice, Proctor appeared at Coach Friedrich's office, still very disturbed about the whole affair. He was determined to quit the managerial post. The coach, who knew Jay's mother slightly (in the local community), had called her early that morning to discuss the matter. He learned from her and also from a teacher at Jay's high school that Jay had experienced difficulty in personal relations before this time. He decided to make an effort to get Proctor to continue, because he felt that this might be an opportunity to help him. The coach knew that he could get most of the team members to "lay off" Jay somewhat. Before offering a careful report of the discussion that took place--which was recorded with Jay's permission--it should be explained that the coach was most interested in non-directive counseling as recommended by Carl Rogers (an authority in this approach to counseling).

Proctor: I suppose you heard about what happened in the pool yesterday before you arrived for the regular session?

Friedrich: Yes, I was sorry that I did not arrive sooner.

P: I have to say this because you have been so nice to me, Coach.

F: You feel that you want to quit because of this incident?

P: Definitely; I don't want to continue, because some of those fellows aren't gentlemen.

F: You feel that they treated you badly?

P: They certainly did. How would you feel if they soaked your best trousers?

F: I would probably be quite upset also. You don't think you deserved such treatment?

Proctor: Well, hardly, I merely walked into the pool and started to put in the lanes when Campbell splashed me.

Friedrich: You feel that he shouldn't have done such a thing?

P: Oh, I know he doesn't like me, but he certainly didn't have to interfere with me when I was trying to do my job.

F: He doesn't like you?

P: He rides me all the time. I guess he feels that I am not doing the various "joe" jobs that he thinks a manager is supposed to do.

F: He doesn't think you're a good manager?

P: I'm sure of that and, for that matter, neither does Porter [another varsity swimmer]. Most of the other fellows are gentlemen, but these two, and I don't like to talk about them, are on me all the time.

F: These two are giving you the most trouble.

P: Yes, that's why I decided to quit, although I didn't want to let you down. I suppose I haven't been a very satisfactory manager.

F: You don't think you've done very well as a manager?

P: In some ways, yes, but in a number of other ways, no. I haven't had the time to do all the jobs that a manager was supposed to do, according to the list of duties you talked over with me.

F: You haven't had the time to carry out all the duties?

P: No, you see, it's very important that I do well with my studies, because my mother is working to help put me and my brother Bob through school.

F: You figured that you had a responsibility to your mother to do well with your studies, and that everything else is secondary.

P: That's true, although I realize that I shouldn't have accepted the job if I didn't intend to carry it out in the best possible way. I did want to continue. I think it's import to face up to these clashes of personality that arise; yet, in this case I just don't think it's worth it.

F: It isn't worth the trouble to convince the squad members that you can take such incidents in your stride and still carry on?

P: I suppose I could have belted him one--if I just could have caught him. But fighting never accomplishes anything; at least it never has for me.

F: I think you're right. 'From the way you say that, I gather that you have had some previous fights with people where it came to blows.

Proctor: Yes, someone was always beating me up in high school. I think I've outgrown that now.

Friedrich: How does your mother feel about this problem?

P: She's quite concerned, but she feels that the decision is mine to make.

F: It is your decision.

P: I want to do the right thing, but I don't want to put up with that sort of nonsense any more. Furthermore, I think the team's sympathies are with Campbell.

F: You feel that, in the main, they are siding with Campbell?

P: Not the large majority, but quite a few I guess. I imagine that most of the fellows are neutral in the matter. I suppose if he doesn't stop riding me, the others will sympathize with me a bit if I control myself and show Campbell that he can't get my goat.

F: You feel that maybe you should try to keep calm and ride it out?

P: At least then I would prove that Campbell and Porter can't chase me away that easily. Maybe I'll take another crack at the job and try to do better. Hey, I had pretty well decided to quit when I came here to see you. I better think it over some more.

F: Well, it is your decision, Jay, but why don't you prove that you can stick it out and do a better job?

P: I think I will. Thanks, Coach.

Proctor did not show up for practice the next day. Coach Friedrich did not know whether he would be back. Barry, who was quite a "card," said with a smile, "I'll really miss him. I'm sorry he quit because of a little thing like that. If he would only apologize, I'm sure we could get along."

Suggested Questions for Discussion

1. Do you think Coach Friedrich should appointed Jay Proctor to the position of manager in the first place?

2. Should a coach try to control kidding of the type that took place on this team?

3. Should a coach try to break up a clique on a squad?

4. Why do you imagine that Proctor seemed to be such a poor manager?

221

5. Do you blame Barry Campbell for beginning to ride Proctor?

6. Do you think the captain of the team should have spoken to Barry about improving his effort?

7. What is your reaction to the "wet trousers incident?"

8. Should Coach Friedrich have allowed Jay to resign from his post without attempting to convince him to continue?

9. Should Coach Friedrich say anything to Campbell and Porter about this incident?

10. Do you think Proctor will carry on with the job?

EASTERN STATE UNIVERSITY (H)

"Coach-Player Relations"
(As reported by two students)

Eastern State University, as a relatively small, semi-public university, had won the conference football championship seven out of the last ten years. This year the varsity team was again favored to repeat as league champions. Although Eastern offered grant-in-aid help to a limited number of athletes in football and certain other sports, such assistance was limited to tuition waivers and a "rumored slush-fund" that was purported to exist through the efforts of certain alumni, local businessmen, and "friends" of the University.

Eastern's first two games were with non-conference teams, the first being won by a narrow margin. The second contest was lost decisively. The third and fourth games were with regular league rivals. Although Eastern was favored in Game #3, they managed to salvage only a tie against what was supposed to be the weakest team in the league. The fourth game was against Riverside University, whose stock had risen sharply after the sudden acquisition of a good quarterback. Riverside now appeared to be the team to beat.

Eastern's coach, J. C. Jonas (known as "The Ram"), was rated very highly by his opponents and by many of the men on his team. As the captain of the team expressed it,

> He was rough and gruff on the outside, but underneath it all he was softhearted and sentimental. Coach Jonas's success is due to his ability in handling players and in bringing out the best in people, rather than to coaching ability in the technical sense of the word.

Coach Jonas seemed to be having an unusual number of player problems this season. A promising sophomore quit, and a key back, Bill Sulyak, also quit the team when the coach changed his position to make room for a promising newcomer. Jim McLeod, an end, became angry when he wasn't used in the first game and told Coach Jonas that he was "playing favorites." He even went so far as to tell him that some of his friends felt that they too were getting a "raw deal."

The team had an unusually large number of second- and third-year men; however, they were starting to work well together. There was a great deal of "kidding and riding" on the team, and the majority seemed to get on well with the coach. Of course, some knew him better than others. They all laughed at his humorous antics, but to outsiders they presented a solid front in regard to their individual opinions of the coach. There was an unwritten rule on the team--as there is on most teams--that each man was to put the team ahead of his own personal desires.

Peter Rodin, a man who was capable of "going both ways" as either a guard on offense or a "noseguard" on defense, came from a small town in the next county. He had originally been a walk-on, and hence had to prove himself before he was offered a grant-in-aid. His parents were from Central Europe originally. He was very serious-minded, a diligent but average student, and friendly. This was Peter's senior year, and he had been on the varsity team since the last few games of his second year. Along the way he had earned letters in track and wrestling also. The wrestling coach had found him hardworking and anxious to excel, but people also liked him (even though they kidded him a lot). Most people felt that Peter underestimated his potential in sport.

During the summer, Rodin had agreed to be best man at a friend's wedding that was to take place on October 15th, the day of the game with Riverside. On Monday, October 10th, he told Coach Jonas of his plans for the following Saturday. On hearing this, Jonas lost his temper and gave Rodin a rough time. The coach was worried about the personnel changes that he would have to make if Rodin didn't play in the important game with Riverside. As time went on, Jonas's anger subsided but he was still upset.

On Tuesday, Jonas talked to Rodin and told him that he was letting the rest of the team down. Rodin thought this point over and decided to call his friend to see if he could locate someone else. His friend wasn't home, so Peter talked to his friend's parents. The conversation was carried on in their native tongue, but Peter had difficulty explaining the situation to them over the telephone. To make matters worse, the long distance connection wasn't too good. In despair, Peter told them to forget his call, and that he would see them on Saturday.

On Thursday, Rodin told Coach Jonas that he had decided to go to the wedding. Jonas became angry once again and said, "If you're not on the train Friday, hand in your equipment!" On Friday, the train pulled out without Rodin.

(Up to this point the case has been reported largely by another member of the varsity team. From this point, the narrative is reported directly by Peter Rodin.)

I have been asked by Dr. E. C. Friedrich, Chairman of the Department of Physical Education at Eastern State University, to tell just how my participation in intercollegiate athletics at Eastern came to an abrupt end.

When I came to Eastern originally, I registered in the physical and health education degree program. I liked football and other sports very much, but I was most anxious to get a sound education. Right away I went out for the football team because I knew that I would enjoy this experience very much. I thought that I knew something about football but, when I got into the thick of things, I realized just how little I really did know. I could see that I had a lot to learn, if I hoped to make the varsity club the next year. I learned my basic football under the freshman coaches, and I appreciated their help a great deal.

In the fall of my second year, I tried out for the varsity team and was doing reasonably well. Toward the end of the season, two other sophomores and I got a break. One regular lineman was injured, and two other senior halfbacks had to attend a wedding on the day of the next game. All three of us did quite well, and stayed up with the first and second teams in preparation for the final game that would decide the league championship. We won that championship game on a brilliant touchdown pass in the last few seconds of play. To me, it was the thrill of a lifetime to have something like that happen to me so early in my athletic career.

In our conference, the track and field championships were held in the fall. I was the team's only entrant in the shot-put event and earned a fourth place in the championship meet. This meant that I had earned two varsity letters in my second year. However, my pleasure was lessened a bit by the fact that my studies had fallen down during the fall season. I always had in the back of my mind that my being at the university was a financial hardship for my parents, despite my grant-in-aid.

In the winter season at Eastern, basketball, wrestling, and swimming dominated the athletic picture. Not having any previous experience with any of these sports, I decided to spend more time on my studies. My grades seemed to pick up somewhat during the period from the end of football to Christmas vacation. During this period we were given fundamental instruction in wrestling in our professional physical education activity class. I really like this sport and was tempted to try out for the team. But then I decided to stay with the books.

After the Christmas vacation, I was approached by the coach of the wrestling team. He urged me to try out for a vacant weak position on the junior varsity team. I accepted this challenge, learned the sport of wrestling quite well, and enjoyed the keen competition and conditioning that it offered. I wrestled for the junior varsity team all season--and again got another break. Somehow I managed in the tryouts to earn the varsity spot to represent Eastern in the conference championship tournament, I won only one bout out of three, but our team tied Branford University, a school with almost five times our enrollment, for the title. To sum it all up, this year was a great success for me athletically, but I failed one of my subjects, and the rest of my grades weren't too high.

My junior year went quite well. I played regular noseguard on the defensive unit of the football team. I didn't go out for track and field in the fall again, because I felt that my schoolwork simply couldn't stand it. I decided to skip wrestling for the same reason, but after Christmas I couldn't stay away. I made the varsity at one of the "heavyweight spots," but separated my shoulder at the beginning of the first match in the championships. I figured that my athletic career was over, but a surgeon decided not to operate, and the shoulder healed very well. At the end of the year, I had passed all my subjects, although there was still considerable room for improvement.

In June of my third year, I was asked by my closest friend back home to be his best man at his wedding on October the 15th. He knew that I played football and asked me at the time whether the wedding would conflict with a big game. I accepted his invitation and told him that I didn't think the coach would mind. I reasoned that it wouldn't be too difficult to replace me for that one game. I expected, as all the sports writers were predicting, that Eastern would be as strong as usual. I recalled also that a couple of other players were permitted to attend a wedding of a former teammate on the day of an early game two years previously. From this, I concluded that I would have no trouble getting a leave of absence for one game so early in the season. My best friend and I ordered our tuxedos together for the big day in his life.

The first game of the season was a non-conference game. On that day, we were minus a veteran offensive guard and an end, who both acted as ushers at the wedding of a former team-teammate.

Two weeks later, we played our first conference game with Branford University. Our new offense was a flop. The tailback was blamed by the fans and the sportswriters for the loss. I didn't blame him, because I felt that the line had bogged down in its protection. You might wonder why I'm writing about this running back, but his subsequent resignation from the team led, I feel, to the turn of events in my case.

The following week our offense was changed radically. The back who was criticized quit after the backfield coach told him that Coach Jonas wanted him to shift to the wingback spot. This position was almost the same as that of a lineman. As Coach Jonas put it, "Bill Sulyak has decided to quit football, so he can spend more time on his studies." In the second conference game, we walked all over our opponent, but for some reason we couldn't score. We were lucky to get a tie. This meant that it was "do or die" on October 15th against River-side!

When should I tell the coach that I couldn't play the next Saturday? I hadn't wanted to tell him earlier, because I didn't want to bother him. I had thought of telling him before the second conference game, but had decided to tell him after the victory. And then the game had ended in a tie!

I talked the matter over with a couple of my friends on the way home, and they gave me the devil for not telling him sooner. I began thinking about it, slowly realizing that I should have told him sooner--but I still thought that he would have no trouble grooming another man to move up into my place for one game. There were a number of good men on the squad just waiting for a chance to take over my slot. Surely for one game they wouldn't miss me.

On Monday afternoon, October 10th, I went to see the coach in his dressing room at the stadium. The conversation went something like this:

"Hello Coach, I don't think I'll be able to play this weekend."

"Why? What's the matter?"

"I was asked last summer to be best man at a friend's wedding on this particular Saturday."

"J---- C----, Peter, not this weekend! This is really a big game for us."

There was a pause. I just stood there bewildered, because I didn't know what to do or say at this point. Coach Jonas sat down in his chair. Without looking at me he said,

"Who's getting married?"

"My best friend back home."

There was a deep silence in the room. He didn't yell or shout (as he often did). There seemed to be a certain degree of anger in his quiet manner. We both remained silent. Seeing an anger in his face that I hadn't seen before, I walked out of the dressing room without saying another word. I went into the players' dressing room thinking that he would get over it soon (as he usually did). I was a little disgusted with myself, and also with his reaction to the matter. Maybe it was the way I just came out and told him. I certainly didn't feel like practicing after that exchange.

I finally went out to the practice field, a little late, just as the coach was walking out, too. He gave me a disgusted look, but said nothing. Many of the players evidently knew about it by this time and began ribbing me, but, in general, they didn't think it was a serious blow to the team. The other player, who was right behind me, began filling my spot--and I substituted with him regularly. I understood the change and accepted it on the grounds that I wouldn't be playing that Saturday.

At Tuesday's practice, the coach asked me in a disgusted tone, "Still weddying?" I was running down to some other players who were doing warm-up exercises. "Yep," I replied, and kept on going.

On Wednesday morning, while I was walking down the corridor in the physical education building, the freshman line coach happened to see me and asked me to drop into his office.

"I hear some rumors that you are going to a wedding instead of the game on Saturday."

"Yes, that's right."

"I'd like to know more about it, if you don't mind. I was talking to the coach this morning, and he was very concerned about your possible absence. He didn't ask me to do anything like this, but I'd like to know why you're going and why you told him so late."

He asked me a few questions about the wedding and then asked me how close I was to the groom. He told me of the seriousness of taking off whenever one feels like it, and that this would only add to the disharmony on the club. The spirit of the team wasn't just what it should be, plus the fact that we were struggling with a new offense. He told me that the club was weak in the noseguard spot, especially for this game.

He went on to tell me that if this were his team, he wouldn't hesitate to drop me from the club for pulling such a trick. He didn't know what Coach Jonas was going to do, but the way he painted the whole picture made me feel like two cents. I told him that I didn't think it was as serious as this. He seemed to understand my predicament and told me of a similar incident which involved him a few years back. I felt terrible, so I decided to get in touch with the groom and tell him I couldn't come.

I placed a call to the place where my friend worked, but they couldn't seem to locate him. I decided then to call my hometown that night and talk to his mother. I thought of a friend who could take my place--one who was a good friend of the groom and just about my size, too!

Before practice that night, I had another talk with Coach Jonas and apologized to him because I had not let him know sooner. He mentioned again that I would be letting the team down if I went. I told him that I was going to phone home that night in an attempt to be released from my commitment and obligation.

In the dressing room before practice, I asked a couple of the other players about the situation; they both agreed that it was a ticklish matter at this point. They went on to say, however, that they saw no reason why I shouldn't attend the wedding. But after this day's conversations with both coaches, my mind was made up. At practice, the coached used me in regular play as if nothing had happened.

I wondered if all of the people at home would understand my situation. After our nightly chalk-talk, I used the coaches' telephone to place the call. I got my friend's mother on the phone and told her that I probably would not be able to make the wedding on Saturday, but that I would get our mutual friend to take my place. I then called my friend, but he wasn't home. I was even more "twisted up." I told the coach on the way out that I hadn't yet achieved my purpose, but that I would call again in the morning.

I couldn't sleep that night because I had made such a mess of things. No matter what decision I made now, I would be letting down either good friends or my teammates and coaches. In the morning, I talked to a few close friends who were divided in their opinions. I placed the call to the intended substitute for me, but he said that he couldn't make it. I then telephoned the groom at his place of employment and explained the whole situation to him. I just didn't know what to say. . . .

Suggested Questions for Discussion

1. What do you think of the team captain's appraisal of Coach Jonas?

2. What is your general impression of Peter Rodin?

3. The details of the events of Peter's "fateful week" seem to differ in the two accounts. Whose story do you believe?

4. Should Peter have declined the invitation to be best man at the time when his good friend asked him in June?

5. What do you think of Coach Jonas's handling of the affair?

6. Was it proper for any of the assistant coaches to have tried to influence Peter?

7. Why do you imagine Peter didn't tell Coach Jonas about his friend's wedding sooner?

8. Do you think Peter should have made a stronger effort (any effort) to locate a substitute?

9. Should Peter's decision be affected one way or the other depending upon whether he lost his grant-in-aid? (Of course, the coaches of wrestling and track and field might be able to help him with such assistance.)

EASTERN STATE UNIVERITY (I)

"Program Planning in Undergraduate
Professional Preparation"
(As reported by a recent graduate)

The undergraduate program in professional preparation
for physical and health education at Eastern State University
began several years after the end of World War II. There
were three male graduates in the first class, all of whom went
on eventually and earned Ph.D. degrees. The second graduating class included two men only, both of whom went on to
highly successful careers at the secondary school level. The
first chairman of the physical education department was asked
to resign just as the first class was graduating. He was succeeded by Dr. Friedrich, who left for another position six
years later. During that period the number of men and women
enrolled in the undergraduate program increased steadily, but
not especially rapidly. Friedrich had been anxious to start a
master's program summers, but that plan was not approved by
higher administration. Despite the fact that the staff was
overworked with both teaching and coaching responsibilities,
it was generally thought that the undergraduate majors in physical and health education received a fine overall university experience. The graduates had no difficulty whatsoever in lo-
cating positions in the field, because they had a solid arts and
science background followed by a strong major program in
physical and health education. Additionally, their laboratory
experiences in physical education were such that graduates felt
competent to coach and teach a variety of sport skills. Interestingly enough, during this period the entire program was so
arranged that the students had only one opportunity to elect
a course--and the schedule was so arranged that this course
had to be Geography 20 (a recommendation from the state department of education).

Approximately fifteen years after the program began,
there was an agreement throughout the state between the universities and the state department of education that brought
about a significant change in many professional preparation
programs that prepared physical education teachers and coaches. Henceforth, the "professional preparation" or "professional education" aspect of the undergraduate program in the various universities was completely the prerogative of physical
education teachers (professors) engaged by departments and/
or schools of education given the authority to certify teachers
in the various subject-matters taught in the secondary schools.

In effect, this meant that the subject-matter unit in the university (e.g., English, history, physical education, etc.) was solely responsible for teaching the discipline itself. Teachers of subjects would be prepared by the departments and/or schools of education. Obviously, this brought about a considerable change (albeit a gradual one) in Eastern's undergraduate physical and health education major program.

When Dr. Friedrich had left Eastern, he had been replaced by Mr. Archambault. Mr. Archambault had been engaged at Eastern just as Dr. Friedrich was assuming the departmental chairmanship. Archambault had been highly recommended to Eastern by the state director of physical and health education. His record as both a sound physical education teacher and coach over a period of years provided significant strength to Eastern's program during its formative years. Mr. Lawrence, another fine staff member who had been instrumental in interesting Dr. Friedrich to come to Eastern originally, was a successful basketball and football instructor and assistant coach. He also taught a number of physical education and sport theory and practice classes.

One day late in the fall (of approximately the fifteenth year in which the undergraduate program had been developing) Mr. Lawrence approached Professor Archambault about a complaint that his fourth-year physical education majors had brought to his attention in class recently. Bob Nowell, the class president, had been the spokesman for the group. He criticized the program of professional preparation for physical and health education at Eastern very sharply. First of all, he pointed out that they were being offered only seven courses directly related to the physical education field as follows: history of physical education, health education, anatomy, kinesiology, organization and administration, tests and measurement, and one annual activities or laboratory course in sport and physical activity skills. On the other hand, they were required to take four humanities options (one each year), three English courses, two biology courses, and two psychology courses as well. Thus, Bob--and he stressed that most of his classmates felt just about the same way--felt that he was ending up with a liberal arts and science degree and inadequate professional preparation in the physical and health education field.

Still further, Bob Nowell went on to explain that the basic problem was compounded and made much more acute by the fact that the physical and health education courses they did receive were poorly taught and typically superficial. For example, the history of physical education course was taught by copying the teacher's lecture notes from the blackboard, regurgitating these facts or opinions on the final exam, and then forgetting everything that a person had memorized. The administration course dealt with principles and ideas unrelated to the practical administrative situation in the field. Anatomy classes were cancelled indiscriminately by the medical doctor who gave the course at the medical school. When it was in session, the class usually consisted of a quick view of the cadaver and then--since the teacher was an avid fan--a thorough analysis of the last varsity football game. The health education course was one in which the instructor presented assorted health facts, theories, and opinions, but ignored the basic methods of presenting these and the really controversial issues to a class at the high school level. In other words, the order of the day at Eastern was a series of courses characterized by a stereotyped presentation of theoretical, easily forgettable, impractical knowledge.

The one, well-taught, practical course offered each year was the activities or sports skills experience. However, it consisted of six to eight different sports (for the men) as follows: football, basketball, track and field, swimming, volleyball, tennis, wrestling, soccer, hockey, group games, and dancing. The first three activities were emphasized for the boys, even though some of these sports were overlapping seasonal sports--like basketball and swimming, or soccer and football. Moreover, some of the students were not interested in teaching or coaching certain of the sports and/or activities presented, and hence felt that heavier concentration should be given in their preferred activities and sports.

Last in the list of complaints presented by Bob Newell was the matter of fourth-year students about to graduate being required to undertake a piece of independent research as part of the required tests and measurements course. Most of the men felt too inexperienced and too pressed for time to do well in such a requirement. Further, students viewed this as an unnecessary, valueless project, because only three members of the entire senior class were even thinking about doing graduate work in the field. All of the others were firmly committed to the idea of teaching and coaching at the secondary level.

Professor Archambault, the chairman, listened to these criticisms, and then decided to call a general staff meeting in order to have these claims presented to the entire faculty. Mr.

Lawrence was very concerned and somewhat upset when his history of physical education course was criticized so sharply. He defended himself by saying that he was too busy with coaching and other duties to always present new facts to his class, or to spend time worrying about the effectiveness of his teaching techniques. The argument was presented that there were indeed certain principles of administration that should be stressed because of their applicability to all situations. The point was made that the medical doctor who taught anatomy was very busy, and actually received no compensation for teaching in the department. Insofar as the health education was concerned, the students had to understand that teaching methods were no longer to be handled by the Department of Physical and Health Education. Next the matter of the activities course was considered, and here it was a question of "personpower," so to speak. In other words, the courses or activities were selected on the basis of what was presumably needed in the schools, the facilities that were available at Eastern, and the teachers whose schedules could be freed from other responsibilities at a particular time. Finally, the tests and measurements instructor argued that a research experience was needed by all, and could be useful to all students no matter what level of education they entered as teachers subsequently. In conclusion, Professor Archambault stressed that (1) the liberal arts and science background would be appreciated somewhat later by the students when they were actually out in the field teaching; (2) more staff was needed to improve the offerings; and (3) graduates who returned for a visit typically praised the background of preparation they had received at Eastern. On that note the meeting ended, but members of the group in attendance were not smiling or joking as they left the room.

Bob Nowell felt that "something" had been accomplished by the very fact that such a session had been held. Professor Archambault had thanked him for coming to present the list of suggestions and recommendations. Nowell wondered if there was anything else he could or should do. He wondered also whether people would be critical of him--and how this might affect his grades or future.

Suggested Questions for Discussion

1. Do you think that the undergraduates in the physical education program were typically receiving "a fine overall university experience?"

2. What are your thoughts about the inclusion of "a solid arts and science background?"

3. Does the absence of elective course possibilities disturb you in any way?

4. What do you think about a situation where so-called general professional education courses are taken <u>after</u> the completion of a physical education major program?

5. Do you think that Mr. Lawrence was wise in bringing the entire matter to the attention of Professor Archambault?

6. Did the list of criticisms make an impression on you (i.e., do you feel that the complaints were valid, and how general do you think the feeling of discontent was?)?

7. What do you think brought the matter to a head in this way?

8. Were the specific responses adequate in your opinion?

9. What did you think of Professor Archambault's summation?

10. Is there anything else that Bob can or should do?

11. Do you think he was wise to get involved as he did?

EASTERN STATE UNIVERSITY (J)

"Emerging from Sport Club Status"
(As reported by a recent graduate)

Intramural athletics at Eastern State University had been operating in a seemingly hit-or-miss fashion for many years. Even so, certain men's sports were very popular, and a relatively few women's sports were carried out regularly with considerable enthusiasm by a number of women students. The gradual increase in student enrollment, along with the beginning of the undergraduate program in professional preparation in physical and health education, were factors that helped to increase the scope of the intramural program.

Responsibility for the administration of the intramural athletics program at Eastern changed hands a number of times over the years. Mr. Jonas had first assigned it to Mr. Lawrence who had many other responsibilities including a role as assistant coach for both football and basketball. Mr. Lawrence used to joke by saying (after he no longer had the responsiblity), "Why even I used to handle intramural athletics out of my back pocket." By that he meant that he would reach into his back pocket for his notebook (while coaching football) to tell some inquiring student that his intramural football game was being played on such-and-such a field.

Shortly after Dr. Friedrich had become department chairman, the intramural athletics program became the responsibility of the department of physical and health education. Mr. Lawton was engaged as a faculty member with the understanding that this program would be one of his major responsibilities, an assignment that he carried out with a great deal of enthusiasm and promotional effort. Approximately five years later, when Mr. Lawton was hired as department head at a distant state university, the intramural program was shifted back under intercollegiate athletics, and Swede Nilsson was invited to return to Eastern again from a post he had been occupying at the local YMCA.

Both intercollegiate and intramural athletics at Eastern State were actually controlled at this time by an athletic directorate composed of faculty membrs and student representative. Even Dr. Clark, the president of Eastern was an ex-officio member, and he showed great interest by coming whenever possible and speaking on crucial issues prior to any balloting. Mr. Jonas, the director of athletics and head football coach, was responsible to the athletic directorate. Mr. Nilsson, as intramural athletics director, worked directly under Jonas, as did Mrs. Lorainis, the women's athletic director. Mrs. Lorainis had assumed this post about two years before the appointment of Mr. Nilsson (when Taylor Washburn had resigned to return to her native city to be near her aging parents).

All students at Eastern were technically members of Eastern's athletic directorate. Every student paid an athletics fee that was used to support both intercollegiate and intramural athletics. Of course, gate receipts were used to help defray these expenses as well. Once a year, on the occasion of the athletic awards banquet, a very brief meeting of the student population was called to elect a slate of approximately four student representatives to serve on the directorate. Theoretically, this gave the students a voice in policy-making for competitive athletics at Eastern, but in actuality gestures such as this were almost farcical.

About three years after Mr. Nilsson took charge of intramural athletics, a group of students decided to see if rugby could be added to the roster of intercollegiate sports at Eastern. They had formed a club, and then had run a four-team league on campus successfully for a period of three years. There was evidently some regulation in the by-laws of the directorate that spoke to the necessity of a three-year trial period before such recognition could be sought. At any rate, the president of the rugby club presented the matter to Mr. Nilsson for consideration. He recommended that a letter of petition be written to Mr. Jonas, who would presumably carry it forward to the monthly meeting of the athletic directorate.

The executive of the rugby club drafted the following letter to Mr. Jonas:

September 15, 19--

Mr. J. C. Jonas, Director
Division of Intercollegiate Athletics
Eastern State University

Dear Sir:

A number of students on campus have operated an informal rugby league on campus for three years. Our initial membership of eleven has grown to between fifty and sixty students. We are convinced that many more students would join our league if they could be provided with a minimum amount of equipment.

We are grateful for the use of the upper field twice a week, but now we have reached a stage where we wish to further our request. As you undoubtedly know, similar groups have been formed in five other universities in the state--all on an informal basis such as ours. At a recent meeting of representatives from each of the groups, it was decided that we should make an effort on our home campuses to form an intercollegiate league.

We are therefore seeking your support in helping us gain such status. We understand that such a matter must be considered by the Athletic Directorate and that, if approved, a limited budget would be needed to get us started. Any assistance that you are able to provide us at both the local level and league level would be sincerely appreciated. Please consider this as a request for your support for this venture. Within a few weeks we will ask you for your comments, and we stand ready to provide any other necessary information.

Very sincerely yours,

Colin Rogers, President
E.S.U. Rugby Association

On October 1st, Rogers went to see Mr. Jonas at his office. After waiting thirty minutes for Mr. Jonas to return from his coffee break, the administrative officer pointed to Jonas' door and said, "He'll see you now." Rogers identified himself and reminded Jonas about the letter he had sent on the 15th of September. Jonas responded offhandedly and brusquely, "Rugby is a great game, but no good at the intercollegiate level because it can't support itself. I can't afford to sponsor it here at Eastern. If some of your group want some good contact, suggest that they come out for football." Rogers attempted to debate the issue with him, but then the telephone rang. At that moment the administrative officer appeared at the door with another person to see Jonas. Rogers left quietly.

Somewhat despondent, but still realizing that he was going to have to report back to his group, Rogers decided to seek assistance from Professor Archambault, the chairman of the Department of Physical Education. (It should be pointed our that Archambault had been an assistant football coach formerly; was present gymnastics coach; and by virtue of his chairmanship was automatically an ex-officio member of the directorate.) Professor Archambault listened to Rogers' presentation; sympathized with the group's plan; and pointed out that interest and conscientious leadership seemed to be evident. Further, Archambault thought that at least an approach should be made to the directorate. He stated that it might not help, but that he would be willing to talk to Jonas about the matter.

When Archambault spoke to Jonas about the talk he had had with Rogers, Jonas was somewhat upset at the tactics that Rogers had employed. He didn't feel that such pressure should be employed. He told Archambault that rugby was too dangerous in his opinion, and also that it would be too expensive for his limited budget. Archambault then decided to argue the case with Jonas more strenuously. He challenged the practice of feeding approximately eighty people on the two football squads each night during the regular season (a period of twelve weeks altogether). Moreover, he stated that those players whose homes were right in the same city could eat their evening meal at home. He argued that even the implementation of his second point would save about two thousand dollars, and that this sum would be more than enough to sponsor the rugby team.

Jonas became angry at this turn of events. He maintained that the university didn't need any more sports, and that "his teams" must be well-fed. "After all," he stated, "they do supply a large portion of our budget through the gate receipts they bring in. How much money would rugby bring in at the gate? You can tell that Rogers that he's going to have to continue to 'bang heads' at the intramural level as long as I'm in charge around here."

Archambault reported the gist of his conversation back to Colin Rogers. Not wanting to be too discouraging, he didn't tell how strongly Jonas had responded. Rogers thanked him for his attempt to be of assistance to their plans. He said that he would talk the entire matter over with his executive once again. Professor Archambault felt discouraged and somewhat frustrated himself. He wondered whether he should take the matter over Jonas's head to the athletic directorate. He rationalized to himself that the students did indeed have a very good case for support.

Suggested Questions for Discussion

1. Who should bear the responsibility for an intramural athletics program in a university?

2. How extensive should an intramural sports program be?

3. Where should the responsibility for a so-called sports club lie--with the intramural program or with the intercollegiate program?

4. If all students pay an athletics fee, what sort of representation can they legitimately expect at the administrative level?

5. What do you think of the method employed by Rogers and his associates to gain more recognition for rugby at the intercollegiate level?

6. Should Rogers have argued more strongly with Jonas instead of going to Archambault with the problem?

7. Should Professor Archambault have injected himself into the situation?

8. Was the point that Archambault made to Jonas about evening training table for local students a valid one?

9. Was Jonas right in maintaining that those athletes who were responsible for a large portion of the gate receipts should reap the rewards of their teams' efforts?

10. What should Rogers and his colleagues do now?

11. What, if anything, should Professor Archambault do?

PART 4
SUMMARY AND CONCLUSION

CHAPTER 7

THE GOAL: A SUCCESSFUL MANAGER

By the time you read this summarizing and concluding chapter, you will probably have read and discussed most of the cases in this text. You have now been exposed to the case method of teaching human relations and administration (or management) as applied to the field of physical education and athletics. It is not possible for us to know if our hopes for this teaching method have been realized. This chapter is, therefore, an effort to summarize some of the beliefs and reactions that have come from other groups similar to yours who have used this material and these cases.

Fundamentally, the reason for this text was the belief by us that decision-making is basic to the task of the manager and that the case method of teaching human relations and administration provides an excellent approach for the program administrator in physical education and athletics. Further, it is our considered opinion that the typical administration course in our field has not given students an opportunity to face the sort of problems that will be encountered on the job.

The book started with a management overview in which we emphasized the steadily increasing complexity of modern society, and how this has necessarily has brought about a managerial revolution with its subsequent effect on physical education and athletics. We explained how today's manager is faced with the necessity of welding action and theory together so that he or she will be able to cope with the prevailing "management of decline" syndrome that will probably remain with us in the 1980's.

Then we traced very briefly the development of administrative thought with special emphasis on the late nineteenth and twentieth centuries. It appears that thought, theory, and practice in administration or management has mushroomed in a seemingly disproportionate manner in recent years, yet many have been disappointed in the inability of administrative theorists to achieve a level of generalization that would enable all managers to carry out their duties as effective social scientists. We discussed some of the approaches that have been applied to administration such as the traditional approach, the behavioral approach, the decision-making approach, and the more recent "ecological" approach that stresses the organization's "ability" to adapt to change and thereby to strengthen and develop itself.

Next we turned to our own situation in North America where organized physical education and athletics during the past one hundred years has gradually but steadily become a vast enterprise that demands wise and skillful management. Keeping in mind that a recognized profession needs an organized body of knowledge based on research, we inquired as to the lack of sound research on this topic in our own field. The above notwithstanding, we pointed out that some organizational structure should be developed--presumably within educational institutions--whereby a body of knowledge can somehow be determined and then transmitted to those who are interested in sport and physical education management as a career. Paradoxically, we pointed out, just when we are criticizing the developing profession for its lack of formal orientation and adaptation to what Toffler has identified as "The Second Wave," we are also encountering his prediction that Second Wave society will gradually but steadily be superseded by the "Third Wave" of change.

Currently Useful Generalizations

You have become aware that it is not possible to consider a particular case in a vacuum. This is why we devoted two substantive chapters to a categorization of the various administrative problem areas that may be encountered. These were not put forward as firm principles for guidance in the solution of the many problems. We simply offered this material as reasonable "currently useful generalizations" based on the experience and insight of us and many other administrators and managers who have been working in the field of physical education and athletics for decades. Prior experience with other problem situations--that which we termed "Knowledge Base Carry-Forward" as a subheading in case analyses--sharpens your discriminatory powers. We form "currently useful generalizations" continually, often modifying what we believed earlier. These serve as indispensable guides as we confront new problems in our work. Before leaving any case, we should always ask ourselves, "What have I learned that will help me in a general way in facing future situations?" Admittedly, we probably carry this out implicitly anyhow, but in this course we ask that you carry out this function explicitly at the end of each case analysis.

That some of you may still have some doubts about the wisdom of this approach is acknowledged. The hope, of course, is that this experience that has been shared with your classmates and instructor will help you to realize eventually some of the goals that you have set for yourself in the exciting realm of physical education and athletics administration.

Learning (and/or Teaching) by the Case Method

In Chapter 4 we considered the problem of learning (and/or teaching) by the case method. There we stressed that the primary objective of a course in physical education and athletics administration such as this was to offer a basic approach to decision-making in which sound human relations was practiced. It is extremely important that the student's capacity to work effectively with others be strengthened. The hope is that through this experience you have been helped to develop an attitude and a point of view toward administrative practice. If you, who have presumably had much experience with team sports and games of all types, can see that group effort means literally "team effort," perhaps you will become a more efficient manager is a society which is stressing, but still exploring, the full meaning of "democratic administration."

Although this book does not for a moment minimize the importance of factual knowledge, we do maintain that the truly important qualities for a successful administrator are: the ability to work cooperatively with others; the ability to think and act responsibly; and the ability to provide an "atmosphere" where co-workers will have an opportunity to work effectively and with true satisfaction as members of the group.

No Fixed Formulas for Specific Situations

By now we hope that you realize that the case plan of instruction is no easy way to learn, although some may still disagree. In addition, it is not an easy method for a good teacher. There are no fixed formulas to use in specific situations. The need is for the administrator to devise with his associates a step-by-step pattern to bring the various factions in a situation into some sort of harmony, so that progress can be realized. As you tackle any case problem or study, we urge you to master all the available tacts thoroughly and to discard all the irrelevant facts and opinions quickly. Keep in mind that what are termed the half-facts can cause you difficulty. Are they true, or aren't they? Or is something a fact in a certain situation? Of course, we must decide for ourselves what the exact question at issue is. Furthermore, we should learn to ask the right questions to get at the basic or main problem.

Once we have settled upon what we think is the main issue in a case, or in any administrative problem we may face, we may then break it down into sub-issues or sub-questions. Some believe that formulating and answering these sub-questions is the best way to arrive at a solution for the main or basic issue. They prefer this approach to another method where pro's and con's are listed on opposite sides of the "ledger" at the outset, although it is generally agreed that this technique can be useful with alternative solutions later in the analysis. Now that you have come to this point in the course, you may have found that there are a number of ways to approach the analysis of a case.

In most cases we have found that there are a number of alternatives that could conceivably guide our actions, but that certain courses of action seem more plausible than others. Thus, it is the seemingly <u>plausible</u> courses of action that warrant careful analysis and exploitation.

It is not necessary, nor even desirable, to memorize conclusions or available facts from a case. What we are trying to develop is the power to think and to plan in a constructive, orderly manner when confronted with a problem that must be met sooner or later. Of course, it is necessary to study a case carefully before discussing it, but it is just as important to think through the results of discussions and to understand that critical questions have been raised.

Some Have Difficulty With This Approach

The chapters describing the case method were inserted in this book deliberately, because some students almost inevitably question the value of the case method of instruction. Our stance has been that students should not be too disturbed, if they have found some difficulty with the case plan of instruction initially. It has been argued, for example, that the number of students finding difficulty had a direct relationship to the maturity and practical experience of those enrolled in the course. An excellent academic record beforehand can't but help, but other competencies are very important as well. For example, we might inquire whether the person is the sort who seems to learn from experience, or has the individual developed the ability to express himself or herself clearly both orally and on paper?

A problem may arise with those people who find it difficult to convey their real thoughts to others and to get them to
trust the sincerity, much less the wisdom, of their words.
This relates, of course, to the establishment of a system of
communication. Through the case discussions that you have
had to this point, you may feel that you have achieved a certain basis of understanding with your colleagues. Further, it
is probably true that class members know a bit more about each
other's reactions to certain problem areas in the field. Nevertheless, if you had to work together with these people on a
full-time basis in a difficult administrative situation, you would
undoubtedly agree further that additional steps could be taken
to help in the achievement of genuine understanding and respect.

Becoming a bit more theoretical in this regard, Barnard,
in his now classic Functions of the Executive offered some wise
words that we can well review today about the establishment of
a system of communications:

> The first executive function is to develop and main-
> maintain a system of communications. This involves joint-
> ly a scheme or organization and an executive personnel.
> The processes by which the latter is accomplished in-
> clude chiefly the selection of men and the offering of in-
> centives; techniques of control permitting effectiveness
> in promoting, demoting, and dismissing men; and finally,
> the securing of an informal organization in which the
> essential property is the compatibility of personnel. The
> chief functions of this informal organization are expan-
> sion of the means of communication with reduction in the
> necessity for formal decisions, the minimizing of undesir-
> able influences, and the promotion of desirable influences
> concordant with the scheme of formal responsibilities
> (Barnard, 1938, pp. 226-227).

This matter of communication, especially if the case method of instruction is pursued in some depth within a person's
total academic work load, may cause considerable difficulty to a
certain percentage of students who "can't seem to get the hang
of it." It has been our experience that many of these people
can be helped with individualized counseling. Eventually, each
student must determine for himself or herself where personal
strengths and weaknesses lie--and then use them in the best
way possible.

When students realize that they are indeed on their own,
the very large majority eventually relinquish the established

habit pattern of relying on the teacher for the answers. Ideally, you should be looking forward to the challenge of more administrative problems or cases in which you can test your mettle. In the vicarious experience provided by the case method, you have been able, as one instructor put it, "to stick your necks out and have them stepped on." In time, the "neck muscles become conditioned to the tread of many heavy feet." Fortunately, only rarely does an individual become discouraged through these vicarious experiences, where the risk of failure is at an almost absolute minimum.

Examinations and Grades

You may now be facing a final examination in this course, a matter which we discussed at some length in Chapter 6. It would seem wise to speak even more briefly about what may constitute a satisfactory examination paper in the case method. It is undoubtedly more difficult for your instructor to tell you clearly and specifically why a paper is superior, good, satisfactory, or unsatisfactory, than if he were teaching, say, algebra or chemistry. Perhaps it will help to tell how superior students approach the material at hand. Basically, they are concerned with the problem of communication and the achievement of a common basis of understanding. They take a carefully defined clinical approach, but they realize that no one can hope to learn all the facts in a given situation. They understand that a person responds not to the facts, but to the facts as he or she sees them. They believe the attitude of the administrator to be most important in determining the behavior of the various staff members. They stress the point that action taken too fast can trigger adverse reactions on the part of subordinates. They refrain from recommending "principles" of administrative action and suggest instead the adoption of basic assumptions that have to stand the test of verification in specific situations. Finally, they realize that people's behavior is governed by many different factors, and that staff members will not always be affected by presumably logical thinking-- hence, any given action on the part of manager or staff member might well be taken in the light of the assumed favor or disfavor of the group.

Poor students, on the other hand, tend to see things as either "black" or "white." Many of them accept any and all opinions of the participants in the cases as fact. Some go to the other extreme and immediately discount any statements or opinions as unverifiable; thus, these students do not strive to analyze the problems evident in the cases. When some students find that they are making little or no headway in the analysis of a case, they "reason" that the particular case at hand does not offer them enough information to gain the insight sufficient to formulate a solution.

From the standpoint of the "science of meanings," the language and logic of poor students show deficiencies. The words and phrases they use in their answers carry no real meaning. They tend to make statements like "the whole answer to this problem lies in the fact that the department head didn't establish good communications," but then they leave it at that and fail to analyze precisely what the problems were and how they could (should) be corrected. Or they may say something like "that coach needs to lie on a couch and tell his troubles to a psychiatrist." Well, maybe he does, but the case analysis is not strengthened by such a flip remark with no real rationale for the statement.

Some seem possessed with the idea that a departmental administrator has two choices: he can get efficiency by being tough, or he can keep his staff members happy but unproductive by being a "softie." Basically, these students seem to come to examinations prepared to think, feel, and act in the same old habitual ways. Students who have truly absorbed the lessons to be learned through the case plan of instruction have learned a new behavior pattern. We all appreciate that examinations bring with them a greater pressure than everyday class sessions; thus, poor students revert to their basic ways of thinking, because they have not yet mastered this new approach. They tend to concentrate on one small area of the total problem. They rarely show an understanding of the administrative process that has developed--with its accrued deficiencies--because of the various problems explained in the case. They grasp for a solution--almost any solution--that comes to them at the moment. Because they are confused, they resort to an authoritarian approach, thus losing the precious opportunity to propose a solution that might better the administrative process currently in operation.

Other poor students see that a definite problem exists; hence, it must be solved immediately. They fail to see--or to take the time to see--all the alternatives possible. "Either the coach should be dismissed, or the offenders should be put on probation." They often set themselves up as "little Gods" and proceed to arbitrate in sepulchral tones. On the other hand, some qualify their statements to such a degree that their proposed solutions are meaningless. Others develop "should" complexes. "The coach should realize that he has been too strict with the team members." "The young women should understand

248

that winning the Bradford game means everything." "The athletic director <u>should</u> be able to see that the coach is under great pressure."

Implications for Clinical Research

There is no doubt but that many graduate students in sport and physical education can find ample opportunities for research in human relations and administration through the use of the case method. Although methods of research differ a great deal in their specific application, basically this descriptive (clinical) research would follow typical research methodology along these lines. This would involve observation with the recording of observed data; generalization to theory formulation; and then testing theory postulated by the establishment of hypotheses that would be subjected to further clinical observation. Since very little experimentation of this type has been carried out in physical education and athletics, students would, of necessity, need to acquire a background in clinical research and case writing. Some students, particularly those who have had little background and seemingly no special talent for statistics, may find the case method technique of descriptive research highly interesting. Here the concern is with the analysis of qualitative factors that most often cannot be measured by statistical treatment.

An earlier effort by Bauer offers a helpful analysis for anyone who wishes to undertake such investigation involving administrative cases as follows:

> (1) detailed observation of administration in process, including events and decisions as they unfold in administrative situations; (2) careful and skillful recording of observations of numerous ongoing administrative situations; (3) penetrating analysis of the data in each recorded observation, and comparison with data from other observations; (4) abstraction of tendencies or uniformities in the process of administration; (5) generalizations of a tentative nature concerning various uniformities or tendencies; (6) testing of generalizations by continued observation, recording, and analysis (Bauer, 1955, pp. 40-42).

This approach could be applied with no special problems to the many areas of physical education and athletics in which elements of management are present. The working relationships consistently become more complex when long range aims and immediately realizable objectives seem to differ. Managerial problems are continually in evidence at all educational levels in the various aspects of sport, dance, and exercise, and no doubt similar problems arise in the other sectors of a public, semi-private, and private nature. It will continue to be true that many more people do not succeed because of their human relations as opposed to their knowledge and working ability. The evidence from business, law, and medicine prove that truly significant help can be gained from employing the case method technique of descriptive research. In a field such as ours, there is every reason to believe that similar gains can be made through its intelligent application.

The Complexity of Any Administrative Situation

Any administrative situation may be unusually complex, because a number of factors may be involved in individual behavior. Such factors as past experience, one's present situation, economic incentive, and personal attitude at the moment all have an influence on behavior. The work situation itself and any changes that are occurring add to the mix. The group code within the organization, which in turn is affected by community standards and societal values and norms, is a fundamental factor as well. Management says one thing, but management does another--this too can have an impact. In some circumstances certain factors indicated above could be the most important determinants of behavior; in others they might well be relatively insignificant. The task as you analyze a problem situation is to gain as much perspective as possible. But you must, while responding to the facts as you see and hear them, keep in mind that each person views a situation differently. Such a realization in itself should often cause administrators to hold back before initiating quick action to meet a problem.

Despite this warning about the wisdom of moving slowly and deliberately in any problem situation, we mus take a moment here to resurrect William James' well-known distinction between the "tough-minded" and the "tenderhearted." James, one of the leading figures in early United States' pragmatic philosophy, meant by this that we must be tough-minded in the way that we think and act in life. McNair picked up on this by applying it to the task of the manager who is confronted with a serious problem in his or her work. "The tough-minded have a zest for tacking hard problems. They dare to grapple with the unfamiliar and wrest useful truth from stubborn new facts. They are not dismayed by change, for they know that change at an accelerated tempo is the pattern of living. . ." (McNair, ed., 1954, p. 15).

A re-emphasis of such an approach seems essential to serve as a reminder that you as a manager cannot consistently straddle the fence in an administrative problem situation and survive. The case method approach can and should be the "hard route," for you must tell others what you have decided should be done in a particular situation. Naturally, others stand ready to challenge any statement that you make--that is, if they feel it represents a belief that they cannot accept. It is, of course, the instructor's responsibility to see that the class settles down to rigorous analysis of the facts and the issues in the various cases. This is most difficult for an instructor if he or she is still to keep uppermost the goal of the nondirective approach. It should be obvious why the instructor generally does a minimum amount of challenging at first in this type of course. It would be easy for the instructor to use the authority of his or her position to get you to accept a predetermined position.

Attitude Is Important

Similarly, the administrator's attitude toward his or her staff is most important. When things go wrong and unrest prevails, almost anything said or done will be looked upon with disfavor by skeptical eyes. Thus, any action--and undoubtedly action must occur within a reasonable period of time--taken to rectify difficulties will have to be considered carefully in light of the reactions that this "remedy" may cause. If the line of communication has not broken down completely, the manager may be able to predict with a good chance of success what effect his intended words or deeds will have. When you assume a new position as an administrator, it is especially important that you make your first moves carefully and with considerable forethought.

Most people are willing to admit that they have certain bad habits. Unfortunately, although they often know what is right, they do not do it as a matter of course. However, when you assume a managerial post, you should commit yourself in a high "batting average" as you seek to solve problems administratively. It is usually wise, for example, to seek the counsel of others on the staff before setting a policy, but many still seem to go ahead on the basis that the "boss knows best." Some other false notions are: staff members will work hard only when driven; the staff will generally respond to what the manager calls "logical thinking"; and what the administrator thinks about them is more important to people than what their colleagues think.

Don't Leave Cooperation to Chance

With every passing year, education is becoming increasingly "big business," and this applies to the "sport, exercise,
play, and dance business" in society at large as well. This
means that management in these increasingly complex enter-
prises cannot expect cooperation among staff members and between staff and management to develop by chance. Why is it
that some coaches perennially have teams where fine team spirit
is evident to all? Why is it that you can sense that a good
spirit prevails in some organizations when you have been in
building only a few minutes? Can this be achieved by telling
people that they must cooperate with others? Is this team
spirit developed by the coach or administrator because he or
she promotes an atmosphere favorable to esprit de corps?

Such an atmosphere can be developed by: delegating
responsibility and authority; by allowing subordinates to participate in policy formation (evidently the genius of Japanese
Theory Z about which we have been reading), which helps to
bring about emotional acceptance to necessary decisions; and
by keeping the lines of communication open. In this way the
administrative burden on top will be lightened, and all of the
workers will develop a feeling of belonging to management.
Granting that such an approach may often be more time-con-
suming, it nevertheless wil pay handsome dividends if handled
correctly in both worker satisfaction and organizational production.

Democracy in Action

We tend to throw around the phrase "democracy in action" too carelessly. As we examine the multitude of organizational problems bubbling up all around us, it becomes obvious that there is a great deal of disagreement as to what is
meant by the phrase "democratic manager." We hear that the
"age of leadership"--at least we we once knew it--is past in
the Western world at least. We are tending away from the idea
of a "born leader" and more toward the view of management as
a team enterprise.

Perhaps now you are ready to take another step forward
--to agree that administrators or managers are made, not born,
that they can be developed in a democratic atmosphere. Certainly there are risks to this approach, but at least everything
is not being staked on the qualifications of one individual, who,
for any number of reasons, may not hold his or her position
for long. The encouragement of this type of participation by

staff members prepares them for a succession of managers capable of carrying on efficiently their predecessors' work.

Moving from the realm of the practical to the theoretical, we believe that here is a way to come much closer to the goal of democracy for which we have been striving. This approach would assuredly seem to be in accord with so-called "Third Wave" management. Now that you have made a good start in this direction, we urge you to continue to use this approach in your work in a tough-minded way. Discuss, debate, argue your way through to decision-making that will make your physical education and athletics organization truly effective. In this way you personally will develop all those necessary attributes for successful management.

References

Barnard, C. L.: Functions of the Executive. Cambridge, Mass.: Harvard University Press, 1938.

Bauer, R. C.: Cases in College Administration. New York: Teachers College, Bureau of Publications, Columbia University, 1955.

Leenders, M. R., and Erskine, J. A.: Case Research: The Case Writing Process, second ed. London, Ontario; School of Business Administration, The University of Western Ontario, 1973.

McNair, M. P., Ed.: The Case Method at the Harvard Business School. New York: McGraw-Hill Book Co., 1954.

Ouchi, W. G.: Theory Z: How American Business Can Meet the Japanese Challenge. Reading, Mass.: Addison-Wesley Publishing Co., 1981.

APPENDIX A

Management Philosophy
for
Sport and Physical Education

(Self-Evaluation Check List)*

by

Earle F. Zeigler, Ph.D.
The University of Western Ontario
London, Canada

---

* This is a 1979 revision of a self-evaluation check list which the author began to develop approximately twenty years ago. Appreciation is expressed for advice from others offered since that embryonic version appeared.

Note: More than twenty years ago such descriptive adjectives as "strong," "weak," "fairly friendly," "friendly," "conservative," and "democractic" were used to describe the philosophies and/or management styles held by various administrators. It was argued further that there was a relationship between the administrator's implicit and explicit philosophical beliefs--his position or stance in regard to life in general, to education, to religion, and even to health, physical education, and recreation. Some twenty years later, we are still concerned about how the man or woman carries out his/her managerial function --whether it be in government, industry, education, or in sport and physical education.

Today descriptive social science of a much more sophisticated nature has recently categorized managers as "the craftsman," "the jungle fighter," "the company man," and "the gamesman"--presumably with some overlapping and gradation among these classification.

This check list represents an effort to give you some insight into your own managerial philosophy.

Instructions: Make your responses directly on this questionnaire check list. Select the descriptive phrases or paragraph which best (most probably not exactly) describes your own belief about your own management philosophy. Circle one letter from each question asked--the response which is closest to your position or stances in regard to the problem, statement, or belief being described.

1. I tend to view the field of management (administration) as the following:

    a. As an art. Many fine managers have never had a course in administration, and I don't believe any courses would help them significantly. In the field of higher education, for example, I approve of the practice where they select the chairman, dean, or even the president, from the ranks of scholars and research scientists. Such a person can learn to administer an enterprise while on the job.

    b. As a developing social science. The behavioral sciences have already turned up scientific evidence about humans and their interrelationships that has provided us with substantive, but embryonic, theory about human relations and the decision-making process. If a person is "armed" with this knowledge, and has had an internship experience, it seems to me that he/she will have a much better chance of becoming a more successful manager--all things being relatively equal. The argument here, therefore, is that administrative practice should be based on the knowledge about human behavior presently available--knowledge which is then used skillfully or artfully.

2. In regard to the manager's image of himself, and the whole question of staff relations, we find that those in charge of programs view their roles differently in respect to the administrator's relations with staff members. As I see it, the manager is,

   a. The person in charge of the organization or enterprise, and one who is somewhat akin to the captain of the ship, the leader of the band, or even the general of the army. Typically, this person seeks advice when needed, and then issues memoranda and other directives to those working below on the table of organization. All work typically in a line-and-staff relationship.

   b. The leader who is ultimately responsible for the output of the organizational system--in education, for example, a system which has as its function the conservation and transmission of the established value pattern of the past (and the present too!). This person has a deep respect for the student's personality and intelligence, for example, and he feels also that the personality of teacher is tremendously important. Personal and social relations are basic, if we want to get the best from people.

   c. An educational leader who is deeply interested and committed to the process of administration in an evolving democracy. This person is really concerned about putting democracy into action to the greatest possible extent, so the staff member will find himself drawn into policy formulation as a member of committees geared to action and decision-making. To deviate from precedent may well be necessary to help some new plan improve the organization. Flexibility and experimentation are the watchwords, because such an open approach is needed in these changing times.

3. A recent study of business executives disclosed that there appeared to be four major types of managers (administrators) functioning within the corporations of the United States. As I think about it, I feel that I would like to function as a manager in the following way:

a. As one who holds to the long standing values of the work ethic, including respect for people, concern for quality and thrift. I am interested in the process of making something work; I enjoy building. I tend to see others in terms of whether they help or hinder my effort to do a craftsmanlike job. I tend to be quiet, sincere, modest, and practical. I would like people to admire these virtues. I find some difficulty in accepting goals which I do not share, because I hold to my own beliefs strongly and (naturally) want to do my own thing in the best possible way.

b. As one whose goal is power. I tend to see my peers as accomplices or enemies. I believe that what I am working for is really important, and I don't mind being viewed as an empire-builder. If I am in a situation where I hold a good deal of the power, I will work to find my place in the organizational hierarchy. Then I will move ahead as best I can whenever the opportunity presents itself. All of life, and this includes work too, tends to be a case of "survival of the fittest," and I intend to be around for some time to come getting my share of "the good life." Some people would say that I see subordinates as "objects to be utilized," but I think that judgment is too harsh. I do my very best to take good care of the people who work for me in the accomplishment of the highest organizational goals.

c. As one whose commitment is to maintain the organization's integrity. I am interested in the human side of the organization--in the feelings of the people around me to the extent that this is possible. My sense of identity is based on being part of a powerful, protective organization. Fundamentally, I am concerned with security, and I am anxious to maintain an atmosphere of cooperation, stimulation, and mutuality among my associates. I believe in being courteous to my associates and loyal to my organization. We can be secure in our posts and still have good performance.

d. As one whose main interest is in challenge. I like competitive activity where I can prove myself to be a winner. I am not afraid to take risks, because I have confidence in myself. I am not afraid either to put pressure on associates to motivate them to achieve beyond their normal pace. I reason that life and work resemble a contest, and it takes enthusiasm and effort to come out on top. If I am enthusiastic, others will catch some of that energizing spirit and make it their own. I want to be regarded as a dynamic person, a winner. And yet I believe in being mindful of the goals of the organization that has provided me with the opportunity for leadership. Thus, I am usually able to submerge my own ego, and what is good for the organization will quite probably be good for me too.

(adapted from the work of M. Maccoby)

4. The administrator/manager usually has an important part to play in staff selection and general appointment policies. If I were making selections, I would,

a. Look for a person who will--in an educational organization, for example--will be a fine teacher with a clear, orderly mind, one who can present his subject-matter thoroughly and completely. This person should not be a troublemaker--one who is going to rock the boat too much. In other words, he should understand clearly that there is a line-and-staff relationship in any organization. However, his opinions are valued, and thus are taken into consideration when decisions are made.

b. Pay great attention to the personality of the candidate when making a selection. His background and credentials are very important, of course, but I want to be certain about his value system. It is very important that he come through to his staff associates--and to his students in an educational organization--as a person who is truly concerned about their growth and development as individuals.

c. Be most concerned that the person I hire is sensitive in the area of human relations. Of course, I want him to be highly competent and scholarly (the latter especially in an educational organization), but I also want a person with originality in his/her make-up--one who

259

will work hard and who will exhibit a certain level of adaptability to a changing world situation where such a quality will be necessary.

5. If the manager/administrator were functioning in an educational setting where his organization was responsible for a total program of sport and developmental physical activity, he would state the following:

   a. I believe that intramural sports and voluntary physical recreational activities should be stressed. This applies especially to team competition with particular stress on cooperation and promotion of friendly competition. Interscholastic and intercollegiate sport competition can be introduced when there is a need, because striving for excellent is important. However, it is important that materialistic influence be kept out of educational programs as much as possible. I believe in a concept of 'total fitness' which implies an educational design pointed toward the person's self-realization as a social being.

   b. I believe that we should allow the individual to choose his/her sport and developmental physical activities based on the knowledge of self--what knowledge and skills he/she would like to possess. We should help the young person to feel at home in the sport and physical activity program--to be "authentically eccentric" as he/she finds ways to commit self to values and people. The extreme overemphasis on winning in this culture should not be permitted to keep a person from selecting a sport according to the values that a person wishes to derive from it. Thus, I believe that the field of sport and developmental physical activity should strive to fulfill a role in the general education pattern of arts and sciences with a goal of "total fitness."

   c. I believe that sport and developmental physical activity must yield precedence to intellectual education. However, I do approve of competitive athletics since they do help with the learning of sportsmanship and desirable social conduct if properly conducted. Still further, I believe in a daily period of physical training for all students to develop and preserve a minimum level of physical fitness. Such daily exercise could be called part of the curriculum, I suppose, but competitive sport, both intramural and extramural, are extracurricular--as is all other physical recreation.

260

d. I believe that intramural sports and physical education classes are more important to the large majority of students than interscholastic or intercollegiate sports and deserve priority if conflict arises over budgetary allotment, staff availability, and use of facilities. This is not to say, however, that I am not giving full support to team experiences in competitive sports. This can be a vital educational experience if properly conducted. Students should have the opportunity to select a wide variety of useful, developmental physical activities, many of which should help to develop "social intelligence" and also bring natural impulses into play. Thus, I am interested in promoting the concept of 'total fitness,' rather than that of 'physical fitness' alone.

e. I support competitive sport and developmental physical activity fully, although such activity does occupy a lower rung on the educational ladder, so to speak. In competitive sport, I believe that the transfer of training theory is in operation with the development of desirable personality traits, but sports participation should always be a means not an end. Thus, I am not only interested in education through the medium of sport and developmental physical activity; I believe also in the need for development of the body in such pursuits.

6. Insofar as my personal philosophy of life is concerned, I subscribe generally to:

a. A philosophy that "the world exists in itself, apart from our desires and knowledge." There is only one reality; that which we perceive is it. "The universe is made up of real substantial entities, existing in themselves and ordered to one another by extramental relations . . ." Man lives within this world of cause and effect, and he simply cannot make things happen independent of it.

b. A philosophy stating that "the order of the world is due to the manifestation in space and time of an eternal and spiritual reality." Mind as experienced by all people is basic and real; in fact, the entire universe is mind essentially. Man is more than just a body; he possesses a soul, and such possession makes men and women of a higher order than all other creatures on earth.

261

c. A philosophy emphasizing that existence precedes essence, and that people therefore decide their own fate. The world of material objects is somehow not the world we live in as human beings. From the context of this human world, all the abstractions of science derive their meaning ultimately. The basic human task is for the man or woman to become an authentic individual.

d. A philosophy embodying the "principle" or theory that nature is an emergent evolution, and that the human's frame of reality is limited to nature as it functions. Thus the "structure of cultural reality" should be our foremost concern. The world in which we live is characterized by activity and change, and this means that we must create the values by which we live.

e. A position that finds speculation about the nature of reality quite futile. Some holding this position would argue that the human should be studied as a symbol-using animal. Then they would proceed to ask what "the universal traits of this symbol-using species" are. Our problem is, therefore, to learn how to improve our use of language--how to analyze the structure of our statements and to apply what might be called linguistic therapy to both our scientific hypotheses and our everyday language.

7. If we were discussing the educational philosophy of the manager/administrator, it would include a statement such as:

a. "The general aim of education is more education." "Education in the broadest sense can be nothing else than the changes made in human beings by their experience." Social efficiency can well be considered the general aim of education. Some holding this position generally go so far as to say that the supreme value in education is social-self-realization, and they are desirous of extending the concept of 'group-centered education' to make it mean such development as part of a world culture.

b. The primary task of education is to transmit knowledge, without which civilization cannot continue to flourish. Whatever humans have discovered to be true because it conforms to reality must be handed down to future generations as the social or cultural tradition. Some holding this position believe that the good life

262

emanates from cooperation with God's grace, and that development of the Christian virtues is obviously of greater worth than learning or anything else.

c. Through education the developing organisms becomes what it latently is. There is a "moral imperative" on education. Education should aid the child to adjust to the basic realities (the spiritual ideas of truth, beauty, and goodness) that the history of the race has furnished us. As man's mind strives to realize itself, there is a possibility of realization of the Absolute within the individual mind.

d. It is probably rather pointless to state that one holds such-and-such an educational philosophy. Man is a symbol-using creature, and it is probably quite ridiculous to think of education as the means whereby young people are prepared for the job market. Educational concepts must be clarified if education is to become truly effective. Both ordinary language and professional education terminology are so confused and confusing that actual "language therapy" is needed to "make education healthy" again.

e. "Even if there is general agreement that a set of fundamental dispositions is to be formed, should the criterion used for the evaluation of the worth of individual dispositions be 'public rather than a personal and private criterion?'" Education should somehow "awaken awareness" in the learner. Students should "constantly, freely, baselessly, and creatively" choose their individual pattern of education.

8. As a manager/administrator, I believe that:

a. There are valid principles of administration that should almost never be violated. Practical rules and procedures can be developed from such principles, and they can be relied upon to provide most of the answers to administrative problems.

b. It is now evident that the idea of practical rules and valid principles create many pitfalls for the manager/administrator. The idea of being able to solve administrative problems in a fairly automatic fashion is ridiculous. The evidence is being gathered from ongoing social science about human behavior. Today's manager/administrator must be armed with a sound knowledge of theory and practice. As Gross has stated so succinctly, what is needed is an "action-theory marriage."

9. After a new staff member is hired, the question often arises about some sort of instructional supervision. In fact, in many institutions such evaluation by "superiors," peers, or students is often required for promotion and merit raises. As a manager/administrator, I would be inclined to:

   a. Hire a competent individual, a "self-starter" who seems certain to continue to be a fine teacher and scholar, and give him/her the chance to "do his/her own thing." I certainly wouldn't be running around checking up on this person and visiting classes regularly for purposes of evaluation. I checked this person out very carefully before he/she was hired. I have every reason to believe that fine work will be done, and I don't wish to infringe on anyone's academic freedom by "breathing down that person's neck" who is trying to do a good job.

   b. Hire a competent individual, a "self-starter" who seems certain to continue to be a fine teacher and scholar, and give him/her the chance to "do his/her own thing." But I believe that a new teacher needs. and often wishes to have, supervision of his/her teaching--especially at first. We need to improve our methods of determining whether learning and education (more broadly defined) are really taking place in the classroom, gymnasium, or on the field. As new evidence becomes available from the behavioral sciences, this information concerning how to be a more effective teacher should be passed along to all teachers, and especially the younger ones.

10. This twentieth century in North American education has been a perplexing affair. Van Cleve Morris has stated, "Whenever a vacuum appears in the community the school has been asked to fill it." As a manager/administrator, my reaction to this is that:

    a. Many of the courses that have been added to the school curriculum, such as home economics, sex education, driver education, and a large variety of other subjects, should really not be part of the school's basic offerings. It is difficult enough just to teach the fundamental subjects well, and this cluttering-up of the curriculum inevitably results in a lowering of

educational quality. Many of these the home, the
ences should be made available by the home, the
church, or some other community agency.

b. The school and the community are working together
as "partners" in every way. This is not a simple matter to decide by saying, "these are essential subjects,
and these others are not." The needs of the child
must be met in the best possible way. If the schools
are better equipped to undertake a particular task,
then boards of education and educators, with the cooperation of the parents, should see to it that a child's
education is complete--that it prepares him/her to meet
the demands that life may make on the individual.

11. Determination of policies and the making of important decisions are most important in the educational world. Realizing that wise decisions should be made, as an administra-
tor/manager I would tend to:

a. Involve as many members of the board of education
and faculty as possible in the formation of policies.
(In a university setting, I would want student representation on all important committees.) If people are
going to have to live with policies, they have a right
to be part of the group that decides upon them. The
same thing can be said for the making of important
decisions which will inevitably affect the future of the
program in which they are involved. A vote should
be taken whenever possible. Of course, the assumption here is that voting implies a responsibility--the
one who votes, or expects to vote--has an obligation
to be as fully informed as possible.

b. Make decisions based on the best evidence available.
I would talk the matter over with the people most
directly concerned, but I also recognize that the final
responsibility and decision are mine. If a decision
backfires, and we are called to task by the higher
administration, I am the one who has to come up with
the answers and the reasons for the failure. Naturally, I would expect to have a good batting average
as far as decisions are concerned, or else I would be
replaced (or asked to resign). All of the preceding
doesn't mean that I wouldn't seek advice from my colleagues. When possible I would ask for a vote on
certain matters, and would quite probably take straw
votes on others. But as the administrator--as the

one who presumably knows more about the problem
than others and who bears the ultimate responsibility
--at the very least in just about any situation of true
significance I should be in a position to cast a strong
veto or to overrule.

12. In regard to the buildings and grounds aspect of institutional management, I believe that:

a. The buildings should be functional and efficient. A
school or university, for example, should be efficiently planned, systematized, and rational. A fixed inter-
ior pattern would be just fine, because our curriculum
by definition does not need to change from year to
year. Despite what has just been said, the physical
situation probably isn't the most important thing; the
most important thing is to have high-quality teachers
who know how to transmit the cultural heritage to the
oncoming generation.

b. What we really need is a structure where individual
freedom and questioning can take place. In the final
analysis, institutional architecture will not turn out
educated people--no matter how expensive it is.
Buildings should be designed for adaptability to un-
expected changes in program. Our curriculum will
quite probably be undergoing continual change, and it
seems quite foolish to always have to add a new addition just to make room for such change. Thus, we
should probably have movable walls, modular construction, and a concept of 'flexibility' insofar as the use
of space is concerned.

13. Having proceeded this far with the self-evaluation check
list, I think that the results of this self-evaluation will
show me to be:

a. Essentialistic (traditional, conservative, etc.)

b. Eclectic (neither strongly one way or the other--from
a total standpoint, that is--stances were not
consistently essential. or progress.)

c. Progressivistic (pragmatic, liberal, etc.)

d. Otherwise (don't see it this way totally--somewhat
existentialistic; more oriented to language
analysis, when considered individually)

Answers: (Read only after <u>all</u> thirteen questions have been
            answered)

1. Management--an art or a social science?
    a. Essentialistic
    b. Progressivistic

2. Manager's image of himself/herself
    a. Essentialistic--very much so
    b. Essentialistic--idealistic educational philosophy
    c. Progressivistic

3. <u>Types of business executives</u> (according to Maccoby)
    a. The Craftsman--essentialistic
    b. The Jungle Fighter--very essentialistic
    c. The Company Man--essentialistic
    d. The Gamesman--essentialistic

4. <u>Staff selection and appointment</u>
    a. Essentialistic--very much so
    b. Essentialistic--idealistic educational philosophy
    c. Progressivistic--moderately so

5. <u>Beliefs about sport and developmental physical activity</u>
    a. Progressivistic--reconstructionistic (Brameld)
    b. "Otherwise"--somewhat existentialistic and progressi-
            vistic
    c. Essentialistic--naturalistic realism
    d. Progressivistic--pragmatic naturalism
    e. Essentialistic--idealistic educational philosophy

6. <u>Personal philosophy</u>
    a. Essentialistic--philosophical realism
    b. Essentialistic--philosophical idealism
    c. Otherwise--existentialistic orientation
    d. Progressivistic--pragmatic naturalism
    e. Otherwise--language analysis

7. <u>Educational philosophy</u>
    a. Progressivistic--pragmatic naturalism and reconstruc-
            tionism
    b. Essentialistic--includes naturalist realism, rational hu-
            manism, and Catholic moderate realism
    c. Essentialistic--idealistic educational philosophy
    d. Otherwise--language analysis
    e. Otherwise--existentialistic

8. Are there principles of administration?
    a. Essentialistic
    b. Progressivistic

9. Instructional supervision
    a. Essentialistic--very much so today because of the
        1960s
    b. Progressivistic

10. Curriculum development
    a. Essentialistic
    b. Progressivistic

11. Policy-making and decision-making
    a. Progressivistic
    b. Essentialistic

12. Buildings and grounds
    a. Essentialistic
    b. Progressivistic

13. You have already given your opinion about your position
    insofar as management philosophy is concerned. Keep in
    mind that you have identified yourself as being either
    "essentialistic," "eclectic," "progressivistic," or "other-
    wise."

Note: Now please tally your answers to determine your posi-
        tion as best possible. Keep in mind, of course, the
        subjectivity of a self-evaluation such as this check list
        is.

        A large majority of your answers one way or the other
        will quite probably classify you are being either "essen-
        tialistic" or "progressivistic." If you find yourself
        fairly evenly divided between the two positions or stances,
        your management philosophy or style may well be con-
        sidered to be "eclectic."

        However, if you find that you have checked the "other-
        wise" category whenever it was available, and further
        that you really felt uneasy with this approach to cate-
        gorization, you could well fit under the "otherwise"
        category (which would probably be either existentialistic
        or geared to language analysis in philosophy).

Secondly, now that you have made this attempt to classify your probable management philosophy, and based on
the tally of responses just carried out, were you accurate in the self-assessment you made in Question #13?
(   ) Yes   (   ) No

Finally, do you feel that this self-evaluation check list
showed you to be one of the following:

   Strongly essentialistic (   )

   Essentialistic (   )

   Eclectic (   )
    (Middle-of-the-road in total perspective,
     but not on individual answers or stances)

   Progressivistic (   )

   Strongly progressivistic (   )

     ?????

APPENDIX B

EASTERN'S LONG, BITTER, CIVIL WAR*

The Alhambra Daily Express. Saturday, March 12, 19--

by Gerry Warren

(Note: This article appeared in the Alhambra Express approxi-
materly fifteen years after Eastern's new physical education building was completed. To help the reader put
everything into some sort of time perspective, keep in
mind that Eastern's Director of Physical Education, as
explained in Eastern State University (A) case, retired
three years prior to the opening of the building; that
physical education and intercollegiate athletics had been
separated at that time with Jonas becoming Director of
Athletics and Robins becoming Chairman, Department of
Physical Education; that Friedrich had replaced Robins
three years later; and that Archambault became the
chairman when Friedrich left after six years in office.
Case I and Case J occurred approximately four years
after Friedrich had left. This newspaper article appeared about five years after the incidents reported in
Cases I and J had taken place. The name of the city
and the newspaper are obviously fictitious, as are all
the names and places recorded in the various cases.
The cases as reported, and the sequence of events
from Case A to Case J, are factual--insofar as it was
possible to obtain the facts.)

Alhambra - The faculty and administration at Eastern State
University are engaged in a long, bitter war of attrition.

The faculty charges that the administration is "parochial,
paternal, autocratic, and complacent," and as a result the university is a "colorless institution."

The administration has been frankly baffled, and until
recently has fought the faculty with aloof silence. It has
answered the gentle probings of the only local newspaper with
a flurry of "no comments," all of which have been faithfully
reported.

270

The faculty wants a larger say in the university operation, a reorganized board of trustees and a reorganized university senate.

It wants to negotiate, as a union would, with the administration for salaries, pensions, tenure, retirement, study leave, and all conditions of employment.

But what the faculty wants most is a share in the government of the university.

The administration has found it can no longer ignore faculty demands, and various committees have been established to study the issues. But the faculty is not convinced that the new administration tactics will accomplish anything.

The faculty demands are angrily presented in three briefs written by professors. Two have been submitted to the Smith-Jones Commission on University Government, an inquiry financed by a large grant from the Ford Foundation. Sir Roger Smith, a British teacher and administrator for more than 20 years, and Donald A. Jones, professor of government at Santa Fe State College, have completed their study of the governing structure of universities. Their findings are to be published next Friday.

Perhaps the most important question they have studied is the role of the faculty in university government. Should universities follow the tradition of universities in other countries, especially those where staff members play an important role in government? Or should universities follow the practice of many institutions where the separation of administration and faculty is carefully maintained?

Both faculty and administration at the University are waiting anxiously, but nervously, for the Smith-Jones findings. The administration has indicated it will use the report as a philosophical guideline for the future.

Of course, tension between faculty and administration is in no way a problem just at Eastern; it is a continuing growing pain for all universities. In recent years, however, it appears that Eastern has the most acute symptoms.

The man who has caused the most pain for the administration with a country club image is a lean, tweedy, middle-aged professor of political science; Dr. Martin Elborn, who is called a troublemaker and radical by his enemies, and a moderate by his friends.

Dr. Elborn dislikes the administration so much, especially Dr. E. G. Clark, the smooth and evasive president of the university, that when he presented a brief to the Smith-Jones commission he refused to do so in the University's administration building because the atmosphere was emotionally unbearable.

The Fearless One, as Dr. Elborn has become known to his colleagues, said in a 31-page brief that the comfortable university of silver-grey Gothic buildings has a long, well-deserved reputation for parochialism, complacency, and not very benevolent autocracy. "Correspondingly, the faculty as a group and often as individuals has been timid, suspicious, fearful, and cynical."

Dr. Elborn has been sincerely disliked by the administration since a report on his brief was carried in the student newspaper, in which he was identified sometimes as Prof. Y and sometimes as Prof. X. Administration officials believed the report was leaked to the paper to embarrass them, and they truly resented the X, Y cloak-and-dagger tactics.

Another, more significant report, was submitted to the Smith-Jones Commission by the Faculty Association committee on university government.

The brief calls for a new name for the university--a reflection of faculty resentment of the Alhambra area establishment, which owns everything from the Turf Club to the local cemeteries--a new board of trustees that would be faculty-dominated, and the scrapping of the present senate.

It charges Dr. Clark with surrounding himself with "yes men" accountable to him alone, which "isolates the faculty from the president and makes his decisions appear arbitrary and ill-founded."

"In a university as colorless as this one, with as little sense of community as it has, the failure of the administration to respond to the new faculty enthusiasm and concern is no surprise."

The new faculty enthusiasm and concern is not really new at all. The professors are becoming increasingly discontented with the university government only because they are in a position to do so.

The timid professor 10 years ago is a dying creature. No longer are professors prepared to suffer silently. Increasing numbers of younger men are becoming professors, and they push harder and shout louder than their predecessors.

Another factor in the increasing discontent is that today, more than ever, university professors are in demand because of the opening of new universities. They know if they get tired of one university they can move to another. The administration is eqully aware of this new mobility.

The target for most faculty criticism at Eastern is Dr. Clark, 59, who was dean of the medical school before he became president 18 years ago. During an interview the alert, chain-smoking president, who suffered a heart attack last summer, was uneasy, evasive, and unhappy about the prospect of publicity.

Dr. Clark, who has been stubbornly silent in the past, answered the charge that he is paternalistic in his dealings with the faculty. "It would be a sad thing if a president were not concerned about the desires and ambitions of men in a community of scholars. But if that means cracking a whip, I deny that."

While Dr. Clark admitted that there has been a lack of communication between faculty and administration, he added: "There is a much better atmosphere today than there was two or three months ago. There is an increased attitude of trust and concern on both sides to solve the problems."

A number of interviews with members of the faculty showed a continuing attitude of distrust on their part, but they admitted that administration officials were starting to listen.

Proof of this was the establishment last September of a board of trustees' committee on faculty relations under the chairmanship of G. B. Shaw, counsel for the commission looking into the affairs of Pacific Acceptance Corporation.

Mr. Shaw recently wrote a letter to Professor J. C. Walters, chairman of the Faculty Association, a quiet, mild-mannered historian. Administration officials contend he is easily led by the more militant faculty members.

"We simply must resolve, and at once, the question of the role of the Faculty Association. You ask to be recognized as the voice of the Faculty. In respect to what matters?"

Mr. Shaw wrote that if it were in respect to conditions of employment, such as salaries and pensions, there would be no difficulty. But if it were in respect to other matters, such as certain appointments or the establishment of a new library, there would be great difficulty.

"It is surely unfair to attack the board for failure to recognize you when you will not or cannot tell us what you mean by recognition."

Professor Walters wrote back that the faculty is trying to establish consultations with the board of trustees on such matters as terms of employment, government and planning of the university, appointments, and any other area of general concern.

"Further attempts at definition seem futile," Professor Walters wrote. "It is in the very process of collaboration itself that the real roles of individuals and groups take shape and grow. At this university the process of collaboration has yet to begin."

And this is where faculty-administration relations stand today.

After the president and his assistants, the faculty most resents the board of trustees, whose members, except for one, are businessmen and belong to Massilon's elite and somewhat quaint establishment. The one, Robert Kingston, is first vice-president of the Massilon District Labor Council.

The most common criticism of the members of the board is--what do they know about education? But an even more serious criticism was made in the Faculty Association committee brief to the Smith-Jones commission.

It suggested conflict of interest on the board of trustees. "Two members of the board, at least, are senior officers of the company which handles the university pension and insurance plans," the brief said.

The two members of the board not named in the brief are J. E. Reading and Matthew Jefferson, both of whom are associated with the Massilon Life Insurance Co.

"I cannot understand the mind with the kind of thinking that would doubt such men as Mr. Reading and Mr. Jefferson, who were senior executives in insurance many years before they joined the board," said Colonel Rupert E. Douglas, chairman of the board.

Colonel Douglas, honorary chairman of Southern Securities Company, one of the state's largest investment firms and a breeder of fine race horses on a 750-acre farm near Massilon, commented on the faculty reform movement: "I don't think it is important, but it is disturbing. It prevents cooperation. Is that a sensible approach?"

He also spoke in defense of Dr. Clark. "I would like to take the opportunity afforded me of expressing publicly complete confidence in Dr. Clark, president of Eastern State University, and Mr. Will Ross, vice-president of administration and finance, and all other members of the administration."

On Tuesday, Governor Robert Johns announced a new appointment to the board. He is Adam W. Johnson, 42, vice-president of the Sterling Company, manufacturers of engineering supplies in Massilon. His appointment to the board is likely to bring a kind of perverse satisfaction to the more militant members of the faculty movement who were predicting their nominee for the board, Supreme Court Justice Lance Laskowitz, would not be accepted.

The faculty is disappointed with the students at Eastern who live a comfortable existence in their broadloomed dormitories, and apparently have no desire or intention of rocking the boat one way or another. They have the distinction of being the only student body in the entire region of the country that voted against free tuition.

But there are a few rebels around. Robert Whitestone, a fourth-year honors program student who was one of two students this year to win a Woodrow Wilson fellowship, said the concept of academic freedom is really "news to the administration here."

Mr. Whitestone, tall, thin, and extremely nervous, said that as long he had been on the Students' Council the faculty has received little support from the student body. He quoted a past president of the counceil who accused the faculty of wanting to be both union and management.

Another student, Sean Jameson, editor of the student newspaper, sat behind his small desk in his office in a campus basement, surveyed his busty Playboy centre-spread pin-ups, and said: "They have operated this university just like a big business. What do they know about education?" He said the administration has gone on for years without considering the faculty and students.

The faculty view of the administration officials, in Professor Walters' words, is that "they think in terms of the nineteenth century. They have a corporation attitude; they are conservative emotionally and philosophically; and they probably wanted to see how far they could go in pushing us."

The administration view of the faculty appears to be: "What do they want?"

And the view of the Smith-Jones commission? Both faculty and administration, perhaps for different reasons, are keeping their fingers crossed.

INDEX

#4